How Hitler Evolved the Traditional Army Establishment

How Hitler Evolved the Traditional Army Establishment

A Study Through Field Marshals Keitel, Paulus and Manstein

Andrew Sangster and Pier Paolo Battistelli

Pen & Sword
MILITARY

First published in Great Britain in 2024 by
Pen & Sword Military
An imprint of Pen & Sword Books Limited
Yorkshire – Philadelphia

Copyright © Andrew Sangster and Pier Paolo Battistelli 2024

ISBN 978 1 03610 602 7

The right of Andrew Sangster and Pier Paolo Battistelli to be identified as Authors of this Work has been asserted by them in accordance with the Copyright, Designs and Patents Act 1988.

A CIP catalogue record for this book is
available from the British Library

All rights reserved. No part of this book may be reproduced or transmitted in any form or by any means, electronic or mechanical including photocopying, recording or by any information storage and retrieval system, without permission from the Publisher in writing.

Typeset by Mac Style
Printed in the UK by CPI Group (UK) Ltd, Croydon, CR0 4YY.

Pen & Sword Books Limited incorporates the imprints of After the Battle, Atlas, Archaeology, Aviation, Discovery, Family History, Fiction, History, Maritime, Military, Military Classics, Politics, Select, Transport, True Crime, Air World, Frontline Publishing, Leo Cooper, Remember When, Seaforth Publishing, The Praetorian Press, Wharncliffe Local History, Wharncliffe Transport, Wharncliffe True Crime and White Owl.

For a complete list of Pen & Sword titles please contact

PEN & SWORD BOOKS LIMITED
47 Church Street, Barnsley, South Yorkshire, S70 2AS, England
E-mail: enquiries@pen-and-sword.co.uk
Website: www.pen-and-sword.co.uk
or
PEN AND SWORD BOOKS
1950 Lawrence Rd, Havertown, PA 19083, USA
E-mail: uspen-and-sword@casematepublishers.com
Website: www.penandswordbooks.com

Contents

Introduction: From the Reichswehr to the Wehrmacht viii
    A State Within the State viii
    Hitler in Control xi
    How to Make a Career xiii
    Co-operation and Clashes xvi
    Welcome to the Book xviii

Field Marshal Wilhelm Keitel: The Blotting Pad

Chapter 1   Introduction 3
    Early life to 1918 4
    Early Interbellum Years 8
    Interbellum Years under Hitler 12

Chapter 2   The Second World War 26

Chapter 3   A Condemned Man 56
    Post-war Interrogations 60
    The Trial 61
    Civilian Interviews 70

Chapter 4   Views of Political Contemporaries 74
    Views of Military Contemporaries 78
    General Histories and their Perceptions 81

Chapter 5   Final Thoughts 84

Field Marshal Friedrich Paulus:
The Eleventh-Hour Field Marshal

Chapter 1	**Early Life**	91
	Background Family	91
	The First World War	93
	Interbellum Years	95
Chapter 2	**War Years**	100
	The Second World War	100
	To the Eastern Front 1942	106
	Paulus's Humanity	108
	The First Offensives	109
Chapter 3	**Stalingrad**	114
	The Horror of the Stalingrad Battle	114
	Stalingrad, The Battle	118
	The Cauldron	124
	Capitulation	140
	Looking Back to Stalingrad	143
Chapter 4	**In Soviet Hands**	145
	In Captivity	145
	After the War	151
Chapter 5	**Divided Opinions**	158
	The Nazi Regime	158
	Views of Contemporaries	160
	Views of Historians	162
	Final Thoughts	165

Field Marshal Erich Von Manstein: The Military Mind

Chapter 1	Introduction	171
	Natural Born Soldier	172
Chapter 2	Staff Officer and War	178
	The Eastern Front, 1941	182
	The Victor on the Battlefield	186
Chapter 3	Turning Point	197
	Dismissal	204
	Post-war	209
Chapter 4	Manstein in the Contemporary Views	213
	Manstein and the Historians	216
	Final Comments	218

Final Observations   222
Notes   225
Cited Bibliography   236
Index   239

Introduction

From the Reichswehr to the Wehrmacht

A State Within the State

The German Army, the Reichsheer (the old name for the German Army until 1919), had enjoyed a prominent role within the state and society until the November 1919 collapse with Germany's surrender after the Great War. Closely tied to the Kaiser, the army was a stronghold of tradition centred around the Prussian officer elite, who basically ruled the entire institution. The surrender and the subsequent Peace Treaty signed at Versailles shook the country and its traditional military institution from its roots, leading to many changes. The transition appeared smooth, albeit not without difficulties.

On 6 March 1919, the National Assembly of the Weimar Republic created a provisional army (the Reichswehr) which consisted of 43 brigades, with the existing Reichsheer to be dissolved following the completion of the demobilisation. The withdrawal of the German forces from the occupied territories, which had started in the immediate aftermath of the armistice, had been almost completed by then with the units returning to their home garrisons, or to pre-designated demobilisation sites. The exception was given to those units whose garrisons were on the west bank of the Rhine River, which had to be demilitarised according to the terms of the armistice, the units having their garrison moved to the interior of Germany. The demobilisation led to the dismissal of millions of men who were rapidly returned to civilian life and unable to find work, and soon realised that their efforts and their sacrifices had been forgotten.

Even though it is normal for armies to reduce in size following the end of a war, the restrictions imposed on the Reichswehr by the Treaty of Versailles led to the creation of a small army compared with its past, a mere 100,000 men. After the transitional army had reduced it was followed by the dissolution of the brigades, which left the army with mere units at regimental level. On 1 January 1921, the Reichswehr was officially created, based on this strength of 100,000 men. The effects of this dramatic reduction in strength can be easily imagined. Millions who had been drafted before and during the war may well have returned, albeit uneasily to the civilian life, but the army also had thousands of career officers who suddenly faced the prospect of losing their jobs, their careers, and their much-vaunted social position. The Versailles Treaty allowed 4,000 officers, the Reichswehr only had some 3,700, which was nothing when compared with the 227,000 officers in the Imperial Army of 1918. Most importantly, of all these, some 38,000 were career officers, while some 15,000 had been promoted during the war. The selection process was note-worthy. Most of the officers selected to join the Reichswehr came from the career sector, with the traditional Prussian elite, the backbone of the Imperial Army, seeing its predominant strength within the army shrink from some 30 to about 24 per cent of the entire officer corps. Most of the other officers selected (which was about three quarters of the officer corps) were mainly chosen on the basis of their experience and accomplishments during the war. Former staff officers were preferred, in fact they were the first choice in the transition, along with those who were decorated, and the actual reduction in the percentage of noble-family officers matched a long-term trend, which had started before the beginning of the war. Hardly any officer promoted during the war or officers with radical political views, whether leftwing or right-wing nationalists, tended to be excluded as well.

It can be seen that in its creation, the Reichswehr was ruled by two factors: the safeguarding of traditional values, and the need to continue along the path demanding innovation which had been started before its birth. The shrinking of the elite Prussian officer corps was a step in the path towards innovation, but it also served the purpose of making space for those staff officers who were considered necessary to create the basic structure of a new future army. By maintaining a lower number of officers than that permitted by the Peace Treaty, the Reichswehr clearly indicated its ambition of creating a highly selected officer corps to serve as the backbone for future development. This sense of the new evolvement played a prominent role in the 1918 post-war Germany, touching upon the lives of all the field marshals mentioned in this study.

As it is well known, the Reichswehr did not restrain itself to the simple duty of creating a defence force, but it started planning for future expansion while developing studies in the field of military innovation. The Army General Staff, formally prohibited by the Versailles Treaty, was maintained with the creation of the Truppenamt (Troop Office), with officers still being trained as general staff officers at the Leaders' Assistant Training School. It was a form of cover-organisation for the prohibited German General Staff. A Black Reichswehr was thereby created, a form of parallel army, which was enabled to conduct studies and experimental weapons, due to the newly developed co-operation with the Soviet Union, the two pariah states seeking mutual support. While staff officers studied the impact of motorisation on the future army, the troops trained using dummy tanks, because real ones were forbidden by the peace treaty. Soon, the traditional role of the army within the German nation was re-established, despite the situation and the restrictions. In 1925 the former Field Marshal Paul Hindenburg was elected president, and even though the 'father' of the Reichswehr, General Hans von Seeckt, had to resign in the following year, the ever-growing power acquired by Kurt von Schleicher (since 1928 head of the Office of Ministerial Affairs) not only established the role of the army within the state, but also secured its ever-growing influence on German politics.

Hitler's rise to power in January 1933 was welcomed by many, but also created a problem. The promise to denounce the Versailles Treaty and to create an effective and strong army by re-introducing the national conscription suited the Reichswehr's aims, which had been pointing in that direction since its very creation. On the other hand, the fact that Hitler could rely on a series of paramilitary formations and his rule appeared to threaten the role and independence of the Reichswehr, which was extremely jealous not only of its position, but also of its own social structure. Clearly it was a matter of keeping the balance, supporting the traditional functions and structure of the German Army, while at the same time granting Hitler the necessary power to enforce those innovations which were deemed necessary, to restore the previous role and status of the military in Germany.

Hitler in Control

The army fear of a possible interference from the paramilitary formation of the Sturm Abteilung, the SA, disappeared following the Night of the Long Knives in June-July 1934. The physical elimination of the SA leadership, first and foremost with the leader Ernst Röhm, and of any opposition to the regime, which also included von Schleicher, guaranteed that the Reichswehr would maintain its independence while being promised a future expansion. Hitler, with unusual caution, proceeded step by step and was very careful in avoiding any possible problem with the army and its leadership. While the expansion programme was developed, Hitler's first step followed the death of von Hindenburg on 2 August 1934. He took full charge as both Reich Chancellor and head of the state, thus becoming Germany's Führer. Hitler had the troops take their oath to him, being supported in this move by the Reichswehr Minister, Werner von Blomberg. The reward was swift, and in March 1935, Hitler sanctioned the birth of the new armed forces with a series of decisive steps. First, on 1 March, the Luftwaffe was officially created, and on the 16th, universal conscription was re-introduced while officially denouncing the Versailles Treaty. The Reichswehr ceased to exist, and Germany acquired new armed forces (the Wehrmacht) with three separate branches, the Heer, the former Reichswehr, the Luftwaffe, and the Kriegsmarine. They were all expected to respond to Hitler as supreme commander of the Wehrmacht.

The composition of the Wehrmacht revealed the balance Hitler tried to maintain between tradition and innovation. The army kept its conventional structure, and its leadership with von Blomberg as Minister of War attempted to maintain its independence. The Luftwaffe, headed by Hermann Göring, represented the most innovative of the three branches, and its creation clearly followed Mussolini's decision to create an independent air arm in 1923. This also happened in Britain with the Royal Air Force, one of the few independent air arms in the world. The Luftwaffe's innovative character, due both to its specific nature and new creation, was compensated by the intake of a large number of army officers, such as the future Field Marshal Albert Kesselring. The Navy was the only one of the services which managed to maintain a degree of separation between itself and the new regime. The rapid growth of the armed forces was welcome, and tensions started to grow within the army itself, when the advocates of the new Panzer Arm clashed with the traditional army officers. They tended to oppose this innovation because it offered the new units too much power by making the Panzer Arm independent. There was a similar debate in Britain over the true value of tanks. For his part, Hitler stood and watched, waiting for a suitable opportunity to take charge.

The decisive moment came in 1938, as Hitler started his expansion programme aimed at Austria and Czechoslovakia. On 12 January, von Blomberg had married Eva Gruhn in Berlin, with Hermann Göring acting as best man. Two weeks later he had to resign following the alleged news that his wife had been a prostitute (or had simply posed for pornographic photos, in fact the evidence varies in the many accounts). On 4 February, the Army Commander Werner von Fritsch was forced to resign following falsely constructed accusations of homosexuality, which enabled Hitler to take the last step. The War Ministry was abolished, and was replaced by the Oberkommando der Wehrmacht (OKW). This marked a major step in Hitler taking control of the armed forces, but it did not represent the decisive step for direct control. It appears that Hitler moved along traditional guidelines more than some generals wanted, the future Field Marshal von Manstein regretted that the Oberkommando der Wehrmacht, was not a proper interforce command which may have enabled sound combined warfare.

In reality, the changes were minimal and only secured Hitler's control on some of the key aspects of the military administration and structure. The Wehrmacht High Command was in fact formed by an Operations Staff which acted as Hitler's personal advisor, but it also controlled the armament production and military intelligence, the Abwehr, led by

Admiral Canaris, which was now under Hitler's direct control. The choice for the man who was to lead the Wehrmacht High Command, was General Wilhelm Keitel, another potential Field Marshal. This appointment was curious because Hitler took him from the army elite, but at the same time assured he chose a person whose Prussian loyalty was beyond doubt. The other changes were minimal, and in order to understand them it is necessary to focus on names. General von Brauchitsch took over as the new Commander in Chief of the Army, the position having not been cancelled, and he soon acquired a new Chief of Army Staff in General Franz Halder, who replaced General Ludwig Beck who had opposed Hitler's plans against Czechoslovakia. The two components, tradition, and innovation, started to merge, the old-style Prussian military ensuring that the Prussian traditionalists and the new generation were more or less shackled to the Nazi party. As some of the biographies provided in this book will reveal, all too often their careers depended upon these two components, neither of which seems to have prevailed in the first years of the Second World War.

How to Make a Career

The human social structure being what it is, ensured that in Germany during the 1930s a circle of relationships of who knows who, would secure a career in the armed forces, more than any actual skill and knowledge. Most of the high-level German army commanders came from the old school, and Hitler never considered replacing them after the fall of von Blomberg and Fritsch. The generals also reacted accordingly, generally supporting and obeying Hitler, but in their post-war memoirs, always claiming to have opposed him. Some names started to emerge, in some cases due to a combination of their skills and Hitler's personal support. This could be the case of General Heinz Guderian, who was an innovator in the traditionalist army officer corps. His rise in command was due to the fact that Hitler took a personal interest in the development of the Panzer arm, thus making Guderian his putative leader and securing his personal career. Other officers relied on the more traditional ways to secure a promotion. General Friedrich Paulus owed his career mainly to General Halder, being in practice his protege, and he only came to Hitler's attention later as he started working on the plans for the attack against the Soviet Union, and he was eventually given a field command. The most interesting case is probably that of Erich von Manstein who, despite his extremely traditional Prussian military background, was himself an innovator and had no friends within the restricted circle of the army top brass. It was Hitler who discovered von Manstein's talent, securing his future career as a field commander. Nevertheless, despite his achievements, von Manstein's brusque personality and his lack of social sensitivity saw both the top brass in the army and Hitler turn against him, resulting in a premature dismissal.

There were those who, to a greater or lesser extent, owed their careers to Hitler. General Erwin Rommel might have been just a first-class field commander, rising at best to command a corps, had it not been for Hitler who secured him the command of a Panzer Division, then gave him command in North Africa. Accomplishment on the battlefield was always a means to secure Hitler's attention and guarantee a career path. This was also the case of General Eduard Dietl, whose victory at Narvik granted him a career path which was deserved. Model, a future field marshal was, to a lesser extent, another general who owed most of his career to his actual achievements, rather than any favour either from Hitler or from the army establishment. This seems to have been the case with many of the Luftwaffe officers, Kesselring being the foremost case, whose only obstacle to a successful career path was Hitler's concern that by appointing him in the highest positions, possibly meant having Göring taking too much control.

As the war started, careers developed all too often beyond expectations. Hitler made his attitude clear when, in the aftermath of the fall of France, he promoted all those who were in the lead and created nineteen new field marshals. Promotions, bribes in the form of gifts and pay rises, and special appointments certainly guaranteed that the army leaders would remain loyal to Hitler and to the regime. The generals (or newly appointed field marshals) did not object but played their part. In the first years of the war the combination of Hitler's leadership and army establishment only came close to a dangerous level of friction once, when the plans for the attacks against France were being developed. The divide between Hitler's role as the commander in chief of the armed forces and the army establishment expanded, as Hitler insisted on attacking France as soon as Poland was defeated. Hitler's policy did not take into consideration two factors. First, the winter and the unsuitable weather, and secondly, the fact that the army was completely unprepared for the task. There was not even a properly prepared plan to attack France, and these issues soon became a matter of debate. By November 1939 both von Brauchitsch and Halder started considering taking some action against Hitler, as he had insisted on compelling the army to attack under unfavourable circumstances. Nothing came out of this disruption and Hitler was able to avoid any confrontation. The possibility of harsh weather compelled the attack to be continuously postponed, until Hitler had to abandon his plans following the Mechelen incident, when a German aircraft with a staff officer aboard landed in Belgium revealing the attack plans.

From February 1940, the attack having been postponed to the spring, some form of debate ensued between the army leadership and Hitler. This was about the plan which, as Hitler noted, was too traditional and unimaginative as it merely reproduced the Schlieffen Plan which had led to the 1914 failure in France. It was on this occasion that Hitler was to discover to what extent even the most traditional army officers could be the bearer of innovation. The development of the *sickle cut* plan, which was a combination of von Manstein's and Hitler's ideas, was finally developed by the army staff which accepted it as the best solution. Nevertheless, Hitler decided not to take risks and von Manstein, who had no friends within the army staff, had no role in the actual execution of the plan. This was a time when neither side of the political and military divide were inclined to clash.

The victory over France in June 1940 ended any possible debate between Hitler and the armed forces. Although a gross exaggeration, the definition of Hitler as the 'greatest military commander of all times' secured his role within the armed forces in a definitive way. His choices would no longer be challenged, nor would his position. Hitler repaid this trust by securing the careers of his military commanders, but ensuring he was able to choose whoever he wanted according to needs. Erwin Rommel had distinguished himself during the First World War, earning the coveted Pour le Mérite which guaranteed him a position in the Reichswehr even despite his lack of staff officer training. Rommel was undoubtedly a good field commander, but he had no friends amongst the army elite, and he only secured command of a Panzer Division in the war against France due to Hitler's personal intervention. His character and his skills were undoubtedly behind Hitler's decision to give him command of the German forces sent to North Africa. This all followed a series of disappointing interviews with other army generals, whose more traditional views hardly suited Hitler's demands. Rommel's swift advance into Cyrenaica was a masterpiece, until he ran into troubles as he attempted to subdue the Tobruk fortress. Facing his failure, the Army Staff sent General Paulus to try and resolve the problem, only revealing Rommel's shortcomings. However, no matter how critical General Halder was of Rommel and his style of command, neither he nor anyone else from the army ever suggested his removal or being given another command; Hitler was in control. By 1941 the mutual agreement between Hitler and Germany's military leadership had become a fact, the two happily co-existing even despite the differences, and diffidence, which were mainly to emerge only after the war, when it was safe.

Co-operation and Clashes

After the war ended most of the German generals, namely, those who survived and ended up in British or American captivity, wrote self-serving accounts justifying themselves. Many of these publications underlined that Hitler was solely responsible for the German defeat, which had been caused by his decision to attack the Soviet Union which eventually led to disaster. The generals claimed to have opposed the idea, as they repeatedly stressed, but this was Hitler's ideal aim, namely the war against Bolshevism in its den. Needless to say, more recent historiography has revealed that matters did not always go that way. The original idea of a war against the Soviet Union came from the army, which considered this as the best solution to defend Germany from a possible Soviet attack. Hitler, as he had with von Manstein, took this idea, and made it his own. The content of the famous 31 July 1940 conference makes this point. Hitler wanted to destroy the Soviet military capabilities in order to be able to concentrate against Germany's main enemy, which was Britain. No opposition came from the army for this idea, either because they supported the policy or were now subservient as a group.

It is most likely that the army staff and its subordinate commands eagerly developed the attack plan against the Soviet Union, which went under the codename *Barbarossa*. Amongst those who developed the plans was General Friedrich Paulus who, due to General Halder, had acquired the position of chief of operations within the army staff. Neither Halder nor Paulus ever objected to the idea of attacking the Soviet Union, and only a few critical voices rose from the bulk of the army generals. The point being that, while Hitler lulled himself in the delusion of being the greatest military commander of all times, his generals had the same delusion of having an invincible army which could defeat a giant like the Soviet Union. In this, Hitler and the army worked in perfect harmony, until some issues started to emerge when the Soviet Union was eventually attacked. The main debates dealt with the aims of the German campaign in the East. Halder, and other generals, focused on territorial gains and aimed at the seizure of Moscow which they thought should have been the primary objective. Hitler instead relied on the more traditional German operational doctrine, focusing on the destruction of the enemy forces. This led to the much-debated decision to fight for Kiev before attacking Moscow. This decision resulted in a huge pocket of thousands of trapped Russians, but it also caused a fatal delay in the attack against the Soviet capital city.

Facing the failure of Operation *Barbarossa* as early as September 1941, the tacit agreement between Hitler and the army started to crack. Hitler's suspicions on the actual capabilities of his commanders grew, and he convinced himself he knew better, which in some areas was possibly correct. This was a turning point best seen in the study of Field Marshal von Manstein. The Soviet counterattack on 5 December 1941 took the Germans by surprise, and led to the first defeat of the German army in the war. Several generals started losing their nerve, and withdrawals took place all along the front. Hitler's reaction was drastic: he removed the now Field Marshal von Brauchitsch and took command of the army. The first clash between Hitler and the army establishment transpired to be to his advantage. Hitler's order to stand fast, as many historians agree, eventually saved the army from collapse, and gave time to restore the situation, even though this only happened in the spring of 1942. Brauchitsch was the first on a list of generals who were removed, and this marked the beginning of a new phase in the relations between Hitler and his army.

Loyalty, meaning the willingness to obey his orders whatever, became the important factor, with Hitler relying on people who could be trusted more than he would with capable commanders. Paulus, who distinguished himself at Kharkov, was a typical example. As Hitler started considering the removal of General Halder and sought another Chief of Army Staff, several names were considered. Kesselring was discarded, as his appointment might have put the military at Göring's mercy, and the same with von Manstein who did not have at the time the proper qualifications. The only suitable name, from Hitler's point of view, was Paulus who Hitler knew to be trusted. It is somehow ironic that Paulus eventually ended up with being associated with Germany's decisive defeat in the Second World War, and he refused to follow the most common military tradition of committing suicide after his promotion to field marshal, because field marshals do not surrender. Paulus was an innovator within the rather traditionalist circle of the German army commanders, but overall this did not play to Hitler's advantage.

Welcome to the Book

Many commanders and field marshals have been mentioned during this introductory chapter and some will be carefully scrutinised in the next book on this subject. This particular study deals with the early part of the

Second World War when to many observers the German military appeared unstoppable. However, in the initial stages of the war the relationship between military command and Hitler remained stable because of the successes, but as defeats for the Germans occurred, Hitler became less sure of his commanders and started looking for other options.

This book explores the lives of three selected and vastly different field marshals, Keitel the bureaucrat, Paulus the planner and failed soldier, and Manstein a military success for a brief time. The first two, Keitel and Paulus are remote in historical terms, and the third, von Manstein has had his reputation somewhat coloured by his own post-war publications and overly keen historians. These selected commanders are explored from their youths and backgrounds, all brought up in the Wilhelmine period with its Prussian traditions, and they all experienced the Great War at one level or another. They held in common the various parts they played in the turbulent 1920s, as the German military tried to rebuild itself under the Versailles restrictions, and their responses to the rise of Hitler are noted. Their reactions to these events at times differ as did their experiences. There is always the danger of repeating the facets of this period, but it is necessary to gauge their personal reactions and the parts they played.

Hitler had set himself up as the one national leader in a country once monarchical and despotic, to a country which after the Great War had initiated a good democratic system, but Hitler turned it into a totalitarian state. He was now cunningly planning to make sure he was totally in control of the military aspects of Germany. To do this he had worked on the traditional military command and it officers, ensuring they were onside either by admiration for restoring German military strength, or by hoping to enhance their careers, and by pure bribery. Above all he demanded total loyalty and obedience to his commands, especially as they were regarded as potential high command.

Keitel was the head of the OKW and was unstinting in his loyalty to such an extent that many of his contemporaries were happy to ridicule him, but he remained faithful only having doubts when the evils of the regime unravelled in the Nuremberg Trial exposures. Prussian tradition had always expected loyalty and obedience which suited Hitler's views. Paulus was of a similar mould, and such was his obedience as an administration and planning officer, Hitler promoted him beyond his capabilities by giving him a major field command at a dangerously critical time. It took time in Russian captivity for this field marshal to realise that his adherence to the dictator had been a mistake. In Manstein, at one time considered a possible high command candidate, was a sound tactician and strategist on the battlefield, but lacking the social requirements of personality and daring to clash with the dictator, he was eventually dismissed by his mentor Hitler, and post-war tried to redeem his reputation in two published works.

All three were undoubtedly driven by personal career ambitions, a belief that Hitler was restoring Germany's greatness, and an unfounded belief that Germany would win. However, they were also in many ways different, and this study, by opting for brief biographies, attempts to provide the reader with insights into who these senior military leaders were, what they were like, what sort of people they became. How far Keitel was aware of the Nazi barbarities remains speculative to a degree, Paulus had moral standards and was not complicit, whereas Manstein was convicted of war crimes, a feature often neglected in the study of this man. The reader must make his or her own judgment based on the presented realities of their lives, and of what they make of these top commanders as men and military leaders.

Field Marshal Wilhelm Keitel

The Blotting Pad

Chapter One

Introduction

Keitel wrote his memoirs in his cell during his imprisonment at the Nuremberg Trial, knowing he would be found guilty on all four indictments. He probably wrote them as some form of vindication to future generations, and to counter the opinions of many of his contemporaries about his role as Hitler's obedient robot. Some observers have described him as Hitler's conduit pipe, others as the dictator's 'amanuensis'.[1] He even described himself as Hitler's mouthpiece.[2] He rose to power because of his organisational skills, his hard work, his sense of obedience, his loyalty if not subservience, which was quickly spotted by Hitler. The dictator selected Keitel because he knew this senior soldier was weak, and being a traditional Prussian officer did what he was told. When he made him Chief of the OKW it was a fraud because Keitel held no real power, he simply did what Hitler required and never objected. The fact that Keitel continued to write his memoirs until three days before his execution, reflected his sturdy if somewhat misled personality.

Personal information about Keitel is scarce, his post-war memoir edited by Walter Görlitz must be read with care for the sake of objectivity. As in any such study it proved necessary to give attention to views about Keitel by his political and military contemporaries, as well as the better historians. Also, of considerable interest are the Nuremberg Trial records and observations by his various visitors. His character is of interest given his closeness to the Nazi regime, and he also provided invaluable insights into the dominating figure of Adolf Hitler. In terms of historical objectivity, he must be evaluated with care, because his final literary efforts were a form of defensive apologia to put him in a better light than the Nuremberg trial, and the biased way many contemporaries regarded him.

4 How Hitler Evolved the Traditional Army Establishment

One of the most interesting pieces of research was the unearthing of a conversation in the Russian archives between Keitel and Hitler, which provided an interesting insight and balance to his memoirs.

Early life to 1918

Keitel was born on 22 September 1882 in the small village of Helmscherode, which was seven kilometres from Bad Gandersheim in the Duchy of Brunswick. He was baptised with the names Wilhelm Bodewin Johann Gustav Keitel. He was equipped with a sound intelligence rating (129) when scrutinised at the Nuremberg Trial, which placed him halfway amongst the defendants, the top rating being 143 to the bottom of 106.[3] He never stood out at school where he was considered an average pupil, and he just scraped through his *Abitur* (end of school certificate).[4]

He was the eldest son of Carl Keitel (1854–1934) who was a middle-class landowner, with some 650 acres. Keitel had a younger brother called Bodewin who would follow him into the army and found promotion through Keitel's patronage. The estates they farmed had started with his great-grandfather who at first leased the estates, then his grandfather who eventually purchased the land, so the ownership stretched back some 150 years. Keitel was always proud of being a Hanoverian with its connections with the kings of England.[5]

His mother was Apollonia Vissering (1855–1888), but she died when Keitel was aged six years giving birth to his younger brother Bodewin. Keitel grew to six-feet-one-inch tall, he was solidly built, with a lifelong characteristic of a jutting jaw and a typical soldierly appearance. He often ruminated on taking over his father's estate, but this only became a reality when his father died in 1934. By this stage, his father had married again, and Keitel's wife was not happy with the new domestic scene, and she was ambitious for Keitel as a leading military figure. There would be times when he wished he had ignored his wife and retired to the estate. He enjoyed horse-riding and hunting but was no farmer, but he was noted for his appetite for hard work, and having inherited the land, he stayed with the army organising the estate from a distance. He renovated the estate chapel, because he had been a Protestant which he remained all his life, but probably out of his sense of tradition rather than Christian principles or values. There were times when feeling depressed he often hankered after the quiet life of the home estate, but 'he believed it to be his duty [to stay in the army], perhaps abetted by the counsels of his ambitious and strong-willed wife'.[6]

He was seen by many of his contemporaries as 'old school', based on his appearance, composure, and traditional obedience to his superiors. At Nuremberg many regarded him as the epitome of the Junker class (noble background), but this was a mistake because he carried no *von* before his name, and he came from a very different background compared with this traditional noble class. His family background was Hanoverian which once indicated an anti-Prussian attitude. The military traditions of Prussia were somewhat alien to his wider family, and their general attitude took the form of a continuous protest against Prussia's annexation of the Kingdom of Hanover in 1866. When Keitel's father had once served as a volunteer in the Prussian Hussars, he was not allowed to return home if wearing the hated uniform. Much later in life Field Marshal von Rundstedt would still

Übersicht

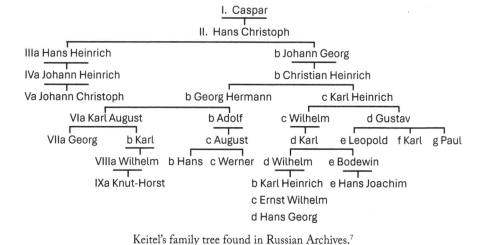

Keitel's family tree found in Russian Archives.[7]

regard his fellow Field Marshal Keitel as a commoner and Hanoverian, indicating that social and nationalistic snobbery was always rife.[8]

As a boy and young man, he was brought up in a Europe which was changing. In central Europe the German, Austrian and Hungarian powers were growing stronger, France had formed a relationship with Russia, while Britain with a world empire tended to stand apart. One of the features of the times was that national military forces were on the increase, and the so-called balance of power was not helped by the emerging nations becoming stronger with neighbour watching neighbour. For so many young Germans the military was an attractive profession because it had social status, and this offered a more interesting life for the young and ambitious. At first, there was the question whether his social class might preclude him, but at that time the army was eagerly seeking more recruits. On first applying in 1899 a regimental doctor nearly turned him down on the smallness of his chest measurements, but he was helped by an uncle who was a senior army doctor, an act of nepotism which 'prevented a humiliating rejection'.[9] He later admitted that 'I became an officer because in Prussia usually an officer was considered more highly than a businessman or other professions', indicating social status was important for him.[10] However, he also recalled that he needed an income while his father lived, because it would mean waiting for his father's death before he gained his inheritance.

He started his military career in 1901 as an officer cadet in the Prussian army, but by joining as a commoner he was unable to join the upper-class cavalry. In August 1902 he was made second lieutenant and joined an instructor's course in the Field Artillery in 1905, then he was attached to an artillery regiment in Wolfenbüttel, where by 1908 he was an adjutant. In 1910 he was made 1st Lieutenant and by 1914 was promoted to Captain.

In April 1909 he married Lisa Fontaine (1887–1959) a wealthy landowner's daughter, who was regarded as much more cultured than Keitel, a man only interested in military matters. She was much more the intellectual, keen on wide reading, music, and overly ambitious for her husband. It was a sound marriage, and from her own correspondence it has been confirmed that she was a strong-willed woman and ambitious.

Because of the financial ramifications of the Great War, she lost her fortune during the inflation years, at a time when they had five children which was why he probably decided to stay in the army, as well as his wife's ambitions for his seemingly important military career.[11]

It was noted that she stood by her husband throughout his life, attending his trial at Nuremberg and keeping her composure when his death sentence by the humiliation of hanging was announced. Much later, in his diaries for September 1938, the diplomat Ulrich von Hassell made the interesting observation that politically his family members were more astute than Keitel, stating that 'his daughter said that many young officers thought the SA Brownshirts should be the first to be sent to the front because they talked too freely'.[12]

The Keitels had six children, one sadly dying as a baby, and two daughters called Nona (1911–1998) and Erika (1912–1943). They had three sons who all followed their father into the army. Karl-Heinz married Dorothea the daughter of General von Blomberg (who later rose to prominence as Minister of Defence), and this marriage will be mentioned later in the text. Karl-Heinz transferred to the Waffen-SS in August 1944 and died in 1968. Ernst-Wilhelm was imprisoned by the Soviets but released and died in 1956. The third son was Hans-Georg who died in 1941 during the Russian campaign, having already been gravely wounded in the Battle of France.

During these years, as a sound young married officer, Keitel was noted above all for his organisational skills, which was probably why, with his trustworthiness, he was selected as adjutant by his colonel. It was even suggested that he was being kept in mind for a position on the General Staff, and so he studied for this possibility, and went on a course to this end in March 1914. This recognition by senior staff of his potentiality was significant, probably based on his organisational skills and sense of obedience so dear to the Prussian tradition.

The course he attended concluded with the start of the Great War. Keitel was on holiday in Switzerland when the first signs of eruption occurred, motivating him to rush back home. He started his war with the 46th Artillery regiment, serving on the Western Front where he was wounded in Flanders with shrapnel in his right arm. On his return he was promoted to captain and then posted to the staff of an infantry division in 1915. His senior officers again started to notice his organisational skills, his sense of duty and ability to cope with demanding work. During this war he met many people who would one day be influential, one being Blomberg, though it has been noted many times that Blomberg and Keitel had little in common as personalities, and even believed that Blomberg did not rate Keitel as highly as others. The Great War tended to be static, and artillery was seen as a major innovation, and it was in this area that many promotions occurred. This importance of artillery caused debate in the interbellum years with artillery men questioning the use of panzer divisions, with a similar debate in Britain over General Fuller's belief in tanks.

Although wounded by shrapnel he saw the effects of war, but he never experienced the bitter hand-to-hand confrontations suffered by soldiers in the trenches. However, it is noteworthy that even at this stage Keitel had again been noted for staff work probably because of his organising skills with his sense of obedience. He was also part of the artillery world which during this war was seen as highly significant and of growing importance. There is no record of what Keitel felt at the Kaiser's abdication, but his wife in letters to her mother referred to this 'shameful exit from the stage after so many bombastic speeches'.[13] Keitel, as an officer, never mentioned this issue.

Early Interbellum Years

Keitel, like many able contemporaries, was retained in the Reichswehr (the official name of the German forces) of the Weimar Republic and helped organise the paramilitary Freikorps on the Polish border. He also lectured at the Hanover Cavalry School and was used in varying ways until 1924, when he transferred to the Ministry of Reichswehr serving in the Truppenamt (Office of Troops), which was the disguised German General Staff, often referred to as the T2 organisation. When in 1925 Field Marshal Hindenburg was made president, there started a gradual movement towards the right-wing, which was welcomed by the vast majority of the traditional military senior men. It was a time when Keitel, in a letter to his father-in-law complained about the dangers of the left-wing, the 'flaming red torch of socialism' which was a common thread running through many in the army.[14] The area in which he worked was concerned about raising reserves for the numerically weak forces, caused by the restrictions of the Versailles Treaty, as the Germans were desperately working in a clandestine fashion to rebuild their military. General Seeckt was reorganising the army so that the seven infantry divisions permitted by the Versailles Treaty could be promptly trebled. The T2 work was to accomplish this and keep an eye on the disputed Polish borders.

It was during this time that Keitel first worked on possible plans for the three forces of the army, navy, and air force to work under a single command structure. This concept of the OKW would come and go, but it was more of a dream world as it was known that Göring, head of the developing Luftwaffe, was looking to be the military supremo, the navy had always valued its independence, and the army had a tradition of being the prime service.

It was during this time that Keitel met General von Blomberg again, and also General Werner von Fritsch. The latter, when Commander-in-Chief of the army, supported Keitel for promotion to various positions. For a brief time in 1927 Keitel was appointed to a field-command, and he was soon made lieutenant colonel in 1929 and assigned to the Ministry of War. He was soon promoted, and back again in T2, but this time as Head of the Organisational Department an area he had worked in before, but now a senior post which he held until 1933 when Hitler took power.

During this time, in 1931, Keitel with others paid a friendly visit to the Soviet Union, because the two internationally deemed pariah states were co-operating on building up their military forces. The Germans, who often arrived in civilian clothes to stop arousing suspicion, were shown only what the Soviets wanted them to see. He was impressed by what he observed in the Soviet Union, writing to his father (29 September 1931) describing the Russian economy and the important status given to their army.[15] He and others were under the impression that the Soviet Union consisted 'of a two-pillar structure of Party and Army, each with equal rights'.[16] This was far from any reality, but the Soviet propaganda worked. The German military were happy to use Soviet Russia and fascist Italy as places to plan and experiment, and countries like Spain, Sweden and the Netherlands for economic reasons were happy to build new types of weapons and resources for the new German military. Even in Japan new submarines were being designed and built under the supervision of the German navy.

During the following year of 1932 Keitel developed a pain in his right leg, which transpired to be a phlebitis or thrombosis which is a serious medical issue of blood clotting. Typically, Keitel continued to walk to his office seeming unperturbed. However, it soon became a serious heart condition and for a time he either had a heart attack, or was in danger from one, which coupled with pneumonia was life-threatening. His wife Lisa developed heart problems at the same time and a period of convalescence was needed. He was in a clinic in the High Tatra mountains (Czechoslovakia) when Hindenburg appointed Hitler as Chancellor (30 January 1933) where Keitel, as a German officer was questioned by the locals about the person Adolf Hitler, who was the twenty-first Reich Chancellor since 1919, and not that well-known outside Germany. Keitel later wrote, post-war, that 'I said that whether he was really suited to be Reich Chancellor seemed highly questionable to me'.[17] For many Germans there was a degree of uncertainty about the figure of Hitler on the national scene, not helped by the fear of the ever-present SA, but criticism was soon repressed by dread of retaliation. The country was experiencing a serious clash between those of the left-wing, especially communists, and a new right-wing version led by Hitler. For military men promising to stay out of politics and only interested in re-establishing the military, opinions were just as divided, but tended to look towards Hitler as an enigma which could be controlled. This was a mistake made by the more powerful nationalistic figures who, like some in the military world, would later wonder what they had unleashed. There seems little doubt that Keitel's wife distrusted the NSDAP and Hitler, and although Keitel veered towards authoritarian leadership, he remained uncertain until he heard Hitler captivate a massive audience with one of his speeches. He was deeply involved in the military's building up a secret reserve which when utilised could triple the size of the army. Keitel never expressed any clear political views, and genuinely seemed apolitical, and according to his wife was overburdened with desk work.[18] However, she noted in a letter to her mother that her husband having heard Hitler 'was thoroughly rejuvenated and full of energy', and it was probably Keitel's own right-wing inclinations which attracted him to Hitler.[19] Like many other military men there was always the hope that Hitler would correct the perceived wrongs of the Treaty of Versailles. In October 1933, Keitel was appointed as a deputy commander of an infantry Division, and in 1934 given command of a Division at Potsdam. He could not, however, have been oblivious to the fact that on Hitler's arrival, even medal-bearing Jewish officers and soldiers were being expelled from the military, that officers and men alike were forbidden to marry non-Ayran women, and the growing mistreatment of Jews on the public streets was obvious to everyone.

It was during this period that his memoirs offer some insight into what has become known as the Night of the Long Knives, although, as in all memoirs, they must be treated with caution. He recorded having constant visits by a SA-General Ernst (who had once been an apprentice waiter) constantly asking Keitel if he needed any help guarding the arms depots, because his SA men were all too willing to assist. Keitel was suspicious and raised the issue as to whether a putsch was being planned, but how aware he was of the politics behind these events is impossible to ascertain. There were rumours that Röhm the head of the SA wanted control of the army as his SA was massive, and it is known that Göring and Himmler had been working on Hitler against Röhm because of his growing influence, intimating a degree of jealousy for their own personal futures. Hitler had every intention of ensuring he was the leader and would not tolerate any interference in his plan, and personally led the night of brutal vengeance resulting in the death of Röhm, Ernst, and over eighty others. When Keitel heard they had all been killed on the spot he later wrote, 'why the guilty parties were not made to stand trial by court martial but were simply shot is beyond my comprehension'.[20] Hitler had behaved illegally by taking the law into his own hands, behaving like a tyrant, and although Keitel wondered why court procedures had not been followed, he naturally accepted the situation. According to Field Marshal von Rundstedt, Blomberg had shown Keitel a list of the men who were to be arrested, indicating Keitel may have been aware of the political background.[21] He had attended a Nazi rally with Blomberg and, like many others, was overly impressed with the sense of order, the marching, the drums, and the banners.

In the spring of 1934, his father died, and he inherited the estate at Helmscherode. He thought about the life on the estate he had often dreamed off and even applied to resign. His wife Lisa did not get along well with her father-in-law's second wife, so Keitel met no encouragement from Lisa to leave the army since it would mean the two women living together.[22] In 1940 he managed to acquire his sister's share of the estate, and also paid his brother off for his part. He had by 1934 intended to leave the army and take on the estate, something which he later regretted not doing.[23] Keitel was evidently valued because of his organisational skills and hard work, and soon heard that General von Fritsch had offered him a command near Helmscherode, evidently an offer to tempt him with home close by, but Keitel selected one at Bremen and withdrew his resignation. At this stage it was seen by some observers that he preferred being in command of troops rather than an important desk in the bureaucracy, but undoubtedly, he stayed on because he enjoyed being amongst the elite and thereby pleasing his wife.

Interbellum Years under Hitler

In 1935 Keitel was recommended to be promoted to major general by General von Fritsch to succeed Reichenau, and thereby appointed Chief of the Reich Ministry of War's Armed Forces Office (Wehrmachtsamt). This was the office intended for overseeing army, navy and air force, the effort to unify the armed forces. Keitel claimed that he wanted to stay in his command, but his ambitious wife Lisa urged him to accept the offer.[24] He was now in a prominent post which would lead to further promotion and the ladder to an appalling humiliating death. Had he retired or stayed as field commander he may have survived the war or at least died under better circumstances. On 1 January 1936, he was promoted to lieutenant general, in time to see the occupation of the Rhineland (7 March 1936). Keitel later claimed that he thought this venture too risky as the French might oppose, which he knew would not have been easy for the smaller German force to resist. Konstantin von Neurath the foreign minister for Germany at that time was brought in to discuss with Hitler the situation, and Keitel was there for the first time. In his memoirs he made no mention of how he felt about Hitler, but he noted that 'Hitler had played with fire and won'.[25] This was to be an issue for Keitel, because like many people success rules out criticism and can create a pathway to disaster.

The Ministry of War's (no longer the Ministry of Defence) Armed Forces Office where he was now working had its own tensions, not least the difficulty of command. It was anticipated that this central office could give instructions to the three services, but it was not a simple task. It had, as noted above, been an idea worked on by Keitel and others for a long time. In Britain, the Chief of the Imperial General Staff also tried to organise co-operation between the three services; it was not always easy, but generally it worked with a few tensions. In Germany, the Army had its own General Staff; the Kriegsmarine as with the Royal Navy in Britain had a proud record of Admirals to organise the fleets; and in Germany the head of the Luftwaffe was Göring who no one would try to override. In his memoirs Keitel recalled the tensions when Blomberg called for the armed forces to hold joint manoeuvres. Blomberg, Keitel and Jodl had all hoped it would resolve any conflict between the services. The army generals promptly opposed any such plans and moves, raising questions and suggesting alternatives, which at times were contentious and quite bitter. Eventually a manoeuvre was successfully enacted in front of international guests such as Mussolini and even the British Chief of Imperial General Staff. It was an opportunity to show growing German military power. They proudly demonstrated their fleet, submarines, aircraft, and the army with their light tanks (machine-guns only). It was obviously an attempt to impress Mussolini, and perhaps even a warning to the British, because under Hitler it could not be regarded as an effort at friendly neighbourliness, even if that were the proposed picture. The chances of a united OKW were always remote (until the final months of the war) which suited Hitler who always worked on the divide and rule principle, leaving him as the top man.

Keitel's status was growing, but not his power, and he was even sent an invitation by Göring to join him in some deer-hunting. Keitel had some social life, possibly more to please his wife, and in an unpublished diary manuscript he mentioned the social functions which he had with visiting foreigners who were sniffing around to see what was happening. He did, however, enjoy the company of Oshima the Japanese military attaché. His work indicated he was closer to the political scene than he always pretended, and along with Blomberg they had instructed that politically suspect officers and men should be dismissed from the military, and the Gestapo informed of their names. A year later they produced a scheme to improve relationships between the Nazi Party and the army; this effort was a result of some tensions which had arisen between army personnel and the SA.

By 1 October 1937, he had reorganised and enlarged the Armed Forces Office with what he considered all the necessary components. Given his propensity for hard work and detail he was probably correct, and he was a key functionary in establishing the work habits of what would be the OKW, but no one had counted on Hitler's desired grip on all power.

In terms of the Far East, Keitel was aware that Hitler had sent various officers to China, regarding it as a good economic resource. However, in seeing Japan as a future ally, Hitler suddenly insisted that the links with China were to be severed, and even Chiang Kai-shek's son, an officer in the Munich infantry regiment was sent packing home. When General von Seeckt returned from China, Keitel had the task of explaining the new policy to him. He recalled how shocked Seeckt appeared, pointing out to Keitel that Chiang Kai-shek was bitterly anti-communist. There was nothing that could be done because Hitler was now firmly in charge.

At a personal family level in January 1938, the engagement between Keitel's son Lieutenant Karl-Heinz and Dorothea (Dorle) von Blomberg was announced. The historian Görlitz said Keitel was aiming at an *entente* with his superior Blomberg, which may well have been true, but these two men had little in common, and there was no warm relationship between them, only business.[26] However, at the time and since, many had seen the marriage as a useful arrangement for Keitel and a pathway to further promotion, how far this was true may never be known.

In the same month as the Armed Forces Office was expanding under its Chief General Blomberg, disaster struck. Blomberg had lost his wife Charlotte in 1932 and remarried a younger wife called Erna (or Eva) Gruhn. Keitel had been aware that Blomberg kept disappearing from the office, dressed in civilian clothes, and wondered what he was up to. Keitel had asked Blomberg's adjutant Major von der Decken who simply and loyally just shrugged his shoulders. It eventually dawned on Keitel that Blomberg intended to marry again. It was a small civil wedding, Hitler and Göring invited as witnesses, but not Keitel, underlining the nature of their flimsy relationship. Curiously, it was almost a secret wedding, no public at all, begging the question whether this was because Blomberg had some knowledge of the problems associated with his new wife.

The honeymoon was broken off because Blomberg's mother was taken seriously ill and died. Fairly quickly after this marriage, Keitel was visited by the Chief of Police, Count von Helldorf who revealed he had a police dossier on Blomberg's second wife, who since 1932 (when Blomberg's first wife had died) had a police record for posing in pornographic photographs and worked as a prostitute. He asked Keitel if the police file photograph was Blomberg's wife, but Keitel had only seen her at Blomberg's mother's funeral, where she had a traditional veil over her face. Keitel unsure what to do, or possibly with other motives passed the file to the power greedy Göring. Blomberg was in a cleft stick: Göring was threatening to go public, and Hitler demanded he renounced his wife or resign, which he did on 27 January 1938. This all provided an opportunity for the senior Nazis to clean their military cupboard and ensure the power was vested in Hitler with Göring and Himmler's powers increased. Later Blomberg would lay the blame for the whole episode at the feet of Göring, though perhaps Keitel might have used his influence to tell Count von Helldorf to lose the file as it was a personal matter. For all their criminal activity it often suited the leading Nazis to be puritanical when it suited them, even though Hitler's possible affair with his niece had been known to some, and Keitel must have been aware of this which for most people would have raised some questions.

This was all to Hitler's liking, because he had every intention of ridding himself of any general who may have taken a stand against his plans for war. Blomberg's natural successor was General von Fritsch, but he was already preparing for a court case under paragraph 175 of the criminal code accusing him of homosexuality (they were known as 175ers). It transpired to be a plot by Göring and Himmler to be rid of Fritsch having rid themselves of Blomberg, thereby creating more space for their influence and ensuring the military followed Nazi policies. Fritsch challenged Himmler to a duel, he was found not guilty but left his command, dying in September 1939 during the invasion of Poland. Keitel did not always appear in a favourable light during these scandals, criticised by General Westphal as the one soldier who had close contact with Hitler, but who 'did nothing to expose and neutralise the vile machinations of Himmler. In the Fritsch affair Keitel failed unforgivably.'[27]

While all these shenanigans were taking place Keitel was summoned by Göring to discuss replacements for Blomberg, and then Hitler also called for Keitel's suggestions. Various names were proposed, but after many discussions, as is well known, Hitler took command of the Wehrmacht in 1938, replaced the War Ministry with the OKW. Keitel was to be its chief-of-staff from February 1938, with Hitler as Commander-in-Chief. Hitler had surrounded himself with men of rank and presumed power, but it was an entire farce as he now controlled all. Hitler assured others that Keitel was not his deputy, he would have no authority to issue orders to the service commands, and he was solely routine administration. He may have probably based these outlines of functions on von Rundstedt's advice who claimed that Hitler had consulted him. Rundstedt had warned Hitler that Keitel knew nothing of the navy and 'he would not dare tangle with Göring's Luftwaffe' and should be army only.[28] The concept of the OKW had fallen apart in its original theoretical premise, and replaced by the politician Hitler who simply controlled all three of the services, and hereafter Keitel's future was focused on Hitler's demands on the long road to the gallows. Hitler had achieved his aim: as one of his many biographers wrote, 'Hitler no longer needed to act – as he saw it – through a maze of restrictive senior figures in the military in order to get what he wanted done.'[29] Hitler was sending out a clear signal that he had no intention of delegating power which was all invested in him. Jodl was one step below Keitel as Hitler's personal Chief-of-Staff. Following the Blomberg affair there was little chance for a unified armed forces command because Hitler had established his dictatorship over the military. On 4 February 1938, after lengthy discussions and interviews, von Brauchitsch had been appointed Commander-in-Chief of the Army, for the same reasons as Keitel because he was much more pliable than his successors.

Post-war Keitel said he had been stunned by being made Chief of the OKW, and agreed he had made mistakes, but he argued, from the moment Hitler took control that any form of restraint or objection was difficult. He wrote that 'it would have been equally impossible for any other general even if he had been far tougher, far more critical and intelligent than I, to have halted our landslide into misfortune.'[30] Keitel knew he was surrounded by critics but no one else, he argued, would have wanted his post, which was probably true. It was not just his being the dictator's blotting pad, but he was now ordained to give Hitler's orders under his signature and authority of the OKW; he was in a bizarre if not misconstrued position of power. On Keitel's recommendation, Brauchitsch had chosen Keitel's brother Bodewin (died 1953) as new Chief of Army Personnel to replace Schwedler.* It was seen as nepotism by some, and this naturally produced criticism from many observers, especially at a time when General Beck and others were demanding that Fritsch be reinstated. The respected General von Manstein was scathing about

---

* Bodewin was appointed as head of the *Heerespersonalamt*, namely as Military Secretary.

all the appointment adjustments, thinking Hitler had been ill-advised, claiming that Keitel's brother's appointment 'was Brauchitsch's first fatal step'.[31] Later Keitel claimed his main concern was that he did not lose Hitler's trust. There was no question that from the earliest of times, Keitel had not only accepted Hitler as the sole ruler, but he had dedicated his professional life to serving him.

In March 1938, Keitel had been aware of the Fritsch trial and acquittal. He heard that Hitler had ordered the false witness and accuser to be shot, but Canaris quietly informed him that this had not happened, implying the witness must have been a plant. A further implication had to be that the prosecution had been planned and plotted by prominent figures in the regime (undoubtedly by Himmler and Göring), but this evident possibility went unnoticed by Keitel, probably out of career motivations. He was very busy as he had been told the Austrian military had to be worked into the War office, a huge amount of work for which he was responsible.

This all started on 8 March 1938, when Keitel had been summoned to the Berchtesgaden, where Hitler was bullying the Austrian Chancellor Kurt von Schuschnigg into the *Anschluss*. Keitel had not been invited to take part in the meeting and had no input. He was simply part of the wallpaper, a silent backdrop. Keitel later admitted that Hitler told him he was invited 'so Schuschnigg would see a few uniforms around'.[32] 'The presence of Keitel and other generals was not lost on the Austrian Chancellor' as their appearance was intimidating.[33] It was all part of Hitler's technique, and this became a habit for Keitel of being the silent but sinister figure in the background. Keitel was the ideal prop with his height, burly build, jutting chin, and stern looks, and for him the 'The Führer became unconsciously a kind of Ersatz-Kaiser'.[34] One of Hitler's biographers quoted Papen's account of this meeting: 'Hitler lost his temper, flung open the door, and, turning Schuschnigg out, shouted for General Keitel. According to Papen, when Keitel hurried up and asked for Hitler's orders, Hitler grinned and said, "There are no orders I just wanted you here."'[35] It was Hitler's ploy to terrify his victim, and Keitel, probably without realising that he was one of Hitler's weapons. It was noted by one of Hitler's biographers that during this time Keitel received many phone calls from generals, including Brauchitsch to persuade Hitler not to take Austria, but:

> Keitel, who was already well aware of the sensitivities of his new boss, didn't mention anything of these calls to Hitler. Even the night before the event Keitel was asked by a General von Viebahn to call the operation off. Keitel explained he could not because he knew it would upset the Führer and mar his relationship with the Army. It was immediately clear that Keitel regarded himself as Hitler's servant and carer. He knew Hitler would be outraged at the caution of the army chiefs, and 'he wanted to spare' all concerned 'that experience'.[36]

After the meeting Keitel was instructed to prepare for the *Anschluss*, so he went to find General Beck as Brauchitsch was away, both feeling somewhat shocked that no plans had been asked for previously. There was no major pre-planning and a high degree of confusion. Post-war he admitted to Colonel Dr Bohuslav Ecer in the Judge Advocate's Office on 3 August 1945, that 'at the bottom of my heart I was a loyal shield-bearer for Adolf Hitler; my political conviction would have been National Socialist'.[37] Even if this meant he was a mere image in the background he remained devoted to his master being impressed by the *Anschluss*, seeing himself as 'an eyewitness to history'. There was a sense of relief that the occupation of Austria involved no bloodshed and did not provoke war; it was seen as a total victory for Hitler.

In his new post Keitel was not the Reichsminister as Blomberg had been, but he was given the status of cabinet rank level, but with no substantive power. Technically in his office, with oversight of all three services, at least theoretically, life was not easy because he was therefore Göring's boss which was sheer nonsense. This overlapping of power was confusing which Hitler always wanted as it strengthened his position as a dictator, using the old policy of divide and rule. Between 1935–39 Keitel was merely the logistics man, the prime organiser ensuring the nuts and bolts were provided and helping to re-establish the German military. It was Keitel who had persuaded Hitler to appoint Walther von

Brauchitsch as Commander-in-Chief of the Army replacing von Fritsch, and Keitel himself was now promoted to Colonel General. In 1939 he was awarded the Golden Party Badge by Hitler, which underlined that Hitler saw in Keitel a party member who would obey, by encouraging his loyalty by giving him a political award which was unusual in German military tradition. This so-called honour may have dated back to the time when Keitel had tried to ease relationships between the Army and the Party. Either way, it was a sure sign that Hitler saw him as a Party man despite the fact he pretended to be above politics. Hitler had rid himself of Blomberg and Fritsch because he believed they stood in the way of his plans; he needed a faithful military servant like Keitel as his formal cover.

On 20 April 1938, Keitel was considered loyal enough to take part in Hitler's birthday celebration. On the same evening he was instructed by Hitler to prepare for General Staff studies for a possible conflict with Czechoslovakia. Hitler informed Keitel that German speakers in that country, left there after the Treaty of Versailles, were being oppressed, claiming his main concern was that the Russians would use Czechoslovakia as a springboard for invasion. Keitel then and later did not have any qualms about the veracity of Hitler's views, and he and Jodl started the work while concealing it from the Army Staff. From this point on there could have been no question in Keitel's mind that Hitler was preparing for war and using himself and Jodl to assist. When General Beck heard about the plans from Brauchitsch he had no doubt in his mind about Hitler's intentions. He promptly wrote a memo that France may well intervene if Czechoslovakia were invaded. Keitel's immediate response was to warn Brauchitsch not to make Beck's views known, because it would anger Hitler and put Brauchitsch into his bad books. Beck had the courage to make his views known, but Keitel, often described as 'the filter' did his best to keep the peace between Hitler and those generals who disagreed with his policies. Beck had principles, but it never seemed to dawn on Keitel that he deemed his first and only duty to please Hitler, and he was too scared to raise issues which should be discussed in the national interests.

The likelihood of a war was increasing, and Göring reported that their Western defence line was not going well in terms of its construction. Hitler was furious, but, as Keitel observed, this construction, which had been started in Blomberg's time, was always considered a 20-year plan. Hitler transferred the gigantic construction to Major General Fritz Todt, and demanded the work was finished as soon as possible. This was yet another clear indicator that Hitler intended hostilities, and a few critics with the necessary courage made their views known. The reaction was immediate, and on 30 September 1938, Beck left his office and Halder took his place. There were considerable internal machinations and chatter as to whether Hitler was going in the wrong direction, and even if he were the right leader. Keitel, somewhat selfishly, was not sad to see Beck's departure because he always believed that Beck had treated him badly, which was probably true, because Beck recognised in Keitel the figure of Hitler's obedient military servant.

The summer of 1938 was taken up with planning an attack on Czechoslovakia, given the code name of *Green Contingency*. The main issue was the question of assembling troops without making public that mobilisation was happening. It was decided to use the old ruse of large-scale manoeuvres which meant they could call up reservists. Keitel thought Halder was good because he managed it without raising suspicions. He described how Hitler poured over the projected plans about Czechoslovakia, demanding the need for armoured divisions to 'thunder' towards Prague. Halder disagreed, telling Keitel that he refused to make such changes. Brauchitsch was asked to talk to Hitler, but he refrained, again clearly demonstrating that even top generals already feared the dictator or were concerned at keeping their status; they did not dare raise objections.

During September 1938 there were the well-known Munich peace discussions started by Chamberlain, with the French and British both alert to the potential dangers. Hitler was aware that Daladier and the French were reluctant to fight over Czechoslovakia, and his experts had warned him that the British military were not ready for any major continental conflict. Keitel was asked to attend but played no part in the diplomatic drama, once again he was Hitler's wallpaper, more like a curious bystander he stood tall and somewhat daunting in the background.

When the diplomatic dust had settled Hitler was still demanding changes, proposing plans to occupy the whole of Czechoslovakia, so Keitel left the Nuremberg rally which he had been attending in order to see Halder, explaining the plans needed to be changed. Brauchitsch said he refused, and Keitel knew he would have to tell Hitler. Hitler demanded Halder and Brauchitsch attend him at Nuremberg where he lost his patience, demanding they did what they were ordered over his demand for armoured thrusts. Brauchitsch co-operated, and Keitel asked, 'Why did you fight with him, when you know that the battle is lost before it's begun?'[38] Keitel was acknowledging, as he would do for the rest of his life, that once Hitler had an idea no one could challenge him or persuade him otherwise. It was dangerous even to raise issues in Hitler's company, and Keitel rarely deviated from the policy of total acquiescence. He later suggested Hitler had wanted to win over Czechoslovakia as an ally, but failed, but such a view by Hitler seems highly unlikely, he simply wanted to dominate.

As such, in late October 1938, Hitler decided to occupy the whole country, although Keitel claimed he did not think a war was likely, which was questionable. They looked at the Czech defence walls which were not unlike the Maginot Line, so they practised on them with the 88-mm anti-aircraft guns which proved highly effective. Working under Hitler as a task master was proving strenuous for Keitel, who wrote that 'with my appointment as chief of the OKW I ceased to be a free man', claiming he had no personal time left, as Hitler was always demanding to see him for one reason or another.[39]

While this was all unfolding, Blomberg with his new wife in Italy, asked Keitel to send his son to him; he was at the time a lieutenant in the Luftwaffe. Keitel obliged and when the son returned, he carried a letter from his father. It was a letter which Keitel felt he had to show to Hitler, because Blomberg had written that he would leave his wife if Hitler would have him back in his military role. Hitler's response was immediately negative, claiming Blomberg had made up his mind, and that was the end of the matter; it was also the end of Blomberg in command as far as Hitler was concerned.*

Keitel felt the whole episode dampened family relations, and when Dorothea and Karl-Heinz married in May, Keitel had to stand in the role of both fathers. Keitel noted that already people were keeping their distance from him, his sons were busy in the army, his daughter Nona worked at home, Erika was a partygoer, and with him always busy it was a lonely existence for his wife. She understood the nature of his work and kept silent, and friends and acquaintances knew that Keitel was hardly a social person with all the secrets he carried. Outside his office his only interest was organising the work done on the homestead he had inherited, including the restoration of the chapel as Keitel was a traditional Protestant.

By February 1939, the machinations over the Czech situation were growing, and Keitel was organising the military, later claiming that senior officers, including himself, were told little of diplomatic interchanges. Despite this claim he witnessed the treatment of Emil Hacha without seeing it as bullying, although when Hacha fell ill because of the pressure, Keitel admitted that he felt sorry for him. Keitel may have been Hitler's choice of wallpaper for this meeting, but Hitler would often turn to Keitel and asked if he agreed, which was always answered in the affirmative.[40] Hitler's triumphant entry into Prague is well known and Keitel kept him company, and saw Hitler drink a tiny glass of beer which was very unusual. Konstantin Neurath was announced as the Protector of Bohemia and Moravia, which Keitel claimed he found 'unedifying'.

The increasing pace of Hitler's bellicose plans for the future became more apparent when in April 1939, Hitler started to raise more questions over Poland. He claimed that he did not want war but told Keitel that 'he who desired peace must prepare for war', and promptly started to demand war-footing by 1 September, avoiding signs of mobilisation. Keitel spent these summer months of 1939 travelling up and down to the

---

* Efforts were made to encourage Blomberg to commit suicide, but he refused. He lived in obscurity during the war, he was found by the Allies, but died from cancer in 1946.

Berchtesgaden, as preparations were made. The work did not worry him or the prospect of war, and in his memoirs, he was more bothered that other attenders had homes or places to work within Hitler's Berchtesgaden. He noted the heads of the Reich Chancery and Party Chancery had their own offices, as did Göring, Ribbentrop, while only the OKW lacked such facilities. Later Keitel found space for himself, but not for the OKW office, which was evidently because of 'Hitler's desire to make all his decisions himself and to sabotage any kind of community of effort'.[41] There were concerns expressed at army level which Keitel later claimed he conveyed to Hitler, namely that the army were still re-equipping, but Hitler always brushed this aside. As the Polish invasion was worked on, the Western defence wall was developing, and Hitler toured the construction with Keitel in his entourage. Hitler had studied the plans, and everyone was impressed by his memory as he seemed to know where he was going. It was also a clear indicator that Hitler had realised an attack on Poland might start a war on their Western borders, and Keitel probably had the same thought, though he would later vehemently deny such knowledge.

Keitel was summoned by Hitler on 25 August 1939, who had been shocked by Mussolini's refusal to join in the projected war despite the Pact of Steel. It was claimed by Mussolini that the Italian king would not sign the mobilisation order which was his prerogative. Hitler was concerned that because of Italy standing back, Britain would back Poland. Mussolini said he needed resources, and when the Germans looked at his shopping directory even Hitler thought the list was deliberately too long. Hitler called Brauchitsch and Halder in, but meanwhile the British and French had renewed their treaty with Poland. Hitler read his demands to Poland to Keitel who thought they were moderate, and Daladier wrote imploring Hitler as an old soldier to avoid war. Hitler's typical response was to regard this message from Daladier as a sign of weakness. Keitel for his part later said the German-Soviet Pact (23 August) would make sure Poland acquiesced, though since the secret protocol had not been made public, it made Keitel's view appear not just unrealistic but like an excuse.

On 30 August 1939, Hitler appointed Keitel to a six-person Council of Ministers for the Defence of the Reich, a form of war cabinet in theory. It was small and intended that way as they would do as the dictator demanded. Keitel was always with Hitler, but this closeness never intimated friendship or close association. The argument over General List and Jodl will be surveyed later in the text, but it is mentioned now to demonstrate that there was no personal friendship between Hitler, Keitel and Jodl, although a degree of growing adoration of Hitler by Keitel.

Chapter Two

The Second World War

Keitel later wrote that as the attack on Poland started there had been no formal declaration of war 'against all our advice'.[1] It was not that Hitler needed any guidance, but he had arranged for what was known as the Gleiwitz incident in which Germans dressed as Poles had attacked a radio station, thus offering the obvious pretence it was a war of defence, which even at the time no one would have believed. Keitel ignored this in his memoirs but knew what had occurred, and he persisted in claiming he was mainly ignorant of what was happening in the political diplomatic world at this time, as the war office had left Berlin for the eastern front. It also became clear during the Nuremberg Trial that Keitel was well aware of the incident, and he was one of the cogs for arranging the supply of Polish uniforms to the SS.[2] He later stated that 'I personally don't hold with such things, of course, but it is the Führer's will and that's that.'[3] All Keitel did at this stage was formally declare war on the Poles but even that was retrospective. Even the prison psychologist noted that when the Gleiwitz radio station was mentioned when talking with Keitel, that 'this struck a sensitive spot and Keitel bristled'.[4]

Keitel later wrote in his prison memoirs that he thought the intervention of Mussolini and Roosevelt could have prevented the prolongation of the war, indicating either shifting the blame or demonstrating he had yet to understand Hitler's real nature. He used the expression that 'we were fobbed off' by Hitler claiming that England and France were unjustified in meddling in what was not their business.[5] Hitler explained that in his opinion any fears about England and France were groundless, England was not prepared, and the French were all pacifists, and it was just a matter of sabre-rattling. News from the western front, according to Keitel seemed to indicate that Hitler was probably right, as they only heard of minor skirmishes after the West declared war, namely the inactivity of the Phoney War.

Keitel then made the claim that 'Hitler seldom intervened in the Commander-in-Chiefs' conduct of the battle' which given that he wrote his memoirs post-war, indicated how flimsy his accounts were, vacillating between painting Hitler in a better light, as if defending his indefensible obedience.[6] As the Polish forces fell back under the onslaught, Keitel with others made several visits into Poland, describing 'the impressive picture of the Polish casualties', and hearing about the death of General von Fritsch shot while talking to other commanders. Keitel just managed to make it back for Fritsch's state funeral and laid a wreath on behalf of Hitler who was too busy. He described how one general had prepared a banquet in the Führer's honour, but Hitler on seeing the lavishness of the meal promptly flew off again, stating he only expected a field-kitchen. Later Brauchitsch confided in Keitel that the meal had been a remarkable success even without Hitler. The founder of the feast was General Johannes Blaskowitz who had protested at the atrocities committed by the SS, and the inhuman treatment of the Poles and Jews. It may well have been Blaskowitz's views more than the banquet which caused Hitler's sudden exit. Blaskowitz was not the only one to be astounded at the treatment of Jews and Poles, and Canaris spoke to Keitel about the situation, but Keitel told him it was the Führer's directive and policy.[7] Some senior officers were concerned it tainted the image of the Wehrmacht, and one of Himmler's biographers expressed it as Keitel not understanding the problem, because 'the Führer had arranged for the SS to carry out the tasks specifically so that the Wehrmacht would not have to dirty its hands'.[8] It is not surprising that Keitel's memoirs refer only to that which he regarded as 'safe'. In the Nuremberg Trial one major witness confirmed that Keitel 'had given the order to do away with General Weygand', which if true indicates a more sinister role than a passive follower of Hitler's orders, as this was evidently an illegal and immoral order, and not part of the German military code.[9] The accusation was later made that Keitel had instructed that General Henri Giraud, who had escaped German captivity, should be assassinated, to avoid assisting any French resistance.[10] Whether Keitel was signing more orders for Hitler or acting on his own initiative is unknown.

Later, in March 1941, Keitel's guidelines noted that the Reichsführer-SS would not be subordinate to the Wehrmacht, most probably because the regular army 'could distance itself from the renewed and extended mass murders'.[11] In September 1941, the infamous massacre of Jews at Babi Yar took place, and Canaris made a formal complaint to Keitel who had to find more than a vague answer, replying, 'These objections accord with soldierly conceptions of a chivalrous war…what matters here is the destruction of an ideology'.[12] Canaris, like Beck, was a man of principle and Hitler's regime had not hoodwinked him, he could see it was immoral and was not in the national interests. Canaris could see through all the drums, banners and all the gloss that Nazism was immoral and illegal, and time and time again he tried to convince Keitel of the truth, but never succeeded. Keitel was all too aware of SS behaviour, and on 9 August 1942 in the Führer's headquarters, Himmler in the presence of senior men, including Keitel, had discussed the question of ethnic policy in the west.[13] Keitel accepted it all on the grounds that he was obedient to the government as encapsulated in Hitler.

In his original manuscripts but not in his published account, Keitel commented on the lack of communications with the invading Soviets, and their concern that the Soviets, who had stopped at the agreed line, had taken the most prisoners. He also drew attention to the Soviet massacre of leading Poles at Katyń, in the full knowledge that Himmler and Hitler were doing the same thing.

As Hitler turned his attention to the West there began the well-known dispute between Hitler and the generals as to when to start this conflict. Keitel found himself siding with his military colleagues. He listed Hitler's reasons but found himself in conflict with Hitler who accused him of conspiring with the generals against him. Keitel offered his resignation, but Hitler turned him down. Others recorded a more heated discussion, describing it as a major altercation during 'which Hitler hurled mad reproaches at Keitel who, deeply wounded, babbled about suicide, and took himself off…after the break, however, all was healed. The incident is not significant. It is at most, symptomatic.'[14] This was a major incident for Keitel and probably marked a significant moment, as thereafter he rarely raised an issue with Hitler which might be confrontational. It was clear that his career came first.

In the occupation of Denmark and Norway, because it involved all three forces, the OKW took a leading hand, mainly through Jodl's planning, whereas the army command had dealt with Poland, and also France but under Hitler's direction. In his memoirs Keitel started to praise the way Hitler handled the military situation. Like many others he had been surprised at the weak allied response and the collapse of the French who had the largest army in Europe. He noted that Hitler's sense of strategy included the armoured break through to Sédan, which originated with General von Manstein's ideas. Keitel thought the OKW was functioning well, although he admitted he was never allowed to make decisions. He had another minor clash with Hitler over the plans to place the administration in occupied Norway away from the military, and he claimed he even walked out of the room. Later when he spoke to the Führer on the matter, he admitted he could make no headway. There was no point in arguing with Hitler, with Keitel writing in his memoirs that Hitler 'really was exercising the Supreme Command and that he was the warlord behind the operation'.[15] Keitel later added that Hitler never detracted from any of the magnificent work done by the General Staff, which is now known to be nonsense. He admired Hitler's attention to detail and his imagination writing 'now, whether I liked it or not, I had to learn to adapt myself to his system,' which he did.[16] Not in the published memoirs but in his prison manuscript, he gave a brief account of his youngest son Hans-Georg who was serving in an artillery regiment in France and who was seriously injured, recovered, but later was fatally wounded in Russia. He was cynical, like many others, that Mussolini joined the war when he deemed it safe, and later became more concerned about Italian involvement. After the defeat of France Keitel declared Hitler 'the greatest warlord of all time' and it was true that 'Hitler succumbed to the delusion that he was a new Caesar'.[17]

In terms of the British, Keitel tried to explain in his memoirs why the onslaught by armour against Dunkirk had been called off, as this was blamed on Hitler by the General Staff. The main concern was that the area could easily be flooded making tanks and other mechanically pulled weapons useless. Keitel claimed the General Staff 'did not have the guts to accept responsibility' and were happy to leave it with Hitler.[18] General Siegfried Westphal in his memoirs thought Hitler had been misled by memories of the Great War, but the sluices in the area were already in German hands, and he noted that Keitel had been sent to reinforce Hitler's orders.[19] The whole question of who ordered the German halt at Dunkirk remains a mystery, with Liddell Hart suggesting that the initial influence probably started with Keitel and Jodl.[20] Keitel described Hitler as 'he who is above reproach of any lack of dash and daring' as innocent, underlining as with many others that at this stage with victory after victory, Hitler was almost deified as a military genius. Keitel toured Paris even being impressed by Hitler's knowledge of architecture.

Keitel conducted the French Armistice under Hitler's orders and demands, and he was pleased to be the master of ceremonies seeing it as the 'climax of my career', but he was only the overseer, and he was not in charge. His emotions, he later claimed were mixed, but like many others he wrote, 'I had a feeling that this was our hour of revenge for Versailles'.[21] Like many Germans, Keitel felt 1918 had been a humiliating and economic disaster, and in his words was now 'blotted out once and for all'.[22] Because of Hitler's seeming successes Keitel like many others tended to elevate Hitler to a perch on Mount Olympus. He also felt a degree of sympathy for his French opposite number General Huntziger, but that was in his memoirs, not in a diary kept at the time. According to the French historian Henri Michel, Keitel, when asked about German refugees in France by Huntziger, suggesting they be left alone, was told by Keitel 'unequivocally that they were warmongers and traitors to Germany and that the extradition of that type of person would be demanded at all costs'.[23] Whether this was Keitel's genuine reaction or Hitler's demand will never be known. Keitel was merely the master of ceremonies as Hitler who took two days away to gloat, leaving Keitel with full instructions.

This was widely known, and Ciano noted that when he was asked to leave the Italian French armistice by Badoglio otherwise it would affect 'the appearance of control which Keitel at Compiegne, did not have'.[24]/*

Keitel, along with others, was later promoted to field marshal, and although he was pleased with the promotion, he later claimed he felt embarrassed because all he had done was sit behind his desk, and as in Poland had only gone to the frontlines when all was safe. Again, as with many other leading military commanders, Keitel was given a gift of 100,000 Reichsmarks which embarrassed him. He placed it in a bank account and left it there, though he never said what others said, namely that this gift was Hitler's way of 'buying them in'. However, there was plenty of evidence that Keitel benefitted financially; Hans Lammers claimed he had a land purchase 'amounting to about one million Reichsmark which was to be added to his estate Herscherede'.[25] The historian Michael Burleigh wrote that Keitel received 764,000 Reichsmark, but the precise figures are difficult to establish.[26] He was far from an impoverished soldier, as a Russian archival source indicated him paying in 250,000 Reichsmark in September 1942. He benefitted financially to a massive extent, and it is known that he increased the size of his land, almost doubling its size.

It was not until 2 July 1940 that Hitler ordered Keitel to announce that the three services were to prepare to occupy Britain, which he signed two weeks later adding the note he expected mid-August to be the time when the plans should be completed.[27] It was then back to the Black Forest to another Todt-built bunker to plan the overthrow of Britain. Keitel noted they were not afraid of the British Army which had been decimated in France, but they were all too aware of the powerful Royal Navy, and the RAF still seemed capable. They realised the English Channel could be potentially dangerous, and, as in Britain, Admiral Pound had warned Churchill it was not the best place to manoeuvre large battleships, this same problem was argued by Admiral Raeder. Nevertheless, they tried to accumulate barges and other vessels to cross the channel, while the

---

* Ciano was Mussolini's foreign minister and son-in-law.

Luftwaffe tried to keep the skies clear of nosey British pilots. It appeared, according to Keitel, that September was considered the best month, and Göring promised to eliminate the RAF in August but failed. More to the point, Keitel, forever in Hitler's presence was gaining the impression that Hitler was having doubts about the whole *Sea Lion* venture. 'The multiplicity of imponderables was too large', in other words there were too many ifs and buts for a clear victory, and Keitel felt that 'Hitler was appalled by the senseless waste of human life'.[28] That the dictator Hitler should be concerned at the possible loss of life was sheer nonsense, and Keitel's views clearly indicated he had lost any sense of proportion when it came to his master. On 12 October Keitel signed one of Hitler's directives:

> The Führer has decided that from now until the spring, preparations for Sea-Lion shall be continued solely for the purpose of maintaining political and military pressure on England.
>
> Should the invasion be reconsidered in the spring or early summer of 1941, orders for a renewal of operational readiness will be issued later. Signed, Keitel.[29]

It was the close of Sea-Lion, not just shelved, but cancelled in January 1942. Keitel spent a few days away hunting and buying agricultural equipment for his farm, and probably in later life wished he had stayed there.

On his return Hitler sent him and Jodl to meet the Italian Marshal Badoglio to see how the Germans could help in the fight in North Africa against the British, but Badoglio turned down the offer for tanks, believing they were not useful in desert conditions. It may well have been, given Badoglio's views, more his distrust of German influence. Mussolini had agreed to air support in this conflict, especially over the key port of Malta. He heard that Hitler wanted to take Gibraltar with Franco's agreement (Operation *Felix*) but Hitler had not realised that both his fellow dictators in Spain and Italy had reservations about Hitler's long-term aims.

However, Keitel was more concerned when Hitler talked to him and Jodl about Russia and a possible war with that country. Keitel pointed out that many of the German divisions were tied down in France and Norway but, as always, Hitler brushed this aside. In a formal interview Keitel heard Hitler's views about the clash of two contrasting ideologies, and that Hitler believed that Russia was preparing to invade Germany. Keitel was still concerned about having sufficient forces, and he quietly spoke to Ribbentrop the foreign secretary, who had been so pleased with his own achievements over the August 1939 pact with Russia. Keitel claimed he then wrote a memorandum on the subject, but Hitler rejected it with anger. Keitel even recalled the tone of his voice, prompting Keitel to offer his resignation, which like the memorandum, was rejected. In a form of justification Keitel's memoirs reveal that he eventually came round to the fact that Hitler was correct about Stalin's intentions, and 'I was forced to concede that he had been right after all in his assessment'.[30] Stalin's greed for power was very much the same as Hitler's but only recognised later. There also probably lurked in Keitel's memory of the Russian army being defeated in the Great War, the purging of Russian generals by Stalin, and the way tiny Finland had managed to fight back. When the German forces were seen gathering on the borders for Operation *Barbarossa*, and spies and diplomats knew what was happening, only Stalin refused to believe it until the attack started. Repeatedly Keitel used the term of a 'preventative attack' trying to justify what was a war of pure aggression. Keitel must have known this at the time and had he and many others bothered to read Hitler's *Mein Kampf*, his 1925 autobiographical manifesto, they may have had a clearer insight into their leader's intentions, especially regarding the so-called *lebensraum* policy. After 1945 as the Cold War started to dominate the political minds, it was again suggested that Hitler was right about *Barbarossa* being a preventative war, but this view was pure political machination. Keitel tried to bolster the view that Hitler was correct by claiming that Russian prisoners-of-war had confirmed this as true, but a starving prisoner will say anything for bread.

Keitel's mind was soon elsewhere as he travelled with Hitler on his pre-*Barbarossa* tour to ensure the doors behind him were secure. He visited Marshal Pétain in Vichy France, then Franco, neither of which were entirely successful, with Hitler stating he would rather have his teeth pulled out than sit with Franco again. Keitel was not involved in the discussions, but he had become a travelling background feature to be seen in Hitler's entourage, always representing German military might. As they were travelling back the news arrived that Mussolini was starting to attack Greece through their client state of Albania. It was another journey to meet Mussolini, and this time Keitel was invited to join the two dictators, but probably for the same reason as he always looked impressive. Mussolini was also able to play these games, and during the meeting a military dispatch was delivered announcing Italian successes. This was undoubtedly at Mussolini's demand, as there were no successes of any significance ever to emerge in the Greek campaign. Hitler this time was correct in his assessment that Mussolini had chosen the wrong time of year to attack, and it would fail. The Italians were seriously short of military resources, and this time Mussolini asked for an armoured division in North Africa. Keitel recognised the fact that at this stage Hitler tended to admire the Italian dictator, and that Mussolini made full use of Hitler, something no German military officer would dare attempt.

It was not long before it was realised that the Italian effort in the Balkans was seriously failing, and Hitler started to investigate ways of sending German troops to assist his Italian friend. This effort to help Mussolini out of trouble occupied Keitel and the OKW, who in cramped offices were now working well, at least according to Keitel. Keitel admitted he worked day and night, never had weekends or holidays, and the only sense of relaxation he had was travelling on different missions when he could not easily be contacted by phone. He was sent by Hitler to places such as Italy, Hungary, Romania, and Bulgaria enjoying the journeys more than the mission.

When the Russian Foreign Secretary Molotov arrived in Berlin, Keitel was present. He later claimed that he heard nothing about the diplomatic interchanges, which was possibly more a line of self-defence in his memoirs. Keitel constantly reminded his readers-to-be that he remained right in believing that Hitler had judged the Russians correctly, and it was a preventative war he was planning. Keitel also noted that because Mussolini had started the Balkan conflicts and needed German help, the attack on Russia would have been more successful than it eventually transpired.

Hitler eventually gave the order for Operation *Barbarossa* in December 1940, though plans had long been under the microscope. Keitel enjoyed this Christmas because he was able to take a break to be with his family on which he wrote notes, but they were removed from the printed edition. It must have been sad as a reflective memory for him because this would be the last Christmas they would ever come together in their home.

Gibraltar still preyed on Hitler's mind, and troops were already being prepared for movement from France, with the Luftwaffe being equally organised. Franco was not agreeable as Keitel noted, he was worried about war with Britain. It was not a direct war Franco was worried about, Britain's resources were already overstretched, but the Royal Navy could create a blockade with Spain, which after its devastating Civil War was heavily dependent on imported food and fuel. It was also a possibility that Franco had looked at the international possibilities, and if Germany fell the repercussions of allowing Germany access to Gibraltar could be immense. Keitel also noted, correctly, that he suspected Admiral Canaris of influencing the Spanish against this venture.*

Hitler promptly dropped the idea and turned back to Russia. When Keitel heard Halder address them all on the plans for *Barbarossa*, he claimed to be stunned at the amount of work which had been done in preparation by the Army Staff. Near the end of March 1941, Hitler had assembled all the necessary commanders to hear his plan in the Reich Chancellery building, and Keitel arranged for all the OKW officials to attend. In his address, Hitler raised the issues as to the reason for war, again as he had done with Keitel, the necessary fight against communism, and rapidly introduced the theme of a preventative war. He then moved onto a highly contentious issue of how the war should be fought, warning his audience that they had to put aside any outdated notions of chivalry, not least because the Bolshevists had long since dropped such outdated

---

* Admiral Canaris, head of the Abwehr (1935–44), was a Hitler supporter until the invasion of Poland, when he became a passive and active resistant element against Nazism.

concepts. The communists ignored the Hague Conventions and they should, he argued, be met with the same fire. He then demanded that Political Commissars were not normal prisoners-of-war and should, be shot on the spot, as they were the backbone of the Soviet ideology, and this action would save German lives. It was nothing short of a political authorisation to commit murder. He added that excesses against Russian civilians would not be a matter of traditional courts martial, and that was left to the discretion of their commanders who knew what Hitler had demanded. Nobody had dared raise any objections to these illegal and immoral orders, but Hitler, suspecting they might, stated as his final words, 'I do not expect my generals to understand me; but I shall expect them to obey my orders'.[31] Having heard or seen Himmler's men in the rear areas restoring so-called order and peace, everyone knew this meant killing civilians and especially Jews, which Keitel never mentioned. Keitel claimed he spoke to Brauchitsch on this matter as it concerned him, and that he and Jodl had tried to raise the issue with Hitler. Keitel wrote that everyone had heard for themselves what was expected, but he had no plans to put it into writing. However, it was circulated by the War Office, and Keitel in his position signed the orders, of which, as he said at Nuremberg, Hitler was the sole author, but because Hitler 'was dead, I alone was called to answer for them by that tribunal'.[32] It was also discovered that Keitel had later signed agreements giving the SS extermination squads permission to operate. Keitel claimed he and Jodl objected, and it is possible that Jodl would have done so more out of jealousy of the SS being seen as military. There is no question that in the planning of *Barbarossa*, all were involved, and none had the courage to object publicly. A General Georg Thomas (one of Keitel's subordinates in the OKW) was asked to explore the economic ramifications of the plans, and he indicated the many problems relating to fuel and rubber supplies. Keitel, on hearing his views dismissed it out of hand, telling Thomas that Hitler would not want to see it, ordering him to produce a more hopeful report. All were guilty of blind obedience to their Führer, expressing their doubts only later in their own defence.

D-Day for *Barbarossa* was set for the 12 May 1941, but other matters had put this on hold. Field Marshal List was marching on Bulgaria, there were diplomatic talks with Yugoslavia to encourage them into the Axis partnership, and the Italians were having problems in Albania even before they reached Greece. Near the end of March, Keitel accompanied Hitler to Vienna where the pact was signed with Yugoslavia, but barely had the ink dried than the Yugoslavian government was overthrown by those opposed to joining the Axis. Keitel and Jodl were called along with Brauchitsch the Army Commander and the Foreign Secretary Ribbentrop to Hitler, who was demanding an instant attack on Yugoslavia. He was evidently furious that all his diplomatic efforts had been overturned by what he saw as foreign rebels. Keitel tried to explain the movement of troops towards the Soviet Union border could not be delayed, that Hitler's suggestion that the Hungarians would help would be weak, and his other idea that List's army in Bulgaria was not strong enough, were all swept aside by Hitler, causing one to wonder why Keitel thought it worth raising in the first place. That this all worked Keitel noted, was the work of the Army General Staff, but he observed that Hitler expressed no thanks. The Hungarian leader Admiral Miklós Horthy was dubious about the help they could offer, but eventually they raised a small army. Keitel praised 'Hitler's dexterity' in persuading Croatia onside, but it was probably more out of fear and growing right-wing tendencies than Hitler. Keitel recalled how their headquarters were in a train from which they successfully guided the Yugoslavian and Greek campaigns, dined with Horthy, and his text effuses a sense of pride the way they handled the Italian military weakness and sorted out the Greek situation. Their main concern was chasing remnants of the British army out of Greece, and then looking to occupy the islands of Crete and Malta. Keitel thought Malta more important which was common sense, but Göring chose Crete probably because it was easier. In Yugoslavia, a bitter partisan war was already emerging.

In June 1941, they were all back in Berlin where Hitler called another meeting about the starting date for *Barbarossa*. Notably he raised the issue of partisans in Yugoslavia using it as a lesson for treating the civilian population too leniently. Keitel indicated in his memoirs that it was about this time it dawned on him that Hitler had a serious obsession about destroying communism. It was a typically biased memoir note, as this must have occurred to him much earlier. By 22 June they all reached the Führer's new headquarters near Rastenburg, the infamous Wolf's Lair, which Jodl described as a mix between a monastery and concentration camp, all the three services were close by for instant communication. By the end of July 1941 Hitler, according to Keitel, felt victory was almost achieved as he believed the Red Army was virtually finished. Keitel noted that Hitler even ordered the resources could be switched in favour of the navy and the Luftwaffe, casting his eye back to the undefeated British. In his memoirs Keitel gave a sketch of life in the Wolf's Lair, and the long and often tedious conferences which always followed, and they all accepted Hitler's line of thinking. Keitel described this as 'this autocrat's disorderly thinking processes and *modus operandi*', written in the safety of his Nuremberg cell.[33] He wrote this after the war, and inadvertently raised the question of why he had not thought this at the time, but took the stance of being the all-too-ready yes-man. Instead, Keitel complained about his workload, and having to deal with thousands of unnecessary trivialities heaped on him by Hitler, who told others to 'ask Keitel'. His name was invoked and used so many times he lost count and sometimes not even known by him, so he claimed. In terms of the OKW life was equally hectic, with Keitel later writing that 'it was designed for Hitler's power and executive authority, with Keitel describing himself as a "chair-borne general"'. After the initial battles tensions arose between Hitler and his army commanders because he suddenly decided to push north and south, and he demanded that armoured forces should be extracted from the drive on Moscow. All the senior military commanders at nearly every level disagreed with this decision, 'except Keitel and Jodl', with Hitler changing an agreed strategy against every professional military judgement.[34]

On one occasion, Hitler, accompanied by Keitel, flew to Army Group Centre to meet the commanders of two tank armies, Generals Hoth and

Guderian.* To his frustration Hitler discovered they outright refused his instructions on the grounds of exhaustion and the need to regroup. Keitel explained there was no way they could check these claims, and Hitler discovered that even awarding them Oak leaves to their Knights' Crosses proved an insufficient bribe. Von Bock the overall commander did not want to lose them and agreed with their arguments. Keitel saw it as a ploy as he believed they were all in disagreement with the overall strategy. Hitler vetoed their next attack to take some high ground in the north based, he argued, on their obsolete tactics of taking the high ground. It was, it appears, more a decision based on his annoyance and as a reminder of who was in charge. Keitel recalled how often he was obliged to listen to Hitler's rantings about insubordinate generals, and there seems little doubt Hitler used him as a sounding board because he was so tame. It also illustrated how some field commanders were prepared to stand up to Hitler, even if men like Keitel obeyed every order without question.

In the meantime, news was percolating through of more serious partisan attacks in the Balkans, and even the resistance fighters in France and Belgium were becoming more active. Keitel blamed it on the British supplying arms and deliberately stirring up trouble. He seemed very much in line with Hitler in his attitude to this type of warfare. Instead of seeing it from the point of view of citizens fighting an oppressor when their army and government had failed, and asking himself what he would have expected from German citizens in reverse conditions, he saw it as the work of 'gangsters, spies, and other skulking vermin'.[35] As such he supported Hitler's draconian measures, and in December 1941 Hitler instructed that Western Europe (except Denmark) should come under the *Nacht und Nebel* Decree (Night and Fog), signed by Keitel. This meant people would disappear into Gestapo hands, either because they were involved, suspected of being helpful, related to a resister, and sometimes just as reprisals and pure revenge. Keitel explained this as 'emulating the enemy in his most degenerate mode of warfare'.[36] It never

---
* Centre Group was directed at Moscow, Group North towards Leningrad, and Group South leading to the disaster at Stalingrad.

seemed to have crossed his mind that Germany was the aggressor, and all warfare is degenerate.

In early June 1941 he was back in Berlin where he met his son Hans-Georg still suffering from his wound sustained in France. He accepted his son's request and had him transferred to a mobile artillery regiment, but with some foreboding. He was right to be concerned as on 18 July, less than two months later, he heard that Hans-Georg had died in a field hospital having been strafed by a Russian plane. He was pleased Hitler wrote a letter of sympathy to his wife, and although Keitel and his wife decided against an obituary notice, Hitler filed one on the grounds that the public should know that even high-ranking generals had sons giving their lives; it was nothing short of political propaganda.

Keitel argued that the OKW, which for some had been dubbed the OKW-Theatre, was often wrongly seen in terms of its function. He argued that the Führer often excluded them from the Russian operations apart from Finland, and the commanders of the Kriegsmarine and Luftwaffe refused to be subordinated to this form of overall control. These informative views of the OKW were contrary to those often held beliefs by their enemies, who tended to see Keitel as in overall charge, informing Hitler of their actions, rather than being instructed by their dictator to every order given. In short, it was Hitler who was not only the motivator, the director, but who always had the last word. It could be interpreted as Keitel's effort to shift the blame, but from other sources and a better understanding of the man Hitler, Keitel's views may have some justification. This was important at the Nuremberg Trial where it was first assumed that it was the OKW which issued the orders, but they were evidently always in total compliance with their Führer.

Keitel was often busy following Hitler's instructions with their allies, Romania, and Finland, and also Italy and Hungary who were constantly seeking military support and resources. In May 1941, he had met the Finnish Chief of Staff General Heinrichs, where agreements were easily made given the Russian attack upon that country. In September 1941 the Hungarian Chief of General Staff, General Ferenc Szombathelyi asked to see the Führer as he wished to withdraw a division (the Fast

Brigade) against the War Office's wishes, given that it was not equipped for a Russian winter. He was given a formal reception at the Führer's headquarters, then passed on to Keitel and Halder to discuss the issues. Keitel gave what he called a banquet in his train carriage to their visitor, and then took him to their headquarters to explain what was happening. He found the Hungarian general somewhat offensive and critical, but when he 'bit back' Szombathelyi became more moderate and even friendly. In early 1942 on Hitler's orders, Keitel returned the visit to Budapest, mainly to try and arrange for the Hungarians to mobilise their home army. It was no easy task with Keitel having to investigate the military resources they needed. It was a friendly visit and Szombathelyi arranged a banquet for him with other generals, and he had personal time with Admiral Horthy, known as the Imperial Administrator. The Hungarians' real fear was encroachment by Romania, and Horthy wondered how the Hungarians would accept that fighting against Russia for Germany would be viewed. Keitel, echoing his master, warned him that the spread of Bolshevism was more dangerous than a local dispute with Romania.

The Romanians were also encouraged to offer more, and Hitler in his politically motivated way awarded Marshal Antonescu the Knight's Cross. In Italy, Mussolini wanted to be seen helping, but was always demanding military resources, even transport to the front lines, and when Keitel saw the Italian troops, he was somewhat scathing about them, especially with their elderly officers. He raised the pertinent point that Italian troops had failed with their attack on the Greeks and wondered how they would cope against the Russians.

Interestingly, Keitel explained how Hitler looked for scapegoats for any failure, even if a disaster occurred because of the dictator's instructions or demands. When von Rundstedt asked permission to withdraw the War Office declined, he was furious in his reply, threatening to resign. This letter was shown to Hitler who had given the orders (not that Rundstedt knew this) and Hitler was enraged, thinking Rundstedt was against him and had him dismissed. Hitler talked to the trusted Sepp Dietrich who supported Rundstedt, so Hitler talked to the discharged general to restore his confidence. There was a similar problem with Field Marshal von Leeb who asked for freedom of action, was refused, his position was overrun, and he asked to resign which was accepted as this suited Hitler. Keitel believed that Hitler's actions were based on the dictator's hopes for his historical posterity in which he did not want to be seen as a failure.

However, a serious disaster was lurking on the horizon as the bitter Russian winter was setting in around German troops inadequately clothed for such bitterly freezing weather, and Hitler's gross underestimation of Russian strength. When Brauchitsch confronted Hitler on this subject with a lengthy argument, which, typically ended in his inevitable retirement. It was within just a day or two that Hitler announced himself as head of the army. A second order subordinated the Army General Staff to Hitler. The ramifications for Keitel were immense; all the administration was transferred to him, but he was totally bound by the Führer's directives, though this element was not widely circulated.

Japan's entry into the war was a major event, but the situation in Russia was looking precarious. There were serious transport problems, the railway systems absorbed time and energy, the winter was making life difficult for frontline troops whose tanks and guns were so frozen as to be useless. Hitler's orders as always, were to stand firm and not lose a metre of ground. In this order he had Keitel's total support both during and after the war, as he compared it to Napoleon's retreat claiming that they would have been obliged to leave their frozen heavy weapons, thereby losing their main means of defence. The commanders in the field evidently knew better. In Britain, Churchill's Chief of the Imperial General Staff, General Alan Brooke, was forever warning Churchill that commanders on the spot knew best and not to interfere. In Russia there were many times when a short retreat seemed the only way, but Hitler always refused, and sacked able commanders such as General Hoepner, General Foerster, and even the well-known Guderian. Keitel was present when Guderian faced Hitler, with Keitel describing Guderian as remaining obdurate as he described the welfare of his troops, but Guderian still had to go into retirement. In his memoirs Keitel was equally obdurate in supporting Hitler's no retreat policy, claiming Hitler's tough plans saved the day. Keitel claimed Hitler was right because he knew what was happening. He was an eyewitness to the confrontations between Hitler and the commanders, but he had no experience of the Eastern front fighting and conditions, and his experience of war was limited to a desk.

As 1942 opened Keitel was dealing with more logistical problems concerning manpower, as troops were being wiped out on the Russian front, ammunition supplies were hampered by poor labour, and in short, the Germans were running out of manpower. Keitel explained how Speer was constantly demanding workers for munitions and building projects, and the war economy was struggling. Keitel described how Fritz Sauckel who was in charge of labour was finding it impossible to fill the gaps in the labour force, with accusations that industry was keeping the best manpower with the less able being sent to bolster army losses. Not once in his memoirs did Keitel mention the slave-labour and concentration camp victims, working under constant threat of death. Keitel observed that these tensions between the various chiefs always suited Hitler, as it was part of his *modus operandi*. Keitel was concerned that the *Waffen-SS* were taking the best recruits, often using bribery to ensure they signed on. He claimed he protested to Hitler on this issue, but he was rebuffed as usual with an angry outburst. Keitel described these manpower issues as an endless tug-of-war, but the reality was that logistically German resources were seriously faltering. Keitel produced statistics which clearly indicated the monthly loss of German troops was massive, and they simply could not be replaced man for man. Hitler had tried to hoodwink the Russians by pretending to swing north, so they responded by putting their manpower there when he turned south. This was a paper game for Hitler, but he had failed to understand the huge resources and manpower of the Soviet Union, and demanded more from his own people when there was nothing more they could give.

This problem meant Keitel remained busy with their allies, trying to make Romania and Hungary forget their mutual distrust of one another and supply troops for the Russian front. He used the traditional argument that Bolshevism was the real menace, but as with Italy, they all demanded weapons, munitions and even transport for their troops. Given the problems the Germans were having with the railways, essential supplies, and even timing, Keitel was faced with an administrative nightmare, travelling around trying to play the military diplomat.

During the 1942 spring offensive on the Eastern Front there were some minor victories which offered a glimmer of hope, with Keitel crediting Hitler for his leadership, but it soon ground to a halt in the Caucasus and Stalingrad. There were flutters in Hitler's dovecote when in the West some of his orders were published revealing potential traitors. It transpired, according to Keitel to be mainly civilians with a Luftwaffe officer called Lieutenant Colonel Harro Schilze-Boyson and his wife, who were duly executed. This was almost a minor tension compared to the friction between Hitler and his military commanders, which was escalating as the Russians started to turn the tables. Field Marshal von Bock's leadership was being questioned, based on the grounds that Hitler thought he was preparing for defence rather than advancing. This started a conflict between Hitler and Halder which led Keitel to believe there would be a leadership crisis. Keitel recommended that Hitler fly out and meet Bock which he agreed to do with Keitel as company. Keitel was taken aback as the meeting appeared to go well with Hitler not exposing his inner doubts, so much so Keitel tried to express them but was ignored. For Keitel, the meeting was far too cordial. He was right about the situation because as soon as Hitler returned, he was raging with fury, and soon Bock was replaced by Field Marshal Freiherr von Weichs.

The next problem was Field Marshal Wilhelm List whom it was claimed by Keitel had stopped SS armoured units from breaking off towards Rostov, other accounts suggest List wished to retreat, all of which irritated Hitler. It was a time of great rage as Hitler accused Keitel of recommending List in the first place, and Jodl who had been sent to see what was happening had supported List's actions. Hitler was beside himself with anger and having developed the habit of eating with Jodl and Keitel, as noted above, refused to shake hands with them, eating lunch alone like an upset schoolboy. Albert Speer in his memoirs observed that 'Keitel skulked about mournfully and displayed great devotion, so that Hitler soon began treating him somewhat more amicably', though Speer's memoirs have to be treated with care.[37] It was not until the end of January that Hitler shook hands with Jodl and Keitel again. It was a matter, as Keitel later wrote in his memoirs, that Hitler had 'a pathological delusion that his generals were conspiring against him, trying to sabotage his orders on what were in his view pretty shabby pretexts'.[38]

Curiously, in the Russian archives are some German documents which record formal conversations between Keitel and Hitler on 18 September 1942. One document was that of Keitel presenting Hitler with possible solutions to issues regarding von Manstein, Jodl's visit to Stalino (currently Donetsk in Ukraine), and his meeting with Field Marshal List which had alienated Hitler from Jodl and Keitel. It appears that Hitler had issued an order [presumably to General List] which Keitel later discovered had made his position difficult. Hitler, later in the conversation explained that he demanded one hundred per cent loyalty from those who worked for him, and the order of which Keitel had been unaware was the one to General List of an advance and not a retreat. It all turned on the need to secure the oilfields to move their produce to Romanian refineries. Later in their conference [page 8 of the record referred to above] Hitler spoke with absolute authority as if he had all the necessary answers explained:

> *Hitler*: Of all these routes I considered the most important one was that over the Tuapse Pass, since only the seizure of the Tuapse Pass offers the possibility to reach Maikop. I have exhaustively explained to everyone that we cannot take it for granted that the refineries there work, which also means we have to transport the oil, and that we possess the certain capacity of refinery facilities in Romania, and that for this reason we had to reach at all costs the Tuapse Pass, as the road, the railway and the pipeline go through there, so that we could transport this crude oil to Romania. This was discussed in full here. Not just once, but rather several times I have made the point that the breakthrough at the Tuapse Pass is decisive, to reach a conclusion.[39]

Hitler spoke with determined authority and working from maps had planned the strategy and the tactics, but failed to understand that the men in the field would have a more realistic perspective. He had sent Jodl who could only agree with General List when he saw for himself the circumstances and as such countermanded Hitler's orders, or as Hitler perceived it, why Jodl gave an order behind his back. It was based on this incident that Hitler said he refused to work with Jodl anymore. There followed this interchange:

Hitler: General Jodl must go.
Keitel: I will not stand up for him, I have always been responsible for myself.
Hitler: From my point of view there is only one person who can be considered, somebody I personally trust and who made his experiences leading at the front. This is General Paulus.
Keitel: Then this is the way you may well take...'[40]

The conversation continued with Hitler reinforcing his point that when he issued an order it must be obeyed, with which Keitel instantly agreed. Keitel's prompt agreement is indicated by his statement that Hitler had obviously resolved the problem by turning to Paulus. Hitler then qualified this by adding that Paulus must first win Stalingrad, and then Halder could also be removed. Keitel instantly agreed that such a move was urgent, but Hitler again reinforced his earlier point that before Paulus replaced Jodl, he must be seen as the victor of Stalingrad. There followed a discussion on the changes in field commanders, including Generals Seydlitz and Ruoff with ramifications for Kleist, Zeitzler, Rommel, and Manstein.

Later, Keitel (page 46 of the document) noted that since his own appointment by Hitler 177 generals had been removed, mostly for age reasons, 66 of whom had been in active or in command positions. It is noticeable in this document record of the meeting between Keitel and Hitler how promptly obedient Keitel was when meeting Hitler. Everything Hitler proposed was immediately acceptable to Keitel, even if it meant major changes for Jodl and other commanders, because as far as Keitel was concerned, Hitler was always right and beyond criticism.

For the sake of painting a clearer picture of Keitel there follows below a brief extract of his opening remarks to Hitler, which serve as an indicator of his personality and sense of total obedience. In places he feels obsequious as Keitel appears to grovel to his master whom, in this very short passage, he addressed as *Mein Führer* six times and moments when he grumbled, grovelled, and agreed Jodl had to go. His reasons for Jodl's departure could simply be trying to placate Hitler following the General List problem, by repairing his own relationship with Hitler, but he was certainly ensuring that he was safely on Hitler's side. The following extract was the start of their mini conference starting at 3.30 in the afternoon (18 September 1942):

Keitel: My Führer! I want to talk to you about personal matters, which are related to the events of the past weeks. I will also report – what you already know – that I came on the day after your meeting with the field marshals, which you had requested, after having been with the Reichsmarschall [Göring], since the Reichsmarschall has replied to specific issues and questions.

Amongst other things he said was that he was not authorised to talk with me. However, on the basis that in this case and with the knowledge I have acquired, as General Schmundt [Hitler's aide] informed me yesterday, I know that you have decided to receive General von Blumentritt, and in relation to this, today, you sent General Schmundt to Paris along with Blumentritt. Allow me to say from my side that I can only be grateful that you have made this arrangement and that the matter is coming to a decision....My Führer! However, from my point of view there are other issues at stake. Since I was not informed, not even about the matter which you have recently discussed with General Konrad, Schmundt only just told me that you have raised some issues which require an answer, and that you would inform me directly since the entire matter is not related to these issues. The matter is, however, related to the situation, as I see it also with regard to the matter of command here at the Oberkommando der Wehrmacht [OKW]. In the past winter and already in the past late autumn, my Führer, the matter has been raised more than once, and from me as well, but you were not ready to appoint, following my suggestion, the then General of Infantry von Manstein as Chief of the Führungsstab, [Command Staff] as it has been mentioned. At the time he was still in command of an Army Corps, then he took over command of an Army in Crimea, was promoted, and is now a Field Marshal. On this matter, the case of Manstein is out of date, I dare say, speaking exclusively of personal matters. In spite of that my point of view is not out of date on the grounds of its basic concept.

My Führer, you have been informed by me, as I must understand it, what came out of the situation in the evening following the return from Stalino of General Steinhuber [handwritten note: amended to Jodl]. I take the liberty then to say something.

My Führer, things have developed during this year in such a manner, that General Jodl was first of all my assistant, I dare say, but as he gradually moved to the foreground, he moved in a more determined way into your command work and in the work made for the overall conduct of the Wehrmachtührung [Wehrmacht leadership]. On several occasions – this is something I must openly admit – I have made it clear to General Jodl that he is not entitled to decision making, nor does he hold any responsibility in that capacity. It had been made clear to you too, My Führer, whenever the situation arose, be that concerning the Commander in Chief of the Army or in whatever critical situation, that you, following my advice, have given me the task or have given me the power or have authority to get directly and at once in touch with these people or organisations, as such, I understood that you expected me to take the initiative in these situations, and that I dealt directly with these matters.

That was the situation back then. I need not remind you that I have already suggested before employing General Jodl in some other capacity and make him act there on other matters, since I have always found and seen the need for that. I do not need to repeat the same suggestion today, since I have discussed the matter with you 3 weeks ago.[41]

Even in the German language the passage can be confusing and rambling, perhaps badly recorded, but it clearly gives a first-hand indicator of Keitel's sycophantic approach to Hitler, as he tries to appease the perceived damage done by Jodl and ensure that Keitel himself can remain trusted by Hitler.

List was dismissed, and Keitel wondered whether it had all started on the political side with Himmler or Bormann. Halder was the next one to fall, with Hitler treating him abruptly and not listening to his views. Keitel had already suggested Manstein as Halder's successor, but it was rejected. It must have felt like living in a totally dysfunctional family led by a perpetually angry boss. In the end Hitler appointed General Kurt Zeitzler as his new Chief of General Staff, the only relief for Keitel was that Zeitzler had once been Jodl's operation officer. However, Zeitzler tended to stand apart from Keitel and Jodl on matters dealing with the Eastern Front as if ordered to exclude them from this major military area.

The Stalingrad crisis was growing, and in his memoirs, it was almost as if Keitel had finally started to question what was happening, not that he would have raised this with Hitler. He had no doubt that if Paulus had been allowed to retreat from Stalingrad and regroup, German victory was still possible. He was correct that a withdrawal from Stalingrad would have been sensible, but it would not have led to victory as he expected, Hitler and Keitel had always underestimated Russian strength. However, Keitel remained loyal, and he blamed Göring for his failure to bring in the necessary supplies, especially as he had promised it could be done.[42]

In January 1943, the time of the fall of Stalingrad and surrender of the Sixth Army, Hitler created a three-man committee of representatives from the forces, the state, and the party. It consisted of Keitel for the OKW, Hans Lammers as Chief of Reich Chancellery, and Martin Bormann chief of the Party Chancellery. The committee was known as the *Dreierausschuß*, the committee of three. Goebbels had wanted to chair this, then later tried to undermine its work.[43] It was all part of a Nazi domestic powerplay, and Goebbels was even able to encourage Göring to join with him to oust Keitel and the other two, 'out of the inflated positions of power they had managed to create for themselves'.[44] This would have been beyond Keitel's comprehension, especially as no one was quite sure why the committee was suddenly formed: it had little autonomy, with Hitler always making the final decisions, and it declined into irrelevance as rapidly as it had been initiated. Stalingrad and the months which followed during 1943, made it clear that Germany was now fighting a defensive war, and the tide of events was turning against them.

On 3 August 1943, Keitel wrote to his wife Lisa about the bombing in Berlin, warning her that the firebombs and storms were more serious than high-explosive devices. He asked that she should leave Berlin as soon as possible, giving her various instructions for her safety. She disobeyed him even though she was having heart problems, and their home was destroyed.[45] On 22 September it was Keitel's 61st birthday and he wrote to his wife again, so pleased that Hitler had invited him into his presence to congratulate him, then to dine with him the same evening, and he also went hunting. However, this was all small joy because Keitel was weighed down with work as Italy had withdrawn from the Axis, and he knew the war was no longer in their favour.

During the well-known plot of 20 July 1944 Keitel was in the room with Hitler and was slightly wounded, and carefully helped the Führer out of the room, dazed but unhurt, with Hitler impressed that one general had remained totally loyal to him. As the historian Knopp pointed out there was a curious and ironic twist in this plot, because Stauffenberg who carried the bomb into the room knew his brief case would be inspected, so he ensured he accompanied Keitel into the room knowing it would ensure a safe passage for him and his bomb.[46]

Once Hitler realised that the explosion was the start of a *coup d'état*, a broadcast was started announcing that Hitler lived, and Keitel was made busy contacting all the various command posts.[47] He played an important role, with Hitler setting up a Court of Honour with Keitel as a member, ensuring many senior officers were dismissed from the military so they could be sent to the People's Court (run by the notorious Roland Freisler), doing so willingly because he had been brought up and trained in the Prussian belief of total obedience and loyalty. To a man like Keitel trying to assassinate the head of government was pure anathema, however, according to one historian there were popular rumours that Keitel may have been one of the plotters, which is simply unbelievable.[48] If true, this may have arisen because Keitel was the epitome of the old school, but such 'old school' betrayal would have been out of the question, and had he known he would hardly have stood in his traditional position to the left of Hitler if he knew anything of the plot. A few weeks after the failed plot Göring and Keitel ordered that all military had to offer the Hitler straight-arm salute, and not the traditional military way.

Later, during post-war interrogations by the curious Allied powers, he was asked what he considered the motives of the perpetrators, to which he gave the speculative answer that they were dissatisfied with the political system and Hitler's direction of the war. He thought that with Hitler's death the soldiers and others would be released from their oath of obedience. This was all too typical of Keitel's mindset, that in breaking an oath all would be solved for the plotters, whereas the resisters knew that the Nazi regime structure, with men like Himmler, Göring, Goebbels, Bormann, and many others, would mean that Hitler's death was only a starting point for the sake of the German nation. His various interviewers were taken aback when Keitel claimed that Rommel, implicated by knowledge of the plot, committed suicide, because otherwise it might have brought dishonour on the officer corps. When they faced Keitel, it was beyond their comprehension that in the middle of a major world war, Keitel should be concerned about such matters.

When on 19 September 1944, Finland signed an armistice with Russia and Great Britain the Finns broke off all diplomatic relations with Germany. Hitler had sent Keitel to meet the Finnish leader Field Marshal Mannerheim the month before, but he failed in the negotiations, not knowing that the Finns were already looking for a peaceful settlement.[49] It was part of the German collapse when allies felt they could leave the Germans to their own fate, and of all people it must have been an error to have sent Keitel, too formal a soldier as a diplomat and known to be close to Hitler. Field Marshal Kesselring had noted in his memoirs that Keitel had failed in his diplomatic abilities, even with the company of the semi-professional Ribbentrop when he had been sent to Italy.[50]

Less than a year later, 20 April 1945 was Hitler's 56th birthday, when he announced the war was lost, but he would stay in Berlin, and fight to the end. 'It was a macabre formality of handshaking and congratulations' as messages were arriving that the Russians were closing in.[51] Keitel and Jodl said they would stay with him to that end which seemed to cheer Hitler up. The fighting was now deep into the Berlin suburbs with Hitler and his staff studying maps in the ridiculous hope that various armies, especially General Busse's Ninth Army and others would save the day. It was a dark and sinister *Alice in Wonderland* in the underground bunker, as they either did not know or pretended that these armies could achieve the impossible against the overwhelming Russian forces. As the birthday wishes were expressed in the bunker, the British and Americans carried out a massive bombing raid on central Berlin, and it was a matter of senior officers having to find their own safety billets. Keitel and Dönitz with their wives watched the bombing from the relative safety of Dönitz's headquarters. On returning to the bunker, they heard that Hitler had been outside awarding medals to uniformed children for their work with the anti-aircraft guns, such was now the poverty of German resources. Keitel summoned up the courage to ask Hitler whether it was time to start negotiations with the enemy, but the reply was prompt with Hitler claiming he would fight to the very end. Keitel was impressed by Hitler's clear and objective instructions, agreeing with Keitel's suggestion that Göring should fly south before communications were cut. What Keitel did not know was that Hitler at this stage was planning his own death for posterity. Keitel organised for his own plane with his personal pilot Funk, to take some senior officials and his wife, along with Dönitz's wife to Prague, from where they could make their way to Berchtesgaden.

The next day (21 April) it was dawning on Keitel that some commanders were not telling Hitler all the facts, as he was, in Keitel's opinion grasping at straws. It did not seem that anyone in Hitler's company dared admit the war was lost. A few years earlier the Germans had stood at the gates of Moscow and thought the war was won, but now the Russians were inside Berlin, fighting in the streets and avenues drawing close to the bunker itself. Jodl and Keitel later both agreed that the optimism pervading the war conferences amounted to sheer madness, which Keitel tried to explain to Hitler. Keitel was rebuked again and told he could fly south if he wished, but with his built-in sense of loyalty he told Hitler he would be staying with him. Keitel and Jodl arranged for key members of the OKW to set out for the new southern and northern centres in preparation. Keitel then travelled with his staff officer around battle torn Berlin, and for the first time found himself near the frontline trying to establish who was where and what was happening. He met General Wenck and explained that he had to break through as it was Keitel's hope they could persuade Hitler out of Berlin, even considering the possibility of abducting the Führer, but this could only have been a pipedream. Wenck was hoping to make it towards Potsdam, and Hitler wanted to know whether he would link with the Ninth Army. Keitel did not know the facts, nor did anyone else as the bunker's inhabitants were now living in ignorance as to what was happening outside. Keitel tried to reason with Hitler who explained, Keitel claimed, that he had been conducting peace talks with England, which was sheer fantasy. Keitel again ventured out to see for himself what was happening, but Hitler forbade him to drive through Berlin because of the dangers. He hoped to fly but that proved just as dangerous, so Keitel investigated the front, but he could hear the gunfire and battle noises encroaching. He was able to communicate with Jodl who was also trying to keep the Führer updated. Keitel again planned to fly in, but it was proving far too risky. He heard that Göring had started surrender negotiations with the enemy which infuriated Hitler who ordered Göring's arrest and execution. Keitel was stunned by this reaction and later blamed it on the hated Bormann.[52] It was fortunate for Göring he was lodged in Berchtesgaden as even at this stage Hitler resented having his authority challenged, and he was struggling in the bunker to be seen as still in control. Keitel probably never knew that Göring had sent him and Ribbentrop instructions to report to him 'unless it was countermanded by Hitler himself', as their world degenerated into one of total confusion and fantasy.[53]

In the meantime, Keitel continued to visit army groups sometimes becoming angry at what he saw, not apparently realising that at this stage everything was out of German control. Keitel was living in an unreal world like those in the bunker. The idea that any rescue or victory could be achieved at this stage was simply beyond belief. When General Wenck had listened to Keitel he reportedly said 'Let the man blather on. None of it makes any sense.'[54] Jodl was living in the same world, explaining to Keitel by phone that matters were becoming acute, which with the benefit of hindsight was an unbelievable understatement. Jodl soon suggested that he and Keitel would have to evacuate their headquarters, but Keitel was reluctant as he did not want to be separated from the Führer. It was a state of total confusion and Keitel was still charging around the various battle zones threatening to sack commanders, which for some may well have been welcome news. He used radio-telephone lines to stay in touch with Hitler and Jodl, claiming the Führer sounded very calm and objective. In the bunker it was a world of fantasy, and when Keitel had sent in messages regarding the hopelessness of the situation some even wondered whether Keitel had turned traitor, and he was holding the generals back.[55] Hitler had asked Keitel when the relieving forces would arrive in Berlin, and Keitel told the truth, namely that the 12th Army was held and could not move, and the 9th Army was also surrounded. Bormann 'dispatched a message to Dönitz accusing Keitel of allowing the forces around Berlin to stand idle for days and urged him to act ruthlessly against traitors'.[56] The so-called rescuing armies, the demands, the accusations indicated not just chaos, but they had descended into a world of fantasy.

While waiting Keitel was told the communication link was down, because a balloon used to transmit messages had been destroyed by a Russian fighter plane. The street fighting was closing in, and he and Jodl with their various personnel made their way to different operational headquarters on an estate at Dobbin, once the home of a wealthy Dutch industrialist. It was here that they met Himmler who was also seeking a new place with his assistants, all of them finally recognising that Berlin could not be saved. They decided to drive north towards the new headquarters where they not only saw the refugees fleeing, but they all had to jump out of their cars when strafed by British fighters. They were hoping to find Dönitz and eventually tracked him down, finding Himmler already trying to join the new government. As May opened, they heard that Hitler had committed suicide. Dönitz promptly refused to listen to Goebbels who had sent a list of the new cabinet members. Hitler's suicide should not have been a surprise if the historian Alan Bullock was correct in stating that Hitler had already told Keitel and Jodl this was his intention.[57]

Keitel with his overwhelming sense of obedience suggested to Dönitz that the Hitler oath was now transferred to him as head of government, giving the modern-day observer the feeling that he was not living in the real world. There was still discussion about counter attacks to drive Soviets back, but they knew they had insufficient forces. Dönitz wanted troops in the east to withdraw quickly, (about a million men) but he consulted Keitel who advised him not to withdraw from prepared positions, so they lost a week of possible salvation for some of their fighting men on the Eastern Front.

Both Dönitz and Keitel agreed that despite his presence Himmler would not be part of the new government, and it was later clear that Dönitz was uncertain about Keitel's presence, placing the signing of the first surrender in the hands of Jodl. It was Keitel who told Himmler that he was not needed, as the new administration moved itself to Flensburg on 3 May. Keitel stayed on for the short-lived Flensburg government under Dönitz. Speer said he grovelled to Dönitz as he had done to Hitler. By 7 May contact had been made with the British Field Marshal Montgomery, and at Eisenhower's headquarters when Jodl, and not Keitel, signed the surrender agreement. It has been suggested that Dönitz did not hold Keitel in high esteem. The next day Keitel was flown to Berlin in a British plane where it was his job to sign another surrender agreement with the Russians, who wanted what they believed to be a major figure of the Nazi regime. In his memoirs he recalled how they were well treated, and the Russians proposed that while the rest of the German delegation would be flown back, Keitel 'was invited to stay'. He argued and protested, and he was greatly relieved when the Russians relented, and he joined the others on the British plane for the return journey. Naturally, the Allies had recognised the Flensburg government only as a means for having an official German authority to sign the surrender papers. Keitel was soon a prisoner-of-war and was then interned at Camp Ashcan in Mondorf-les-Bains. Jodl succeeded him as Chief of Staff until 23 May.

Chapter Three

A Condemned Man

Once a mere prisoner with no standing or position, Keitel entered a personal hell when he was obliged to face serious charges at the Nuremberg Trial on all four indictments. He also realised that many of his one-time colleagues and comrades were not only unsupportive but had derided him during the war years, but now they did so openly and in full public view. He was not so much detested as scorned, and from his notes and observations it was clear that he knew he would be found guilty, and he was more interested in saving his reputation as he thought it ought to be, than avoiding execution.

Hitler, Himmler, Goebbels were dead, and Göring was often regarded as their representative at the trial, which meant his time as a defendant was much longer than any of the others who were indicted. However, Keitel was also regarded as a major component as he was beside Hitler from before the war to the bitter end. It was known that Hitler took command of the armed forces making Keitel Chief of the High Command of Armed Forces, so he was in effect Hitler's military staff. He had been placed in a vulnerable post, and he was never in danger of removal because no one else would have wanted his post. In the Allied camp during the war years, they regarded his role with more significance than it deserved.

There was of course a degree of hypocrisy in the trials, and when some claimed it was victor's justice it was true that the Russians tried to conceal their own crime of the Katyń massacres. The Western Allied aerial bombing was continued past the time when it was necessary, in Sicily there were massacres of Italian prisoners-of-war by two of Patton's soldiers, and this happened in many places during the duration of the fighting. No war is clean, and it is the nature of war that accepted laws and conventions are broken. However, such was the devastating impact of a world war unleashed by Hitler, including many untold massacres, the Holocaust, hostages and reprisals, medical experiments on selected victims, with so many crimes it would take a whole volume to list. As such, the Nuremberg Trial was believed essential to cauterise the wounds, trying to establish some form of peace if not reconciliation. During Field Marshal Kesselring's trial over the questions relating to the brutal repression of partisan activities in Italy, Hitler's orders were to 'wage war with the most brutal means' but it was Keitel's signature which carried this message.[1] There seems little doubt that Keitel personally detested partisans when in office, but he was now facing the fact that he had signed orders which were immoral and illegal. Like many other commanders, Keitel had regarded partisans as criminal, describing the French resistance as mere social garbage, not considering the issue that they were patriots stepping in where their army and government had failed. He signed one on 16 October 1941 which read, 'It should be remembered that a human life in unsettled countries frequently counts for nothing, and a deterrent effect can be attained only by unusual severity'.[2] He never saw the reality of the consequences of his orders, and later expressed regret he had not visited the frontline. When shown during the trial the films exhibiting the brutality, he simply hung his head in pure shame. When talking at a mealtime break Keitel admitted that 'I am ashamed of being German…I'll never be able to look people in the face again.'[3]

Keitel was indicted under all charges, and it is necessary to take a brief look at why he was arraigned. Keitel may have been Hitler's wallpaper, standing in the background, but he attended the February 1938 Schuschnigg conference, and he organised the military arrangements and initialled Case *Otto* which Hitler had issued.* He also initialled Hitler's directives for the attack on Czechoslovakia, and was present when Hitler announced he would attack Poland. He was involved in the discussions over taking Denmark, and in the operation for occupying Norway, this was placed under Keitel's personal guidance. Keitel also signed the orders for the attack on neutral Belgium and the Netherlands. He was fully

---

* Case *Otto* was Hitler's preparations for the *Anschluss*.

aware of plans in the Balkans including Greece, and while he claimed he opposed the attack on Russia he signed Case *Barbarossa*. He was not a key motivator or instigator, that role belonged to Hitler, but he was fully aware that he was serving a man who was preparing many wars of aggression, when he could either have opposed him, or like others stepped back. Keitel understood the ramifications and knew he would be found guilty.

He also realised that he fell under the indictments of war crimes and crimes against humanity. In August 1942 it was Keitel, under instruction, but who signed the directive that captured paratroopers or commandos were to be transferred to the SD which later in the trials was declared an illegal organisation.* On 18 August the same year, it was Keitel who confirmed Hitler's Commando Order, later acknowledging he knew it was illegal, but Hitler could not be stopped. The same happened when in September 1941 he issued the orders for the ruthless treatment of Soviet prisoners-of-war. As noted previously, Admiral Canaris protested about the slaughter of Jews, but a handwritten note of Keitel's reply read, 'the objections arise from the military concept of chivalrous warfare. This is the destruction of an ideology. Therefore, I approve and back the measures.' He admitted he quietly agreed with Canaris, but all he could do was use Hitler's words in defence of an action he knew was immoral and illegal. He was aware of the Einsatzstab Rosenberg looting of art, and General Erwin Lahousen (a high-ranking Abwehr official) testified that as early as September 1939, Keitel had told him that Polish intelligentsia and Jews were to be liquidated. Another signed order on 16 September demanded that attacks on German soldiers in the East should be responded to by killing 50 to 100 communists as a reprisal. When the Reich Commissioner in Norway, Terboven held that sabotage could only be stopped by the relatives of the saboteurs being shot, Keitel replied that he agreed.

During May or April 1941, before the start of *Barbarossa* he passed on Hitler's orders to kill the political commissars, and there should be

---

* SD was the *Sicherheitsdienst*, a form of intelligence agency for the SS.

no courts martial if civilians were killed. In Oct 1942, he signed the infamous Commando order, having already applied his signature to the *Nacht und Nebel* decree (December 1941). He was fully aware that Russian prisoners-of war should not have been used in the war industry, and citizens as slave labour were forced to work on the Atlantic Wall, and he knew Sauckel was obtaining slave workers from occupied countries.

It was clear that Keitel knew all the plans for Poland and Russia and the wars of aggression. He also knew of unfair arrests, assaults on human rights, mass murder, the massacres committed by the *Einsatzgruppen* and never protested. He ignored objections by some field commanders as if he knew best by following the tradition of obedience. He never raised these issues in his memoirs but never denied them when raised in court, and his only defence was he adhered to obeying superior orders and loyalty to the head of government, which for the court was no mitigation.

If he felt under attack from the prosecution, who declared his dedication to his work as criminal, he also felt damaged by many of his colleagues who related either publicly or privately their views on Keitel. From very early on he was widely known as the 'yes-man', but then sycophancy was well-known in the army where upper ranks were like class distinctions, and obedience expected. This was very much a characteristic of many countries, but the proud Prussian treatment took this sense of obedience, loyalty, and honour to its lowest possible depth. Despite this Keitel still stood out from many others, and he gathered a variety of nicknames all focusing on his inbuilt propensity to obey his master whatever the instruction. He had soon acquired the nickname of *Lakeitel*, which was a pun derived from *lakai* meaning lackey. Göring it is claimed, said he had a sergeant's mind inside a field marshal's body, another group of peers knew him as the 'blindingly loyal toady' of Hitler. Another nickname *Nickgeselle*, reflected a popular metal toy for children of a nodding donkey. For a proud soldier such as Keitel these charges and the opinions of colleagues placed firmly before him, would have been devastating as he was obliged to face the reality of his attitudes and beliefs.

Post-war Interrogations

The Nuremberg Trial provided the opportunity for the Allied powers to gain a more substantive view of Keitel as a person, and his role within the Nazi-German war administration. Prior to the trial, it was decided 'to arraign Keitel as the token for German militarism' but this was modified by the inclusion of Jodl, Raeder and Dönitz', known as the military men.[4] As the processes for the trial were debated the defendants were put through a series of interrogations, all of which provided some insights into Keitel's thinking. He may well have tried to avoid some issues, but the general impression appears to be that he was straightforward in his replies. In the Document entitled '10 OKW', he was questioned on the 27 June 1945 by personnel from the USA Strategic Bombing Survey.[5] He stated that he believed Hitler had not expected the Polish occupation to lead to another war, which indicated a degree of naivety in Hitler, or more probably in Keitel's understanding of the dictator. He noted that the lack of aggression by the Allies in the Phoney War indicated that France and Britain were not very determined. He talked of the debate within the OKW as to when the attack on the West should start, noting that Hitler wanted it earlier on the grounds that by the spring the Western Allies would be stronger, and it was believed that Dunkirk had not been a success for the British. After the Dunkirk evacuation, there was a belief in Germany that the war had ended, but knowing the English were mobilising with American support made Operation *Sea Lion* more probable. These were, he pointed out, always decisions made by the Führer, who always stated 'I want to think this over for twenty-four hours', confirming that Hitler was the single controller of German military policy.[6] The bombing of Britain was discussed, with Keitel stating the Luftwaffe was meant to hit ports and resources, tactical bombing, but the British had started bombing cities first which was largely true.

He was questioned about when the Russian campaign emerged as a possibility and admitted it was probably as early as November 1940. More interesting was his opinion about how Hitler drew a distinctive line between military and politics, which he may have hoped would throw him a safety line, as the wars of aggression were a political and not a military decision. He discussed the lack of will on the part of the Italians, the power of the allied air force during the Normandy campaign. He always returned, almost cunningly for Keitel, to stating that the OKW and therefore himself, had very little influence as the Führer decided all military decisions.

The Trial

The trial was more forcible and demanding. Nearly 80 years later the records of these proceedings have provided a source for understanding this rather vague and enigmatic field marshal. His name occurs very often even when he was not the court's central interest at the time. This arose because his authorising signature was to be found on many documents, especially those of a questionable nature, and he was often mentioned because he was frequently present when 'this or that' was being discussed. There are many photographs of Hitler at various meetings with Keitel standing near or in the background, and when around the map table he is nearly always on the left side of the dictator. His presence and signature on multitudinous documents for many observers was condemnatory in itself. Like Göring and Jodl, Keitel appeared under the legal microscope in basic and drab uniforms without their ranks or any insignia, and they were challenged on the role they played. It was also noted that Keitel 'sat stiff and impassive', soldierly as he had always done.[7] At one stage it had been thought that Keitel would stand in the place of the dead Hitler, but Göring was soon established in this role, which made his trial time the longest, though Keitel's case was also lengthy.[8]

During the trial in December 1945, for eleven days when Keitel was not the subject of interest, he was mentioned 181 times, but mainly as being present or because he signed orders.[9] He was represented by Dr Otto Nelte who had been a business lawyer acquainted with his wife's family, and 'who found it difficult to follow his client's way of thinking'.[10] Undoubtedly Nelte, like others, found Keitel's presence at critical meetings and his endless signatures as all self-condemning in the eyes of the court. There were one or two more curious notes revealing Keitel's role. Whenever Nelte, his defence lawyer had the opportunity to offer a defence, he rose to his feet. When General Erwin Lahousen, a high-ranking Abwehr officer who was part of the German resistance to Hitler, was in the stand, Nelte asked if Keitel had asked about the political views of those serving in the Abwehr. Lahousen claimed that Keitel stated he would not tolerate any officer who did not believe in total victory or who did not have 'unswerving loyalty to the Führer and much more besides'.[11] This clearly indicated that Keitel was seemingly more politically active than is often assumed, and Nelte did not seem to have been helpful for Keitel in this line of questioning. The prison psychologist noted that Keitel 'was evidently suffering from loss of face after the damaging testimony of Lahousen,' but it would later become more condemnatory for him.[12] It was a distressing time and Keitel along with Papen refused to see their wives when the opportunity arose. Keitel was depressed and said he was aware of his disgrace and 'I just couldn't face her.'[13] The disgrace he felt was not apparent on his entry to the court proceedings when he had declared himself 'Not Guilty', but like others felt highly disturbed at seeing the films of the concentration camps.

Keitel often had angry interchanges with Göring who bullied his fellow defendants to such an extent, he was eventually kept isolated at his own lunch table. Keitel would try to refuse to respond to Göring's jibes by sitting stiffly, looking ahead, and totally ignoring him. However, it was apparent that because of who he was in terms of seniority, Keitel still tended to see Göring as the senior man who must be obeyed. When Paulus made his unexpected arrival as a witness, Keitel joined in the general melee led by Göring by condemning him for turning against the Führer, which he would himself eventually do once he realised where his Führer had led everyone. Amongst the military defendants Jodl tended to be his best supporter, occasionally Dönitz, but most accused him of being weak.

Nelte did his best under difficult circumstances and with a complex unbending client. Keitel's numberless signatures and knowledge of what was happening dominated the accusations. The Commando Order occupied the interest of the Western powers, but the Soviets wanted more on the subject of *Barbarossa*, especially concerning the preparation for the invasion, and the instructions entitled 'Order Concerning the Exercise of martial Jurisdiction and Procedure in the Area *Barbarossa* and Special Military measures'. Keitel's signatures on these documents alone were sufficient to gain a conviction. Nevertheless, as Keitel acknowledged, he had known some orders to be wrong and tried to oppose them, but gave them his full backing once Hitler had made his wishes known. He argued that he might be accused of weakness and guilt but not of disloyalty or dishonesty.[14] Keitel later explained that 'I did not execute such orders – I merely transmitted them. But after all, that is only a legalistic technicality and there is no use trying to dodge the issue in such petty argumentations.'[15]

However, as noted above, when challenged by Canaris that orders were illegal and against German military tradition. Keitel told him that such notions arose from old fashioned chivalry, but now they were destroying and ideology, 'and, therefore, I approve such measures and I sanction them'.[16] He later admitted he had passed on illegal orders, but he did not think them criminal because he was following the soldier's code of obedience. He was asked by Justice Lawrence if he had ever put his protests into writing for Hitler, which Keitel said he had done once, but he had no evidence at his disposal to prove this incident. Keitel's claim that he obeyed orders was backed by the argument that he had little real authority. This style of argument was used by other defendants such as Funk and even Jodl.

Sometimes the prosecution did not help their case. The French did not provide the necessary documents or evidence, and thought Keitel exercised control over the occupation armies, which Nelte never hesitated to point out. There were problems with the witness Hans Gisevius who claimed Keitel held one of the most influential positions in the Third Reich, admitting he did not influence Hitler, but he did over the OKW and the army.* There was some dispute over this, but many ordinary

---

* Hans Gisevius was in the Intelligence service, part of the German resistance and escaped the 20 July plot retributions by fleeing to Switzerland.

field officers often believed that Keitel was not looking after them. The thrust of the main argument formulating around Keitel as well as Raeder, Jodl, Ribbentrop, and Göring was their sense of total obedience to their criminal leader, namely that 'Hitler's every decision and order for the preparation and waging of wars which they knew in fact to be aggressive', and this proved to be an accusation impossible to avoid.[17] The Russian prosecutor Rudenko ridiculed them by addressing them as noble-minded simpletons. In terms of preparing for an aggressive war the military defendants such as Keitel had nothing to offer in mitigation. Later, under cross-examination, Keitel tried to argue that aggressive war was a political and not a military matter, and as a military non-political man he had been brought up to obey the political leaders of the country.

In further cross-examination, Keitel spoke of his disapproval of the attack on Poland, his surprise the French and British did not attack, his misgivings over the attack on France and later Russia. He constantly admitted he had signed orders for aggressive war, for barbarities knowing they were illegal, stated that he accepted the consequences, but he was only following his soldierly duties by obeying orders issued by the head of State. Some of his fellow defendants admired his frank honesty, others were embarrassed or annoyed. He had constant rows with Göring, and Schacht said, 'I cannot spare Keitel and the others the embarrassment, but I must show that they did not have to obey that maniac Hitler'.[18] Time and time again Keitel's argument remained the same that he had signed orders he knew to be wrong, which did not endear him to many of his fellow defendants and did not impress the court. When asked by a prison psychologist whether he thought Hitler was the real murderer, 'Yes, of course!' he replied emphatically with a wave of both fists, 'But that doesn't mean that I too should be branded a murderer'.[19]

As in any trial the truth does not always emerge, but Nelte did his best to paint Keitel in the best possible light. In March 1944, some 76 Allied officers escaped from their prison camp, for which Hitler reprimanded Keitel, because Hitler regarded such escapees as a danger. According to Nelte, Keitel refused to hand over some recaptured prisoners to Himmler, also arguing that Hitler did not give the order to have such men shot.[20]

It is quite believable that Keitel and Jodl would not have wanted men shot for escaping, it is equally possible that Himmler would not have gone against Hitler's orders, and Keitel was the apex of obedience. This incident was painted by Nelte to put Keitel in the best possible light, and there are many varied and conflicting accounts of the 'behind the scenes' discussion on this incident.

When the possible assassination of Giraud mentioned above was raised, Keitel admitted he did not know what to say, he knew he would be questioned, 'but I was only doing my duty'.[21] The general defence for Keitel was that Hitler gave the orders and Keitel simply passed them on. Speer in his interviews made the pertinent point that although Hitler dictated the decisions, it was not known by the people at large or even the fighting soldiers, 'They thought that the basic directives came from Hitler, but that Keitel and other high officers were responsible for the details', which probably reflected the Allied opinion.[22] Speer later added that the army's hatred was directed more and more towards Keitel. This view of how Keitel was regarded was given more substance by the SS General Erich von dem Bach-Zelewski, who in conversation, claimed 'that the war against Russia was planned by Keitel, Göring, and others. The cruel misdeeds against civilians were intentional.'[23] Another comment came from Field Marshal Ewald von Kleist who said Keitel's instructions 'were the orders of a stupid follower of Hitler'.[24] This widely held concept of Keitel's input probably reflected what the Allies thought to be the case during the war.

Nelte, as part of Keitel's defence, argued about the traditional role of the soldier, noting that there had been 'repeated references here to the concepts of soldierly conduct, obedience, loyalty, performance of duty, and patriotism. It is my belief that all men recognize these concepts to be good.'[25] Nelte admitted that not all these notions were unequivocal, and good and evil ran through all these beliefs, but raised the issue as to who should judge. Although Keitel was Hanoverian and not Prussian, he had been trained within the codes of the Prussian military. Seven months later Nelte kept trying to hammer the point of soldierly obedience as a defence. He quoted the time that when Keitel was in the witness box giving evidence on the Russian campaign, that he stated regarding the ideological orders (killing commissars etc) that 'I knew their content. In spite of my personal misgivings, I passed them on without letting myself be deterred by the possibility of serious consequences.'[26] Nelte admitted that throughout the war years Keitel had been popularly seen as the 'yes-man', by acting as Hitler's willing tool, thereby betraying the armed forces. Nelte described this as a distorted picture, and the orders regarding strategic operations did not apply to Keitel. Nelte noted that:

> The principle of obedience has been changed in military life into one of absolute obedience and embodied in the oath of allegiance. This is equally valid for the general as for the common soldier... The defendant Keitel not only grew up in this school of thought, but during the 37 years of his military service, up to 1938, including the First World War, he had become convinced that this principle of obedience is the strongest pillar upon which the Armed Forces, and thereby the security of the country, rests. Deeply imbued with the importance of his profession, he had served the Kaiser, Ebert, and Von Hindenburg in accordance with this principle. As representatives of the State, they had to a certain extent an impersonal and symbolic effect on Keitel; Hitler, from 1934, at first appeared in the same light to him, that is, merely as representing the State, without any personal connection, in spite of the fact that his name was mentioned in the oath of allegiance.[27]

What Nelte said was correct, but whether blind obedience to illegal or immoral orders was justified by tradition, was for the international court another matter, albeit a vexed issue. Keitel, while being in the defendant's box under cross-examination clearly stated that 'I can only say that fundamentally I bear the responsibility which arises from my position for all those things which resulted from these orders, and which are connected with my name and signature.'[28] Keitel may have hoped that some matters were not raised, but even the most cynical could see that he was not lying as some defendants had done.

It was, Nelte noted, clear that Hitler had recognised Keitel's views as being those of a person he could rely upon. He quoted Jodl who had explained that Keitel's conscience pricked him, that he often raised objections, suggesting alternative orders. During the American cross-examination Keitel had acknowledged he knew some orders were illegal, but he could not contravene the orders of the Supreme Commander of the Armed Forces. Nelte pointed out that every soldier who had appeared before the tribunal had mentioned the duty of allegiance. Nelte accepted that 'the Charter cannot clear him by referring to orders given by his superiors or by his government…at the beginning of my argument I asked you to determine whether, independently of the terms of the Charter, the principle is unimpeachable that the standard determining right or wrong cannot but depend on a national concept'.[29] Later Nelte argued that:

> Dr Stahmer has pointed out that no one acting under or on account of pressure can therefore be a conspirator. I should like to modify this for the circle to which the Defendant Keitel belonged. To say that the defendants belonging to the military branch acted on account of or under pressure, does not accurately represent the real circumstances. It is correct to say that soldiers do not act voluntarily, that is, of their own free will. They must do what they are ordered, regardless of whether or not they approve of it.[30]

Nelte continually appealed to the fact that Keitel was first and foremost a soldier who, like every other military man had to obey orders, even though he accepted that they led to atrocious behaviour.

Nelte tried to find areas in which Keitel had never signed orders yet still appeared implicated, stating that Keitel as Chief of the OKW never issued orders concerning the exploitation, administration, or confiscation of economic property in occupied territory. This may have been true, but it did not avoid the issue that Keitel's name appeared on numerous documents which for most people were immoral and illegal. The French prosecution had attacked Keitel over the massacres at Oradour-sur-Glane and Tulle, and Nelte argued that there was no substantive evidence to support such a prosecution, and that Keitel had no direct part in such atrocities, and no orders with Keitel's signature had been found to validate the argument. His main thrust in this example was to raise the issue that it was all too easy to blame Keitel for matters he supposedly knew nothing about. However, there were many issues which Keitel could not deny and which he instinctively knew to be wrong, although he claimed to have played some part in rectifying matters. For example, although Keitel believed that he had succeeded as far as possible in safeguarding those in question, the Night and Fog Decree had disturbed him. Keitel did not deny that he knew this decree was incompatible with international law. Keitel, in modern parlance, was an 'office-wallah', and claimed that he had no idea that the Night and Fog Decree meant concentration camps and how they were eventually treated. However, in France alone thousands of people simply disappeared under the Night and Fog Decree, and 'ignorance is bliss' was an unacceptable argument. It is also known that Canaris kept him informed of what was happening, often sending him documents of atrocities dressed up as if prepared by enemy agents, knowing Keitel found complaints from German officers to be unacceptable.

Nelte was a strong and respected advocate, and he raised the issue that despite his high rank and position he was not legally responsible for the orders, but this did not hold any substance for the court, as the lowest ranked soldier could argue that when ordered to throw Jewish babies in the fire or smash their heads it was a matter of orders from above.

Throughout the trial the question of Keitel's signature was raised, begging the question as to whether he fully understood what he was ordering, and raising the question as to whether it was him simply signing Hitler's orders. Keitel also pointed out that the signed documents never used the first person, signifying he was the courier for Hitler. The question of forced labour, the treatment of Jews and all areas of immoral and illegal incidents were raised, and whether Keitel played any part. Insofar as the Tribunal regarded Hitler's military staff as guilty, Keitel accepted responsibility in his role as Chief of the OKW. Nelte argued that Keitel never possessed any direct influence on the terrible occurrences in the camps and workshops. However, he also argued that Keitel denied any knowledge of the intended wars of aggression, which was confirmed by Admiral Raeder, but which was understandably difficult to believe. He further argued that Keitel tried five times to leave his post, with Jodl confirming this and adding that Keitel had even contemplated suicide.* When asked during the trial why he had not considered refusing to obey orders and revolt against Hitler, it became clear that for him with his background and tradition this would have been high treason. His soldierly attitudes, Nelte argued were so deep:

> He did not hear the warning voice of the universal conscience. The principles of his soldierly life were so deeply rooted, and governed his thoughts and actions so exclusively, that he was deaf to all considerations which might deflect him from the path of obedience and faithfulness, as he understood them. This is the really tragic role played by the defendant Keitel in this most terrible drama of all times.[31]

In this closing statement Nelte was uncomfortably close to the truth of his client.

Keitel was, as he anticipated, found guilty on all four counts, and he lost the argument to be shot as a soldier, and he was to be hanged like a common criminal. Only the French jurist de Vabes was against executing him. As one of the judges noted, there were too many connecting lines in Keitel's case associating himself with the worse aspects of the criminal Nazi regime, from aggressive war to barbarities under his personal signature.[32] His hanging was not well done, the platform was almost too small for him to drop through damaging his face, and it was a long-protracted death for hanging, taking over 20 minutes. His final words were '*Alles für Deutschland! Deutschland über Alles!*' In his book Telford Taylor who observed the trial wrote 'I shed no tear for any of them, but gave a thought

---

* That he threatened to resign five times is often mentioned, but later Keitel claimed three times, see Gilbert G M, *Nuremberg Diary* (New York: Da Capo Press,1995) p.26.

to Keitel, who had finally seen and acknowledged the reasons for his fate in a dignified way'.[33]

Civilian Interviews

The pre-trial interrogations and the trial itself offered may insights into the character of Keitel and his role, but the reported conversations from various psychiatrists and psychologists revealed much more. For many of the defendants, including Keitel, these visitors were seemingly not part of officialdom. They appeared as friendly guests, almost priest-like, broke the monotony of cell-life, and Keitel always welcomed them and relaxed, resting on his bed smoking his pipe and enjoying the chat. When the prison psychologist called in on Christmas Day, Keitel was almost excited, telling him that 'I thank you from the bottom of my heart for this Christmas visit. You are the only man I can really talk to. A most happy Christmas to you,' he then snapped to attention and bowed from his waist.[34] Those unaccustomed to his military tradition and manners may have found him somewhat obsequious, but the once proud staunch field marshal was now humiliated, ashamed, broken, but remained determined to retain his standards.

He revealed a great deal more than he did in the trial and even in his memoirs. He explained, for example, that ordinary soldiers could be party members, he added 'that he never became one insofar as he knows'…however, he admitted 'sending in a donation to the party at the time and date for enrolment in the party'.[35] This was almost a confession that he was more political than he had previously intimated. He thought German soldiers were good and decent and only did things wrong out of military necessity. Quite how he could describe massacres which were a prominent feature of the trial as military necessity is bewildering, as to justify the killing of Russians for ideological reasons was immoral. He had been moulded by the Nazi leader and had not recognised this even in his personal writings. However, in private, he soon admitted that 'I was in it up to my neck by the time I realised the way things were going. What could I do? I could not resign in time of war; if I refused to obey, I would be killed. Or I could commit suicide. On three different occasions I *thought* of resigning, but it was impossible.'[36]

He added that he had always wanted to be a country gentleman, 'but look what a muddle I got into merely because I was weak and let myself be talked into things. I am not cut out for a field marshal.'[37] His visitor noted during this part of their conversation that 'Keitel is the wooden soldier, the wooden ingratiating smile, yet suffering from the human woes of love of attention, desire for approval.'[38] He often reflected on his personal sadness, noting that between 1938 and 1945 he only saw his home twice, and did so in 1942 to bury his thirty-year-old daughter who died from pneumonia and who had been his favourite child. He also ruminated that his son Ernst-Wilhelm was a captive in Germany, and he had never heard anything of him since.* His other son was in an American prison-of-war camp in the Darmstadt region, his home had been destroyed and his wife now lived in his old home in Braunschweig.

When the subject of Blomberg was raised his visitors soon realised that Keitel found the subject uncomfortable. They thought the problem was that his 'old friend' was embarrassing because of the marriage scandal, but despite their children's marriage they had never been close. When asked about Blomberg, Keitel responded that he was a gentleman and a good man, militarily efficient, but when he took over from Blomberg he added 'that was the beginning of my unhappy time as a soldier'. From that time on he met Hitler several times a week, as beforehand he had only seen him occasionally from a distance. His visitors observed that Keitel was always dignified and composed, but that his hands started to tremble when on the topic of Hitler. Keitel explained to them that 'really I was a chief of staff without responsibility and without knowing what Hitler really wanted and without being told by him'.[39] Keitel claimed he had tried to resign several times but was bluntly refused, he had sharp clashes with Hitler, but even if Keitel had taken his own life, Hitler would not have stopped. He agreed that Hitler was demon-like, but in so doing inadvertently raised the question as to why such a man should

---

* Ernst-Wilhelm was later released but died in 1956.

be obeyed. Keitel claimed he never heard of the brutalities and Jewish prosecution during the war and given the rarefied office situation, this was a possibility, given that he never socially mixed much in public or with frontline soldiers. On the other hand, it could be argued that one would have had to be blind and deaf not to know what was happening, because it was so very public as the humiliation of the Jews on the public streets was so widespread. Keitel explained that Hitler had the ability to convince others he was right, adapting his speeches and powers of persuasion to whomever he was addressing, a feature noted by many others. Keitel explained that Hitler said he expected three things from his selected generals: first, ability for their position, secondly, that they report the situation truthfully, and finally they must be obedient.[40] By obedience, Hitler meant total compliance in a way which would be unacceptable in any civilised world.

Keitel spoke more openly and freely than he would do in the formal courtroom. He blamed the Treaty of Versailles with its economic ramifications and humiliating demands for the rise of Nazism, with which most today, historically, would have some sympathy. He explained how Hitler wanted a middle Europe joining German speakers into one nation, then explaining that Austria was small and could not exist without a German alliance. It was a conversation that at times appeared as wanting to justify the past, other times a sense of regret, sadness, and little joy. Given the life he had led, and the ramifications it was not surprising, but these more friendly conversations drew more out of Keitel with his conflicting emotional problems and offered some insight into the man.

Keitel was badly affected by what was happening to him, telling one visitor he was spiritually in a bad shape, saying 'I am dying of shame. It is disgraceful – horrible! I had at least counted on the honourable record of the Wehrmacht, but now the Wehrmacht is to be disgraced.'[41] When he heard about the atrocities and the involvement of the Wehrmacht in places like Warsaw, he was genuinely distressed, not least because one of his sons had been attached to the SS. He further admitted in the privacy of his cell that he should have left his office to see for himself what was happening. He became almost emotionally dependent on the medical visitors, giving them more of his inner feelings that he did in court or with his fellow defendants. He was stunned that the Prussian military code he had upheld all his life was seen by others to be corrupt, and that Hitler had no idea of what the Prussian tradition meant. He was soon blaming Hitler for committing suicide and thereby avoiding taking the blame, and having explained that, told his visitors 'Don't tell the others [defendants] I just had to get that off my chest', further signifying the weakness in his character.[42] As the trial moved on he became even more vitriolic about his one-time Führer, and he would often become heated waving his arms for emphasis, stating that Hitler 'did not tell us the truth! That is my absolute conviction, and nobody can tell me differently. If he did not deceive us by deliberate lies, then he did by deliberately keeping us in the dark and letting us fight under a false impression.'[43]

Keitel had one British visitor who was cynical or realistic about Keitel's plight. It was an M19 intelligence officer called Airey Neave who had escaped from Colditz. He had been interviewed by the Gestapo and had many friends killed during the war, and he was naturally feeling bitter about the field marshal who had signed the orders. Neave described their first meeting when Keitel 'sprang to attention like a ramrod…in his face a look of weakness. His stupid eyes were frightened…carpet slippers! I had been made to stand barefoot on the stone floor of a Gestapo prison.'[44] Neave was especially angry about the Commando Order and the killing of escaped prisoners, and he made a specific reference to the American guards, who on looking at Keitel felt the same way as he did. Neave is mentioned at this point because although the prison medical visitors tried to see inside Keitel, Airey Neave was only interested in the outside man and what he had done. For such one-time enemies, Keitel's reputation was obnoxious, there was no debate over whether he had just signed Hitler's orders as a functionary, as far as men like Neave were concerned, and with some justification, Keitel was a field marshal who had signed immoral and illegal orders leading many people to their untimely deaths.

Chapter Four

Views of Political Contemporaries

Ulrich von Hassell was a diplomat of the old school, and although he joined the Nazi Party as soon as he became aware of their intentions, he opposed them, and he was executed following the 20 July Plot. Keitel was not a major feature in his diaries, but Hassell's views on Keitel are clearly expressed. Hassell was astonished that Keitel held the view that Britain would not declare war if France were attacked. Hassell decided that Keitel was politically uninformed, and he told his friend Weizsäcker that 'Keitel was simply too stupid to understand such things.'[1] A few days later (29 September 1938) he added that 'there is a growing recognition that Keitel is weak and completely lacks judgement. Stauss [a friend] thinks he is simply incapable of understanding matters.'[2] This lack of understanding of international politics was underlined by Hassell, when he heard that Keitel had proposed that the minute the Germans marched into the Low Countries, Italy would enter the war, which they only did when Mussolini deemed it safe.[3] Later, when Hitler had taken full control of the forces, Hassell noted that during the drive south on the Russian front (1942) he had shut Keitel out completely, a man 'who by his servility had had heaped upon himself the heaviest guilt. When asked about the situation recently Keitel replied, "I know nothing, he tells me nothing, he just shits on me".' Hassell was aware that after the General List affair, Hitler had virtually taken Keitel and Jodl off the Russian front plans. Around his sixtieth birthday Hitler showed Keitel the door, but a few days later he skulked back in.'[4] Hassell was not part of Keitel's circle or involved in the military machinations, but he had sensitive ears in all aspects of German life during these fraught years and was a confidante to many senior figures.

On the other hand, Goebbels was part of the Nazi leadership, and only showed interest in Keitel when it touched upon his area of propaganda. He wrote in his diary that 'Keitel has been too lax in giving the Wehrmacht permission to listen to foreign radio broadcasts. I have put that right.'[5] It was clear from this entry that Goebbels and the traditional Keitel lived in different worlds, which in terms of Nazi political leadership would normally leave Keitel remaining alien. Goebbels was pleased when following a request regarding the propaganda units, Keitel wrote for him a full brief about military discipline, which would have been an easy task for Keitel because that was the only life and tradition he understood.[6] However, one of Goebbel's staff produced a report condemning the work of these units used by the Wehrmacht, which confirmed Goebbel's demands that Keitel and Jodl 'now intend to take steps against the monitoring of foreign broadcasts in the Wehrmacht', which most probably indicated Goebbel's fanatical desire to keep all such actions under his own wing.[7] Goebbels was highly sensitive to any interests or people which touched upon his area of work or his importance. He was having problems with the head of the Wehrmacht propaganda, a Colonel Hesse, observing that Keitel was for sacking the man whereas Brauchitsch was for keeping him.[8] Goebbels' mistrust of the propaganda wing of the Wehrmacht went back as far as 1935 when pursuing military and home-front propaganda.[9] Keitel probably had no idea of Goebbels' powerplay machinations and sense of self-importance. Goebbels did not have a high opinion of Keitel; when he heard he was meeting the Italian military commander Badoglio at Innsbruck he wrote, 'I hope he does more with Badoglio than utter simple platitudes.'[10] As far as Goebbels was concerned Keitel was only Hitler's secretary in military matters, and as cynical as he was with this observation, he was close to the truth.

Himmler left no diary or memos and a search of all his biographies reveals little about his personal views of Keitel. On a basis of historical insights, it was clear that from the invasion of Poland and onwards, there were protests by Wehrmacht officers and others about the barbaric SS treatment of Jews and Poles, creating an ongoing friction between Himmler's much vaunted SS and the German army. This issue may well have reverberated between Himmler and Keitel, who later on behalf of Dönitz was given the task of telling Himmler he was not needed anymore, but it was very different while Hitler lived. Keitel knew that Hitler held Himmler in high regard, and Himmler realised that Keitel was in Hitler's company most of the time, and out of pure safety both probably kept their distance from one another. It seems certain that there was no love lost between them and no mutual respect. One was a dedicated fanatical Nazi and the other a highly traditional military man of the old Prussian order.

Göring's views, being Göring, were better known as he had scant respect for most of his colleagues, and like Himmler was often jealous of those who were close to Hitler. 'Keitel and Lammers he hated – mere secretaries – for worming their way between himself and Hitler.'[11] He also probably knew that Keitel was one of his critics for not mobilising his forces well enough in the early years and at Stalingrad. In many ways it was like any office where jealously over the boss and rumours abounded, creating complex divisions, a state of affairs Hitler welcomed under his policy of divide and rule. While the Stalingrad disaster was unfolding 'Goebbels and Speer, were both committed to undermining the influence of Bormann, Keitel and Lammers (The Committee of Three)', which all typified the nature of the Nazi rule around Hitler.[12] They were hoping for Göring's support who 'was contemptuous of Lammers and Keitel – 'nothing but the Führer's secretaries'.[13] This certainly appeared to be the way Hitler viewed Keitel, as one of Hitler's biographers wrote, 'for the head of the OKW he [Hitler] appointed a man who was to prove quite incapable of withstanding him, even if he wanted to'.[14] Hitler was always changing men for one reason or another if they showed any signs of disagreement with him. Later, at Nuremberg, Göring in conversation said that 'Keitel, who although he was called a field marshal, was a small person who did whatever Hitler instructed' which may have been true but also reflected Göring himself.[15]

Many comments were made by his contemporaries at the Nuremberg Trial, most of them unflattering and tinged with the circumstances of the stress of the day. When Dönitz claimed that Keitel was at least an honest man, Franz von Papen retorted 'an honest man without a mind of his own. But anyway, an honest man', with Hjalmar Schacht adding 'an honest man but not a man at all'.[16]

Speer in his memoirs mentioned Keitel many times, but it must be recalled that Speer had managed to convince everyone at the trial he was a reformed man, and his memoirs were all part of his self-justification. However, he had noted that Keitel would speak up in favour of Hitler's decisions when other military personnel were present, but otherwise he had remained silent, adding 'that constantly in Hitler's presence he had completely succumbed to his influence'.[17] Allegedly, Speer wrote, that Hitler had told him that 'Keitel was as loyal as a dog' which embodied the sort of person he wanted in his entourage.[18] Speer had noted that military men with their background tended to remain 'distinctly dispassionate', but for that reason 'the Byzantine flatteries of Keitel and Göring seemed all the more obtrusive.'[19]

In Italy, Germany's closest ally, the political feelings towards Keitel were boldly expressed by Ciano in his diary when quoting Mussolini: 'Keitel is a man who is happy that he is Keitel', then Ciano added 'the opinion expressed by Bismarck [German diplomat in Italy] is more to the point, Keitel is imbecilic'.[20] Ciano who was gathering a distrust of the German allies spoke with many of them in an open almost dangerous way, and whether this reflected his or other opinions is difficult to pinpoint. Later, Ciano in his usual cynical and amusing style, related a time when Hitler was giving one of his boring monologues, described how Jodl after an epic struggle had fallen asleep, and 'Keitel was reeling, but he succeeded in keeping his head up. He was too close to Hitler to let himself go as he would have liked to do.'[21] In a curious and unintentional way Ciano's humour put his finger on the reality of Keitel's position, he was always close to Hitler like a dog on the lead, and always attentive to his master's whims and wishes. In the allied camp Keitel was rarely a focal point of interest, but it was assumed that as Chief of the OKW he had formidable powers. It was only after the war that it was realised that Ciano's amusing anecdote was closer to the truth.

Views of Military Contemporaries

Some of the views of his military colleagues have been gleaned from their post-war observations and must be treated with a degree of circumspection. This arises because their later views were often written to justify themselves or try and throw these military leading officers into a better light.

During post-war interrogations, General Heinz Guderian explained, 'Keitel is basically a decent character. He was absolutely overpowered by Hitler's personality, and he considered it as his duty to approve of everything that Hitler said. I have never had occasion to observe that he would oppose Hitler in anything.'[22] Guderian's observation reflected the views of most of the German military commanders, knowing that Keitel was Hitler's mouthpiece, and few thought otherwise. One of Hitler's adjutants, Nikolaus von Below, said that when von Seeckt 'was in charge, it's doubtful whether Keitel would have got any further than a major'.[23]

In a biography of von Rundstedt, it was noted that Rundstedt thought Keitel 'was a mere cipher and message carrier, and that it was not worth being anything but courteous to him'.[24] Later Rundstedt became more critical, denigrating Keitel and Jodl 'as mere yes-men'.[25] In his papers Rommel related the time he had flown to see Hitler to try and explain why it was essential to evacuate North Africa, which was sound common sense. He had hoped for a sensible discussion with Hitler, Keitel, and Jodl. However, Hitler flew into an uncontrollable rage, and as Rommel noted in his papers, his 'staff officers, the majority of whom had never heard a shot fired in anger, appeared to agree with every word the Führer said'.[26] It was noteworthy that Rommel had at least noted that they were brought in, intimating that he knew full well these men had little choice but to agree with Hitler, especially when he was in a rage. In a similar manner General von Senger und Etterlin, one of the more educated and morally inclined generals, who rarely commented in his memoirs on Keitel, noted that the directive came from him and 'it can be deduced Hitler' agreed, and it was probably his order.[27] It was not just generals but often their wives too who were aware of the situation, as Field Marshal Paulus's wife Elena Constance 'had nothing but haughty contempt for men like Field

Marshal Keitel'.[28] His wife later expressed the opinion that had Paulus eventually won Stalingrad, he might have replaced Keitel, and yet up to the stage before the fall of Stalingrad, Paulus had always obeyed even the most stupid military decisions which Hitler demanded.[29] Paulus had thought at one stage that Hitler was militarily able, but later observed that 'under the influence of an incessant stream of fatuous flattery from men like Reichsmarschal Göring and Field Marshal Keitel, he really came to regard himself as a military genius'.[30] He was directly critical of Keitel, mentioning that Hitler must have planned Operation *Sea Lion*, as Keitel 'had no creative ideas of his own, and confined himself...to accepting Hitler's ideas and intentions and passing them on'.[31] When German plans had fallen into enemy hands, Paulus was summoned to meet the furious Hitler, and he observed that Keitel had drawn up a 'summary of the charges which he had himself drafted'.[32] However, although Keitel had done the work it was evidently under the Führer's instructions. On the other hand, Paulus noted that when later Hitler wanted General Heim shot, 'he was saved only with great difficulty by Field Marshal Keitel'.[33] However, Keitel could not be regarded as the man who was able to placate Hitler's outrageous responses, as Field Marshal von Manstein recalled a time over a failure in the Ukraine, when Hitler wanted the general killed, but he had heard from Zeitzler that 'even Keitel advocated the immediate shooting of the senior German general'.[34]

Manstein was critical of the whole concept of the OKW, stating that Hitler 'had relegated the OKW to the status of a military secretariat'.[35] He noted that everything depended on the Führer's intuition, with Göring and Keitel showering adulation on Hitler, while Brauchitsch and Raeder did so with a sense of resignation.[36] Manstein was highly respected (but not necessarily liked) among the senior German army staff, and General Heinz Guderian once made the effort to persuade Hitler to replace Keitel with Manstein, but soon discovered it was totally unacceptable. He realised that 'Keitel made life easy for Hitler; he sought to anticipate and fulfil Hitler's every wish before it had been uttered.'[37] Guderian was brave enough to challenge Hitler on why the attack in Russia was so necessary, but Keitel interrupted pointing out that it was for political reasons, upholding his personal belief that soldiers obey their politicians by quoting Hitler to him.[38] Guderian refused to follow the obsequious attitude of Keitel, and he later pressed to replace Keitel suggesting that 'by this act he could get rid of the obscure confusion of command functions that now reigned' but admitting it was a total failure as 'Hitler refused to part with Field Marshal Keitel'.[39] On one of Guderian's persistent challenges Hitler completely lost his temper, and after the meeting Keitel reprimanded him, warning him that he could have given the Führer a stroke. He refused to listen to Guderian's belief that any statesman should be prepared to be challenged.[40] It would appear that Keitel also saw himself as Hitler's emotional carer. For his part Guderian came to the well-known conclusion that Keitel was 'in a state of permanent hypnosis...or of resigned acquiescence'.[41] As Guderian concluded his post-war notes, he was gracious enough to admit that Keitel 'was basically a decent individual who did his best... but he soon fell under the sway of Hitler's personality'.[42] It appears that Guderian was one of the better commanders, and he was also astute in human nature, as he had seized upon Keitel's issue of obedience and loyalty as having been transformed into a form of hypnotic spell.

One field marshal who tended to stay loyal even after the war was Kesselring, who concluded that Jodl was an able strategist, but Keitel, with whom he had less to do, stated that 'his instructions relating to the creation of new units or replacements were based on Führer's orders, which, if arguable, could not be altered'.[43] Once again portraying Keitel as Hitler's conduit pipe, Kesselring's one time Chief of Staff, General Siegfried Westphal was deeply experienced, having also been chief of staff to Rommel and von Rundstedt, and his views on Keitel were highly critical. He wrote that 'Keitel exemplifies the fatal consequences which may follow when a man is placed in an important position for which he is completely inadequate...he lacked all moral courage.'[44] Westphal further noted that the OKW as an apparatus was held in contempt, retelling the joke that OKW stood for *Oben kein Widerstand* (no resistance at the top). Westphal observed that the German leadership had no council as it had during the Great War, in the OKW there was only Hitler's military staff, who all lacked real authority.[45] Westphal made the important criticism that while Jodl had occasionally visited the front lines, Keitel never made an appearance.[46] On a more conciliatory note Westphal, when referring to the Night and Fog decree stated that 'Keitel was certainly not a bad man, but his fear of the demon whom he served suffocated the urgings of his conscience', and added that many were surprised he stood the strain of working for Hitler for the whole war, like others commenting on Hitler's hypnotic powers.[47] Westphal once was outspoken in Hitler's presence, and Keitel escorted him from the room telling him he was lucky, because 'if we old fools had said even half as much the Führer would have us hanged'.[48]

These insights of Keitel's military contemporaries tend to vary little; most are contemptuous with the occasional possibility that behind Hitler's mouthpiece was possibly a decent sort of person, but generally Keitel was held in contempt. In Britain at a prison-of-war camp for officers (Trent Park) bugging devices were used to gather information and opinions. Sönke Neitzel in his book edited and published many of the conversations.[49] Keitel was mentioned about sixteen times, sometimes in passing, otherwise in the same derogatory terms as reflected above. It was basically the same pattern in Liddell Hart's book on speaking to German generals post-war.[50]

General Histories and their Perceptions

Nearly every historian dealing with the Second World War and the Nazi regime hardly differ in their views of Keitel, some expressing their views directly, some emphasising the point by repetition, some by a few references then ignoring Keitel's existence. Richard Overy in his biography of Göring describes Keitel as being like Hess, 'who were merely Hitler's echoes'.[51] Michael Burleigh wrote of the time when Blomberg told Hitler it was Keitel who ran the office, with Hitler replying, 'That's exactly the man I'm looking for', with Burleigh adding that 'He would treat the OKW like a Dictaphone'.[52]

In his massive 900 page volume on the Second World War, *A World at Arms*, Gerhard Weinberg mentions Keitel only six times, maybe indicating that he was not worth the effort. The French historian Henri Michel in his similarly massive volume barely mentions Keitel, but he does drop some heavy hints as to his character and role. According to Michel, Keitel was supposed to have said 'The Führer had informed Jodl and me once and for all that politics were none of our business…we were not always in agreement with his decisions at the operational level, yet we always carried them out to the letter'.[53] Michel also quoted one of Keitel's orders in July 1941 when he wrote, 'the army must spread terror so as to nip in the bud any temptation to resist'.[54] It may be that when Michel wrote that Keitel issued the Night and Fog decree he missed the possibility that Keitel was only the signatory of Hitler's instructions, but this does not obscure the fact he was signing illegal and immoral orders. William Shirer's massive tome mentions Keitel many times but only in passing, and like the rest of the world, unsure whether it was Keitel who issued the orders or whether he was doing so under Hitler's demand, in many incidents an unresolved conundrum. Shirer is nevertheless in agreement with most historians, accusing Jodl and Keitel of being 'yes men', and pointing out that Keitel was also known as 'tell-tale toady', always keeping Hitler informed even as to what his colleagues thought.[55]

The historian Richard Evans mentions Keitel a few times, again mainly because he was there, passing on or giving instructions and of little importance. He described Keitel as 'sycophantic' who after the 20 July Plot bomb exploded, he 'burst into tears, crying: "My Leader, you are alive, you are alive!"'[56] Antony Beevor like Evans only mentions Keitel in passing, but he offers a curious insight when after the bombing of Dresden, Goebbels suggested they killed the same number of Allied prisoners which appealed to Hitler, but 'calmer voices prevailed, including Keitel, Jodl, Dönitz and Ribbentrop'.[57] Norman Davies barely mentions Keitel, twice in passing, and then commenting that Keitel was 'Hitler's closet adviser… lacking talent and backbone, he followed his Nazi masters slavishly'.[58]

On the other hand, in his history of the Second World War Andrew Roberts refers to Keitel many times, and early on in his work wrote that Keitel 'was selected on the basis of his sycophancy and his solid lack of personality and intellect', quoting Keitel who had explained 'all his orders originated from Hitler'.[59] Roberts pointed out that Keitel accepted in court he had no idea of Russian resources and strength, yet that was his task and he was no strategist.[60] The OKH generals despised Jodl and especially Keitel for making no effort to stand up to Hitler, 'accusing them of cowardice'.[61] In his appraisal of Keitel, Roberts is almost scathing, accusing Keitel of confusing facts about weapons and resources with strategy, observing that 'because a train-spotter can take down the number of a train in his notebook, it doesn't mean he can drive one'.[62]

It was impossible to find in the general histories any deviance from the theme that Keitel was a mere sycophant whose sense of obedience made him Hitler's main tool, and by signing all Hitler's orders he seemed to give them military authority to those unhappy to receive such instructions for military or legal reasons.

Chapter Five

Final Thoughts

In mapping out Keitel's life there are only a few conclusions which can be drawn, but his closeness to Hitler's presence revealed many aspects of Hitler's dominating influence not just at the political level, but over the military scene. Hitler was not just issuing orders to occupy another country but taking control of the plans, and at a sudden whim changing them as in *Barbarossa*. He also dictated the details of how a battle should be fought, and when a local commander objected or protested, they knew there was the danger of being sacked. Time and time again he refused permission to retreat even when his commanders knew it was sheer common sense, and no number of individual protests would change his mind. If anyone had the right to question Hitler, most assumed it would be his top military man Keitel, who was simply brushed aside despite his occasional threats of resignation and even suicide. The politician Adolf Hitler, whose only experience as a soldier had been as a corporal in the First World War, dictated when war was to be declared, how it was to be planned and then instructed details in the various battles. When his orders led to disaster Hitler blamed the commanders. Keitel drew to attention the number of generals and high-ranking officers he sacked, often at a whim, and anyone even suspected of treachery from his point of view often landed up in disgrace or executed. In Britain, Churchill often came up with what can be described as 'madcap' ideas, but he had to pass them through the British version of the OKW, the Imperial General Staff. His top man was the Chief, (CIGS) and for most of the war Keitel's British counterpart at face level was Field Marshal Alan Brooke. In Britain it led to many contentious debates between the politician Churchill and his military adviser Brooke, but Churchill, unlike Hitler, never demanded total obedience, and accepted military advice despite his annoyance. Brooke also frequently challenged Churchill over his interference with field commanders, something no one would dare with Hitler.

It has been claimed with some substance that Hitler appeared to have a hypnotic effect on those whom he met, an ability to draw even highly ranked and strong-minded men under his spell. In terms of Keitel, with his sense of military obedience, it seems that after Hitler's early military successes this all turned into a form of slavish devotion. Many of Keitel's contemporary critics perceived this weakness which led to his nicknames and mockery behind his back. This was amply demonstrated in the text with the reference to the German documents relating to conversations between Keitel and Hitler. It was not simply a matter of Keitel treading carefully with the dictator who was like a ticking time-bomb, but a genuine adoration which persisted until the revelations of the Nuremberg Trial. For many generals, especially as the war became one of defence and survival, there was, naturally, a high degree of pessimism, an element which was dangerous to raise in Hitler's presence. Rommel told Keitel that Hitler was living in a world of fantasy and the only hope of preventing chaos was to end the war in the east, which Keitel promised to raise with Hitler, but adding 'I know there is nothing to be done'.[1] Rommel was right in so far that in the closing months of the war Hitler and his confidantes were living in an unreal world. Keitel recognised that Hitler was, in modern parlance a dangerous 'control freak', yet persisted in serving him to the bitter end.

It has often been suggested that Keitel had a limited intellect, a nervous disposition which made him easy for a man like Hitler to manipulate. Those on the outside may have seen Keitel as a powerful and strong figure, his stern looks and posture would have helped, but for many he was just Hitler's lapdog who did what he was told. At the Nuremberg Trial Göring said that 'Keitel's role was a very thankless one in which he came between the millstones of stronger personalities'.[2] There seems little doubt that Keitel appeared to have a weak temperament, but this was undoubtedly the reason Hitler selected him for the post. A Manstein, Guderian, Rommel, and many other military commanders would not have lasted long in Hitler's company, which explained why there were no competitors for Keitel's post.

In the post-war trial situation, much could be discovered about Keitel's personality, and more to the point he had to confront his beliefs and work over the previous years. Keitel tried to explain that he was not the originator of the orders he had signed, but he could not avoid and accepted the fact he had signed them even though he had doubts. During the interbellum years General von Seeckt had always demanded obedience, first to Seeckt, then to the Weimar Republic, and all this was Keitel's legacy along with his background and Prussian military training. For Keitel, Hitler was the new form of monarch who had to be obeyed to the last iota of his demands. He also argued he had no influence and just passed on the orders from Hitler. He was the traditional product of the Prussian military ethos, and although he was by nature not an evil person, he stepped into the world of immorality and criminality because of his training in total obedience.

He had sat behind his desk for most of the war, travelled on Hitler's instructions to meet major figures in Nazi allied countries, but never into a serious war zone until the very last weeks of the war. He hung his head in shame at the films of the concentration camps, must have known that the Commissar Order, the Commando Order, and the Night and Fog Decree and many others would lead to outright barbaric behaviour. If the ordinary foot-soldier argued he was ordered to throw babies into the fire or smash their heads against walls, the excuse of such orders could not be accepted in any normal court. A criminal might argue that he killed a family because his mafia boss had ordered him to, but he would be guilty for doing it as would the mafia boss when caught. If the mafia boss had asked the local priest to convey his orders to the assassin, then the priest would also be guilty of murder if he were aware of the instructions. Keitel signed orders which amounted to criminal and totally immoral consequences, and his attendance at so many major planning meetings, with all his signatures providing so many connecting lines with the evil of the Nazi regime, he knew in his heart of hearts he would be found guilty. Keitel by his constant attendance with Hitler knew what was being planned, what was happening, and he only needed a modicum of intelligence to foresee the consequences. Nevertheless, he rarely raised an eyebrow as he transmitted orders, never allowed his subdued conscience to interfere, and any sense of morality he jettisoned as he transmitted Hitler's orders.

As his lawyer Nelte argued, Keitel's sense of obedience was so deep he 'did not hear the warning voice of the universal conscience'. Many observed, even his critics, that Keitel was fundamentally a decent man, Jodl said at times Keitel's conscience was pricked, and although he was scorned for his weakness and obedience if not adulation of Hitler, few found him personally unpleasant. Keitel was the product of a morally corrupt system which exists in many countries, namely that obedience to orders comes first and foremost, despite any moral misgivings. It took the findings of the Nuremberg Trial to establish that immoral or illegal orders ought not to be obeyed. Obeying military orders was a central theme of the Prussian military code, and Keitel was deeply immersed in this way of thinking, he was the product of the system, and the Nazi regime took this way of thinking to its apex or rather nadir. However, some brought up in the same tradition knew when to protest, even though it meant losing their jobs and even their lives. The system was corrupt and Keitel by adhering to it without question, having the weakness not to protest when he thought matters were wrong, was found guilty. Keitel was wrong but a pitiful case, even as Telford noted he passed a thought for Keitel who had recognised his errors. Only the French jurist de Vabes was against executing him, and this writer cannot help feeling that like a rehabilitated drug-offender can teach others not to follow his past, a reformed Keitel could have been encouraged to write and speak on his mistake of total obedience as a lesson to future generations.

Field Marshal Friedrich Paulus

The Eleventh-Hour Field Marshal

Chapter One

Early Life

Background Family

Friedrich Wilhelm Paulus was born on 23 September 1890 in Guxhagen, and grew up in Kassel, Hesse-Nassau a province in Prussia, a name now discarded. Many writers frequently refer to him as *von* Paulus, but he was not aristocracy, nor even mild nobility, and like other German field marshals such as Kesselring, Keitel, and Rommel, he came from what is best described as a middle-class background. Nearly all the Russian sources tended to address him as *von* Paulus, because there was a Soviet belief that all high-ranking German officers came from noble stock, but it is a mistake often made by many western historians to this day. It has been suggested that Paulus later liked to insinuate he arose from noble stock, but there is no reliable evidence for such a claim. Whenever his name is mentioned today, with or without *von*, it is always linked with the battle of Stalingrad, one of the more important strategic defeats for Nazi Germany, and for no other reason is he regarded as highly relevant. However, he remains of interest because of his sense of blind obedience to Hitler and his eventual turning against the dictator.

His father Ernst Paulus could be described as a white-collar worker, starting his career as a bookkeeper (some claiming he was just the cashier) updating records of the finances for a reformatory institution (an approved school) and later progressing to be the Chief Treasurer of Hesse-Nassau, later moving to Marburg. He was evidently an ambitious man who worked his way through the social strata to a reasonably respected position, but never carried *von* before his name. He had married Bertha who was the daughter of Friedrich Nettelbeck who was his superior in the reformed school. They were what the British designate as middleclass and up and coming civil servants. His son Friedrich Paulus, destined to be a field marshal under unusual circumstances, had a brother called Ernst and a sister called Cornelia but generally known as Nelly.

Friedrich Paulus had the usual social problems of those days, as he was neither wealthy nor of the nobility class. He attended the Kassel High School, successfully passing his final examinations in 1909. When he applied to join the Imperial German Navy in the same year, he failed to gain admission, as the navy still tended to be more driven by social class than the army and demanded less manpower. He pursued his ambitions by reading law at Marburg University (Philipps University), mainly jurisprudence, but he never gained a degree. He lived in a society where military officers were deemed to have a higher social status than even lawyers and doctors, and after just one year's study he heard the army was enlarging, and he was offered a place. The army had various criteria for officer training, but undoubtedly looked to the sons of the civil service class accustomed to serving. He joined the 111th Infantry Regiment as an officer-cadet in February 1910, and his career followed the traditional course for those who were successful in the initial training.* In 1910 he was an Ensign, at the end of the year a 2nd Lieutenant, and after further training in a military school gazetted Lieutenant (August 1911). The 111th Infantry was part of the 28th Infantry belonging to the Corps of the 7th Army, with which he was still a junior officer when the Great War started.

He was a tall figure and like others of the same build very conscious that he stood out, the classical figure for a military man. This along with his class-origins, probably explained why he was forever conscious of his appearance, always dressing correctly, precisely, and neat in his appearance, so much so his friends thought 'he was obsessed by his turn out and his fellow officers called him *der Lord*.[1] His need to be well presented remained a feature for him most of his life. Being in the Prussian military carried its own social status, more so than Britain and most other countries. While in the initial stages of army training, he met his wife to be, as she

---

* The 111th Infantry Regiment had the earlier title of Markgraf Ludwig's 3rd Baden Regiment.

had two brothers serving alongside him in their regiment. They were Romanian and came from a family with a diplomatic background and royal Boyar connections, which may have been another reason some write *von* before his name. It was unusual for aspiring officers to marry foreign wives, but the royal connections may have helped. When the Nazis came to power it was not considered correct to marry foreign wives, but it was apparently no disadvantage for Paulus. While on a Black Forest holiday with the two brothers, Paulus met their sister, which eventuated in their marriage on 4 July 1912.

His wife, Elena Constance Rosetti-Solescu was evidently extremely attractive, said to be a member of the Rosetti family, causing a slight ripple amongst his colleagues and friends. Elena Constance's Romanian noble stock also meant she had a wealthy background. Correspondence revealed that he and her friends called her Coco, and they had a daughter called Olga born in the year of the Great War, 1914, and twin sons Friedrich and Ernst Alexander born in 1918, the last year of that war.* Both entered the army and became captains. Friedrich died at the Anzio landings in February 1944, while Ernst saw action and was wounded on the Eastern Front. He later wrote the preface to Walter Göerlitz's book about Field Marshal Paulus, and he managed to stay in touch with his father in the post-war years. Paulus and Elena's marriage lasted, but they were parted by his imprisonment after Stalingrad and never met again as she died in 1949 in Baden-Baden, though he insisted before his own death that his cremated remains should be buried with her. The Paulus family reflected the tragedy of the war years.

The First World War

When war was declared Paulus was Adjutant of the 3rd Battalion of his infantry regiment. For most of the war he was a regimental and then a staff officer, experiencing both the east and western fronts if only by being there. When the Great War started Paulus's regiment was part of

---

* Olga married Baron von Kutzschenbach and died in 2003 in Baden-Baden.

the thrust into France, and he observed the action around Vosges and Arras in 1914. He was ill for a time, and he had to leave the front. He did not return to his own regiment but was transferred as a staff officer to the *Alpenkorps*, which was a provisional mountain formation, the size of a division and rumoured amongst the enemy to be one of the best. He was appointed as a Regimental Staff Officer to the highly prestigious unit called the 2nd Prussian Jäger Regiment, with which he remained until the end of the war. It has been noted that 'His primary virtues were his conscientiousness, his skill in getting on with his superiors and his ready adaptability'.[2] He was well known for pondering the facts presented to him to avoid making a mistake, spending hours over a problem to avoid any errors. He would be covered in smoke from his habit of enjoying cigarettes and lived off coffee when at his desk. His experience at the frontline was limited, 'for seven weeks he directed a machine-gun detachment on a relatively inactive sector of the Russian Front in 1916', and many observers have often pointed out his weakness as a field commander was due to his lack of experience.[3] After the war he finished as a captain on the staff of the 48th Reserve Division. In 1918 he received the Iron Cross, Classes II, and I, which was more of a routine decoration for service, and having been promoted to captain he must have felt secure within the military world he inhabited. He was from these early times regarded as a man of good manners, known for arduous work, dedication to the task in hand, and he was popular. His pleasantness and manners endeared him even to his superiors. During the war he had seen service in France, including Verdun, Romania, and Serbia, he may well have seen the attrition of the trenches from a distance, but as a staff officer he probably never experienced it at first hand. At the end of the war, he observed the flight of the Kaiser and the collapse of the highly traditional world in which he had been nurtured. German life had been turned upside down and inside out, but he stayed in the army which had become his life.

Interbellum Years

The war concluded with his survival, not even wounded, but Paulus had next to no direct battle experience or any real form of field command. It was noted that he was good at desk work, but when he was given a command post-war, 'the directing staff reported "this officer lacks decisiveness"'.[4] After the Great War he became a brigade adjutant with the Freikorps, one of nearly 4,000 officers called to this task. A report on his work as adjutant stated:

> A typical General Staff Officer of the old school, of good physique, extremely well turned out, modest (at times over-modest) a pleasant young man, with excellent manners and a good mixer. He is, admittedly at pains to avoid making enemies, but he is an exceptionally good and enthusiastic soldier…he is slow but methodical in his office work… displays a marked tactical ability…he is too fond of working at night and sustaining himself with coffee and cigarettes.[5]

As the years unfolded this proved to be a reliable description, as did the earlier staff report that 'he lacked decisiveness'. In other words, he was good behind the scenes at planning and other necessary office work, but his lack of combat or field experience was short of the necessary experience for a field commander. He was a man of theory who took time to think through problems, whereas battlefield reactions need to be quick and decisive.

As is well-known the Treaty of Versailles had limited the army to 100,000, with many other military prohibitions, but the Germans clandestinely rebuilt their military structure, mainly under the guidance of General von Seeckt. Seeckt was a typical officer of his place and time, and he was determined to re-establish German military power. It has been claimed that when Seeckt first met Hitler in 1923, he said, 'we were one in our aim; only our paths were different', and these paths soon alienated von Seeckt who never trusted Hitler's methods or his intentions for Germany.[6] Seeckt was looking for military efficiency, with Paulus at his level soon rising in recognition for his military abilities in organisation. The new structure remoulded itself with a major emphasis on mechanised force with which he often became involved. He was again noted for his height and competence but never regarded as inspirational, often a major element required in a good field commander. He was known to be always industrious, consumed with a hobby of studying Napoleon's invasion of Russia, which given his future was ironic. In October 1922 Paulus was instructed to attend a course for General Staff Officers in Berlin, (known as the R-Course for promising staff officers) studying land-surveying and topography, which was naturally all clandestine. It was here he was given the 'Latin nickname *Fabius Cunctator* – the "waverer"', which was not forgotten by some colleagues.[7]

The following year in 1923 he was made Captain and posted to the General Staff of Reichswehr Group Two in Kassel, and from 1924 to 1927 he worked as a GSO (General Staff Officer) in Stuttgart, followed by two years of regimental duty with the Infantry. This was followed with spending time with the 5th Division instructing tactics and seeking to be a *junior leader*, a vague and inhouse title because 'the training of general staff officers being at the time forbidden by the Versailles Treaty'.[8]

In the autumn of 1931, he was transferred to the Ministry of Defence in Berlin as an instructor in tactics. These were difficult days in Germany because of the political uncertainty, the Weimar Republic was struggling with dangerous street battles between communists and right-wing groups. The Weimar Republic had an excellent basis as a democratic system, but it was unfairly associated with the humiliation of the Versailles Treaty, and as a system struggled with the burden of coping with the violent political extremes which were formidable. Paulus, like many other officers followed the tradition of keeping above politics, knowing that they were reconstructing German military strength after the Great War with the prohibitions of the Versailles Treaty. In February 1931 he was promoted to major on the General Staff, just as Hitler was emerging on the centre stage. Paulus's wife was not enamoured by the brown shirt thugs, and the historian Göerlitz wrote that to 'decent people like Paulus, his [Hitler's] uncouthness must have been repellent'.[9] However, although Göerlitz may have been right in this speculation, Paulus started to appreciate the values he perceived in Hitler, especially in his attempts to re-establish German power and a sense of authority. Later, he always addressed Hitler as the leader, *mein Führer*, and at times admired him. It was not until he was in Russian captivity that he started to open up with criticisms about Hitler which, again speculatively, may possibly have been simmering below the surface but subdued by his inbuilt obedience. He seemed to have no doubts about Hitler's supremacy and ability before the Russian campaign. From various sources of information, it appears that his wife never felt comfortable with the Nazi regime. When Hitler came to power Paulus was still a mid-ranking officer, but under the Nazi regime his promotions increased.

In April 1934 as Lieutenant Colonel Paulus, he took command of the Motor Transport Section, which was transforming into a motorised reconnaissance unit, while also developing other well-known projects of motorisation. Just over a year later, promoted to colonel, he became Chief of Staff to the headquarters of the Mechanised Forces in Berlin, planning for the use of tanks in warfare, which would be important in the years to come. Tanks could be used defensively, but they were more of an offensive weapon, and one opponent was General Ludwig Beck who recognised the dangers of an unnecessary war. Beck resigned in 1938 unhappy about Hitler's plans, and he had the courage to criticise and resist the dictator, his resignation pre-empting his dismissal. He went into retirement, ostensibly, but stayed in touch with military friends and plotted for Hitler's overthrow, committing suicide following the 20 July Plot which he had helped to organise. It has been suggested that Paulus and Beck had similar characters and backgrounds, but not their thinking processes, as Paulus seldom questioned instructions.

Beck's successor as Chief-of-Staff was General Franz Halder who had similar views, regarding Hitler with a degree of scepticism, which has been suggested was possibly why he later chose Paulus as his own Chief-of-Staff. This seems unlikely at this time, and Paulus was more likely selected because of his polite nature and industriousness. Sadly, Paulus never kept a diary or wrote his memoirs, was known to be tight-lipped, at times showing little emotion, and this remains speculation but possibly with some validity, but it was also a time when Paulus may have started building some personal faith in Hitler. This new posting indicated that Paulus was regarded as a competent staff officer, and in February 1938 he was appointed as Chief of the General Staff to General Heinz Guderian of the new XVI Army Corps. Guderian later wrote that his Chief of Staff was Colonel Paulus:

> Whom I had known for many years; he was the finest type of brilliantly clever, conscientious, hard-working, original and talented General Staff officer, and it is impossible to doubt his pure-minded and lofty patriotism. In later years, the foulest slanders and accusations were to be levelled at the unfortunate commander of the Sixth Army destroyed at Stalingrad. Until such time as Paulus is himself capable of speaking in his defence, I cannot accept any of the charges made against him.[10]

Guderian's assessment of Paulus came after the war, but it probably reflected many other commanders who saw in him a skilled staff officer who was loyal to his country, though there were a few officers with a growing uncertainty whether being loyal to Germany meant trusting Hitler. However, Hitler seemed to grow in Paulus's estimation as success followed success.

Another influence on Paulus was Field Marshal Walter von Reichenau, a prominent Nazi officer who hated deskwork which was Paulus's love. This suited both men as Reichenau would rather be outside and active, while Paulus kept his office running well. Reichenau has been described as Paulus's mentor, who was now beginning to fall more and more under the influence of Hitler; it would be Reichenau who would later suggest to Hitler that Paulus should take over the Sixth Army.[11] Whether he was Paulus's mentor is questionable, but Paulus certainly gained a better reputation for being associated with Reichenau, who had a much vaunted reputation for his thrusting leadership and successes on the battlefield.

Just before the Second World War the *Anschluss* with Austria, the taking of the Rhineland, and Sudetenland all occurred, and Hitler fulfilled these deeply held German dreams without bloodshed, and his popularity rose, and probably increased Paulus's admiration of the new leader.

Chapter Two

War Years

The Second World War

Paulus's wife Elena saw the attack on Poland as unjustified, but for Paulus it was a matter of military duty, but her views must have unsettled him. Later she would express similar misgivings about the attack on Russia, their one-time ally and collaborator, but none of this appeared to disturb Paulus whose duty it was to obey orders; other considerations did not count for him, not even his wife's opinions.

Paulus remained in his post until May 1939, when he was promoted to major general becoming chief of staff to Field Marshal Walter von Reichenau, with whom he saw service in Poland. Reichenau led the Tenth Army, which was later renamed the Sixth, and later saw action in the Low Countries. Reichenau admired the younger Paulus, probably because of the efficient way his office was run. Reichenau was often brutal, once ordering men to be shot who went absent without leave or breached his disciplinary code. He would often fight at the front and did not lack courage. In a letter to Paulus on 27 September 1941, Reichenau described how he had led the fighting: 'I was right up in front every day of the battle…I put speed into 44 Infantry Division's attack by personally leading the assault.'[1] In this statement he may well have been relating to the well-known time he led his men in an attack by swimming ahead of them to cross a river. He was an unusual and robust officer, and as a senior commander he led by example, but for others such individual heroism put the key person in danger. Paulus worked with him, and when King Leopold decided to capitulate, it was Reichenau with his Chief of Staff Paulus who dictated the various terms and agreements in their headquarters. The next surrender Paulus experienced, as the historian Beevor noted, was his own capitulation at Stalingrad.[2]

While serving under Reichenau it appeared that Paulus had 'played a part in the practical preparations and planning for Operation *Sea Lion*'.[3] The Sixth Army, which had done well in Poland and France, was now destined to be part of Operation *Sea Lion*. It was planned to leave Le Havre and head towards Brighton and Hove, which would have involved a long dangerous sea crossing. Reichenau's reputation as a fighting commander was ranked high, and as noticed above, continued to enhance Paulus's reputation by mere relationship. Paulus was again noted for his good manners and was popular, and after the battle for France was called to Berlin in the late summer of 1940, to be deputy chief of staff to the German General Staff of the Army, (OKH), Colonel-General Franz Halder.

It was at Zossen, the headquarters of the OKH, that Paulus was Halder's major planner for Operation *Barbarossa*; he was not one of the first organisers as he worked on some initial ideas of General Erich Marcks. Hitler was obsessed with invading Russia, using the excuse as some doubtful senior commanders thought, that it was a preventative war, because he had postulated that the Russians were planning to invade Germany, which few believed had any veracity. After his retrieval of German land before the war, the rapid success in taking Poland and defeating the French who had the largest army in Europe, even the better military minds at this time were beginning to think Hitler was a military genius, and critical questions were soon shut down or not asked. There were tensions between those in the Supreme Headquarters (OKW) operating under Hitler and supported by Keitel and Jodl, with the OKH, the army leadership. Paulus even complained once when he was giving an address to all the staffs, Jodl made a point of yawning out of boredom.[4] As noted in his earlier army reference, Paulus was not a man to make enemies, but he complained about it later. On 19 December 1941 when Brauchitsch Commander-in Chief of the army was dismissed, Hitler assumed total command. Halder was never sure about Hitler and eventually landed up in concentration camps such as Flossenbürg and Dachau, accompanied by his wife and under suspicion but not ill-treated. There were constant tensions about invading Russia, especially later, when Hitler without appropriate consultation, suddenly dictated that it was not the thrust on Moscow which was to be the main attack, but the flanks north and south.

As a student of Napoleon's campaigns, Paulus had raised the question of war in a Russian winter, and the vast expanses of Russia's terrain, but Hitler demanded this was not an issue to be raised again.[5] According to the French journalist and historian, Pierre Galante who had many discussions with General Adolf Heusinger, who was a senior planning officer at that time, it was Paulus who 'took it upon himself to point out the disproportion between the endless expanses of the Russian plain and the comparatively meagre forces that the Wehrmacht would have at its disposal', which was to prove all too true.[6]/* Paulus also raised questions over the possibility of long-stretched supply lines which was to prove all too valid, especially to Paulus himself in the years to come.

It was clear from different accounts that Paulus was not only a lead figure in the *Barbarossa* plans, but at this stage he was a realist about the situation. In his biography of Field Marshal Karl von Rundstedt, Charles Messenger refers to Paulus who at the planning stage raised the questions 'over time and space and pointed to the vast preponderance of Russian manpower...he queried the popular assumption that Stalin's purges had resulted in poor quality leadership...and conducted a series of war games to examine these questions...'[7] Rundstedt and many others agreed with Paulus, and although they were critical few dared raise these issues with the always angry dictator.

German troops were soon massing in the East leaving many wondering what was happening. On the Russian side many were convinced the Germans were about to attack, even the British and many others had worked out Hitler's intentions, but only Stalin refused to believe this to be true, not even believing his own dependable spies. Even at home Paulus's two sons knew something was about to happen, and his wife expressed the view that an invasion of Russia was unjustified.[8] These domestic views

---

* General Adolf Heusinger was respected even post-war, and in April 1961 was appointed Chairman of the NATO Military Committee in Washington, DC.

would have been difficult for Paulus who based his conduct on military secrecy. However, in these reported family discussions Paulus never argued that 'it was a question of forestalling Soviet aggressive intentions', which would have been the uncomplicated way out.[9]

In his memoirs Manstein noted that the *Barbarossa* plans were being drawn up by General Paulus, adding that 'the basic concept of a campaign plan should be born in the mind of the man who has to direct the campaign', a view held by the British Field Marshal Montgomery when the invasion of Sicily was being discussed.[10] Later, after *Barbarossa* had started, Manstein was visited by Paulus from the OKH, and he explained to his visitor 'how run down our Panzer Corps had become in a country which was most unsuitable for the use of armoured troops...and drew his attention to the disadvantages of scattering the Panzer troops'.[11] Manstein explained the best move was to withdraw the entire Panzer Corps and use it against Moscow, and Paulus tended to agree with him. Manstein knew that Paulus had raised the issue of the vast expanse of Russia at the planning stage and decided it was safe to talk with him. It was Manstein's constant view that the planners should be the intended commanders.

Paulus's work for Halder gave him a wide perspective of the developing conflict. Under Halder the Army General Staff were constantly issuing directives and organisational changes. Halder's references to Paulus are immense and provide an insight into the workload of both men. Paulus even provided a new detailed and necessary map of Russia showing the road conditions which Halder thought was excellent.[12] Later in the same month Paulus participated in a report on the British and their military strength, or lack of it, making them unlikely to assist the Russians for whom they already held a deep distrust. It was also widely known that the British main concern was the Eastern Mediterranean.[13] Paulus had been involved in the proposed *Sea Lion* plans for the invasion of Britain, and as such would have been seen as a key element in the planning departments.

Paulus was often used when needed for semi-diplomatic military missions. In late March 1941, a group of Yugoslavian officers had rebelled against their government's adherence to the Axis. Paulus was immediately selected and 'hastily dispatched to Budapest to coordinate the military measures to be taken by the satellite forces against the isolated Yugoslavs'. Paulus was not only regarded as an excellent planner but as a trusted emissary.[14] This episode ended with Operation *Punishment*, when in April Belgrade was bombed killing 17,000 people. Two days later Paulus was speaking on the phone to Halder from Vienna.

In May 1941 Paulus was in North Africa because the High Command had become concerned at Rommel's activities, conducting the strategy as he personally considered best.* 'Halder tried hard to bring Rommel to heel, sending out his deputy' Paulus to assess the situation.[15] Halder would have been aware that Paulus had been a brother officer of Rommel in the 13th Infantry regiment while in Stuttgart, and undoubtedly hoped this would influence Rommel. Paulus immediately pointed out the key issues of managing sufficient supplies to Rommel, which was the main cause of Rommel's concerns. However, Rommel, often critical of the High Command's strategy, was told by Paulus that his rapid and unplanned advance through Cyrenaica had caused the British to withdraw their troops from Greece, 'a move which had been entirely contrary to the intentions of the High Command'.[16] This was a wrong criticism Paulus had to convey, because the British troops had left Greece due to Yugoslavia's rapid collapse and also on Greek advice. Many months later Paulus would understand Rommel's frustration with High Command intrusions. When Paulus had expressed the views of the High Command, he then sanctioned a fresh assault on Tobruk. Paulus and Rommel having once served together would have made the mission easier, but it was a problem over which High Command wanted total control, while Rommel tended to follow his own military instincts. This individual determination to assume total command of his own forces would make Rommel famous and even admired by the enemy, a lesson from which Paulus never learnt. Rommel belonged to the old school which expected the commander on the spot to be the most able to understand what should be done next. Modern communications, the telephone, radio, and so forth changed this

---

* It has also been suggested that Halder was concerned that North Africa was more a secondary theatre of operations given that *Barbarossa* would demand large forces.

to a degree, with the top command hearing what was happening, and making recommendations or issuing instructions from hundreds of miles away from the battle scene. Paulus, by being sent to Rommel, was part of this development, and later in Stalingrad would suffer from Hitler's instructions even down to minor details, which had a major impact on Paulus and the war. In Britain, Churchill's Chief-of-Staff Field Marshal Alan Brooke, was forever telling the prime minister not to interfere with commanders in the field, while in Germany no one dared contradict or criticise Hitler which could lead to dismissal or even worse.

Paulus had been wanting a command posting and played with the idea of recommending a change of leadership in North Africa, himself replacing Rommel, but his wife was not sympathetic, telling him to 'keep your fingers out of that pie! It will not do you any good to be put in the bag in Africa'.[17] His wife appeared more astute than her military husband.

Paulus called in to see Mussolini on the way home, with Halder evidently placing considerable trust in Paulus, writing 'I am glad he is there to act as a guardian of our ideas, which also have the blessing of the Führer.'[18] Later in May, Paulus was in Paris having had a talk with the senior command in France over the use of railways for moving troops, he was the 'trusted nuts and bolts' man.[19] Halder liked Paulus, and they were drawing close, as when on Halder's birthday celebration, it was Paulus who gave the speech.[20] A few months previously Paulus hosted a lunch for Halder and Reichenau, indicating he was regarded as part of their senior social circle.[21] There was only one criticism by Halder of Paulus, when the latter supported a request by Guderian which Halder did not appreciate, writing 'he is completely under the spell of Guderian's lopsided ideas', but generally Paulus was Halder's right-hand man.[22] However, it should be noted that Paulus and Guderian had been close, with one historian noting that Paulus 'was a disciple of Guderian'.[23] Halder used Paulus whenever he was worried about unfolding events, sending him to the Russian front to make Halder's views known face to face with the commanders on the spot.

Under Halder, not only did Paulus have the widest possible knowledge of the different theatres of war, but he was noted for his major input in preparing not only the plans but many of the details for *Barbarossa*. Halder appeared reliant on Paulus's hard work and appreciated him. Later, when Paulus was a field commander in Russia, Halder noted Paulus's early successes in his war diary with a sense of pride. As the early months passed, he noted that 'Paulus, irrepressible as ever, went ahead and overran the enemy', later that 'Paulus is advancing at a promising rate in the direction of Stalingrad…Paulus is whittling down the pocket and making good strides'.[24] Paulus even sent Halder photographs of the battle in Kharkov, but Halder's time in office was limited.[25]

To the Eastern Front 1942

The invasion of Russia had started on 22 June 1941, and as the early months passed, there were rapid advances by the German armoured divisions, and half-a-million Russian prisoners were taken at Kiev. During these early successful stages there was little to do at the OKH, and Paulus was sent on a tour of the Russian posts to assess the ongoing situation. Despite the early successes it was already becoming clear that the issue of long-supply-line problems was going to be serious. Reichenau, like Halder, appeared to admire Paulus's work and complimented him on his plans, with many seeing Reichenau as one of Paulus's patrons. Reichenau was commander of the entire Army Group South, having replaced Rundstedt. He asked that Paulus should take over the Sixth Army as it was too much work for one man. Whether this new command post was suitable for Paulus whose battlefield experience was extremely limited, will always be raised and questioned, not least because his previous experience and main functions had hitherto been behind a comfortable desk with pens and maps. While it is true that some well-known outstanding commanders had successful careers from similar backgrounds, Paulus would be somewhat lost, and be heavily dependent on the advice of others, and even more dependent on Hitler's directions. Nearly all field commanders have had to make on-the-spot decisions with the classic example of Nelson's blind eye. It has often been the case that because field commanders can see the circumstances of the day for themselves, their judgements are often better balanced than the theorists away from the action. It was an abrupt change to Paulus's military career and life, and Reichenau's advice to Hitler was seriously flawed.

Reichenau, although admired for being capable and tough, also had a reputation for being brutal, issuing the notorious orders to kill political commissars and any civilians considered a threat, including Jews. A few days after Paulus's appointment to command the Sixth Army Reichenau fell seriously ill after a cross-country run exercise, and while being transported back for hospitalisation his plane crashed and he died in January 1942. His medical man Dr Walter Flade, a friend of Paulus, wrote and described the crash which was evidently a pilot error from which Flade escaped.[26] Curiously, in another letter Dr Flade wrote about Reichenau that 'I found it difficult to make him understand that even his robust constitution is not indestructible', which said much about Reichenau's tough approach.[27]

Paulus, now promoted to full general, until this time had never commanded in combat anything larger than a battalion, suddenly found himself promoted to commander of the Sixth Army as from 5 January 1942. This was not long after Reichenau's death which had undoubtedly shaken him as much as this unexpected promotion. A field command post by its very nature tends to be an isolated position, especially with the responsibility for men's lives and the political demand for a victory.

His senior ADC Colonel Wilhelm Adam recalled Paulus's early nickname when, as a younger officer, he was known as the 'Cunctator, [procrastinator] the waverer. His sharp brain and his invincible logic impressed all his colleagues...to his subordinates, Paulus was a benevolent and always correct superior'.[28] At this time General Fedor von Bock had taken command of the Army group and was now faced with some wintery conflicts. Colonel Heim was Paulus's first Chief of Staff and described his appearance as 'well-groomed and with slender hands, always beautifully turned-out with gleaming white collar and immaculately polished field-boots, he presented such a contrast to his rugged and always deliberately battle-stained predecessor'.[29] Paulus made a point of visiting all the battlefront headquarters, speaking to officers of all ranks to gather an understanding of the situation, but he would never follow his predecessor in leading an infantry charge.

Paulus's Humanity

He also differed from Reichenau, a well-known Nazi adherent, in his approach in humanitarian issues, lacking the political and racial hatred characterised by Nazism, which historically should place him in a better light. Reichenau had fully co-operated with the *Einsatzgruppen* in killing Jews, and when ammunition was short had suggested that only two bullets were necessary for killing a person.[30] At least Paulus removed his Sixth Army from the mire of mass murder, and never faced any war crime tribunal. Paulus may have been inexperienced in battlefield command, but he was known to be level-headed and also humane. There is one account which has survived and explained that a young soldier accused of faking a bad leg was given a death sentence for cowardice, but Paulus on being notified stepped in and ordered an X-Ray which proved the leg was broken, and instead of a firing squad the young man was released and sent to the hospital.[31]

When later Paulus went to Belgorod, his aide de camp Adam recorded that he was shocked to see civilians hanging from the gallows as a result of Reichenau's orders. Paulus demanded they be removed, and instructed such orders should be rescinded, asking the rhetorical question as to 'what had happened to the Hague Convention?'[32] The historian Henri Michel noted that he stopped the execution of Soviet commissars and Jews in his sector of responsibility, indicating a different moral basis from the Nazi regime.[33] This did not mean that there were no atrocities because the ideology of such actions was embedded in the Nazi regime. There were no SS involved in the Stalingrad battle, but when Wehrmacht soldiers 'reached a hospital for mentally handicapped children in the city, they promptly shot all the ten- to fourteen-year-old patients' but not under Paulus's orders.[34] Often some of the soldiers had been imbued with the Nazi doctrine of pure hatred. Hitler had 'decided the entire adult male population of the city would be killed and the women and

Field Marshal Wilhelm Keitel.
(*German Federal Archives*)

Keitel with his field marshal baton, 1942.
(*Bundesarchiv, Image 1011-811-1888-37, Photographer Wagner*)

A receipt from Deutsch Bank for 250,000 Reichsmark, 1942. (*Russian Archives*)

Himmler and Milch speak to Keitel while awaiting Hitler in Berlin, 15 March 1942. (*Bundesarchiv: Image 183-J00683/CC-BY-SA 3.0)*)

Keitel, Rommel and Dr Robert Ley at a ceremony in Berlin, 1942. (*Bundesarchiv, Image 1011-705-0262-06. Photographer Mahla*)

Hitler meets Claus von Stauffenberg (pictured far left) at the Wolf's Lair, with Keitel in attendance (far right), 15 July 1944. (*Bundesarchiv, Bild 146-1984-079-02/ CC-BY-SA 3.0*)

Keitel formally surrenders. (*Photographer Lt Moore (US Army), National Archives and Records Administration*)

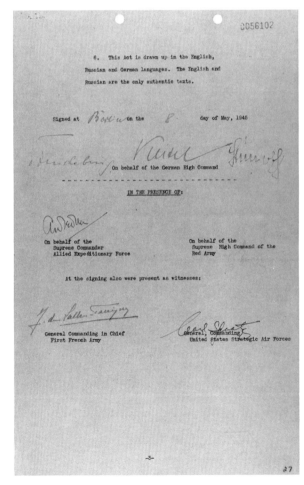

Act of surrender signed by Keitel. (*US Government Archives*)

Keitel as a prisoner. (*Harvard Law School, Harvard University*)

Keitel at the Nuremberg Trial, 24 November 1945. (*Harvard Law School, US Army Signal Corps Photographer*)

Keitel's detention report. (*US Government: Museum of WWII*)

Field Marshal Friedrich Paulus.
(*Bundesarchiv, Bild 183-B24575.
Photographer Heinz Mittelstaedt,
CC-BY-SA 3.0*)

Paulus with Chief of Staff Schmidt and Adjutant Adam taken by Russians. (*Photographer unknown, possibly Georgi Lipskerow. Bundesarchiv Image 183-FO3 16 0204-005*)

Elena Constance Rosetti-Solescu, Paulus's wife. (*Ancestry web*)

Halder with Brauchitsch (right), October 1939. (*Bundesarchiv, Image 183-NZ27722/ CC-B4-SA 3.0*)

Field Marshal Walter von Reichenau with his Chief of Staff, Paulus, August 1941. (*Polish Archives*)

Hitler Conference, Paulus third on Hitler's right, Keitel as always on his left. (*Bundesarchiv, Image 1011-771-0366-02A/CC-BY-SA 3.0*)

German tanks and equipment destroyed or frozen to the ground. The Russian winter was ruthless, and the Germans were poorly equipped for this battle, unlike their opponents. (*Ukraine Archives*)

The Russians closing in with bitter street fighting in temperatures well below freezing. (*Bundesarchiv, photographer unknown*)

The breadth of the Volga is immense.

Paulus at Poltava. (*Bundesarchiv, Image 1011-021-2081-31A. Photographer Heinz Mittelstaedt*)

Paulus at the point of surrender. He looks haggard and mentally exhausted. (*IWM in public domain*)

Paulus arrives at Soviet 64th Army on Volga Delta to sign surrender, 1 February 1943. (*Russian Archives*)

Paulus greets Colonel-General Heitz (suffering from cancer) and other officers after capture. Wilhelm Adam is standing to his right. (*Russian Archives*)

Paulus at a press conference, 2 July 1954. (*Bundesarchiv, Bild 183-25343-0001/CC-BY-SA 3.0*)

Erich von Manstein, 1938. (*Bundesarchiv, Image 183-H01758/ CC-BY-SA 3.0. Photographer unknown*)

Manstein near Donetz, May 1942. (*Bundesarchiv, Image 146-1991-015-31A. Photographer Mittelstaedt*)

Manstein at Kertsch, May 1942. (*Naradowe Archiwum Cyfrowe*)

Manstein views ruins of Sebastopol, July 1942. (*Narodowe Archiwum Cyfrowe*)

Manstein in the Ukraine with General Hans Speidel, 1943. (*Bundesarchiv, Image 1011-705-0262-06. Photographer Mahla*)

Manstein (first from left) surrounded by officers, including General Werner Kempf (first on the right) during an inspection of units from the *Armee Abteilung* on the Eastern Front. (*Narodowe Archiwum Cyfrowe*)

Manstein at his command post in July 1943 along with General Karl Hollidt (behind him). (*Narodowe Archiwum Cyfrowe*)

children deported'.³⁵ Quite how Paulus would have reacted to such an order must remain speculation. He was aware of the Commissar Order of 1 March 1941, that the political officers were to be shot, and another called the *Barbarossa* Jurisdiction Order. This directive gave soldiers the right not to fear judicial recriminations if they treated citizens badly, including the knowledge that Jews were to be exterminated. It is known that Paulus was humane enough to ignore and stop such orders in his sector, which was disobeying the Führer's orders. The question remains if these orders, which he obviously found repulsive, did not cause him to pause and think about *mein Führer*. Even at this stage he knew that Hitler was capable of mistakes or avoiding the truth. For example, Paulus knew that a map published by the Americans showing Russian industries was denied as a lie by Hitler, but he explained to a colleague that 'Yes – the American map agrees with our own latest information. And as far as I am concerned, I must also say the Führer is also wrong when he says: "Hit the Russian a few cracks and he'll collapse"'.³⁶ Paulus also observed that the Ukrainians had a fear of Stalin, and he observed that if they were better treated their sympathy and support for the German forces could be won. Even Reichenau had felt this, but Hitler never listened. It was a time of tension both in what was happening and what must have been an internal conflict in Paulus's conscience. His ADC Adam observed he had a twitch in his face, which was to become more noticeable when under pressure, this had probably been caused by a previous car accident but as with many people, this often occurred when under pressure.

The First Offensives

At the time when Paulus had assumed command, the Russian forces had pressed forward towards Poltava creating a deep bulge. His first action was to move his headquarters to Kharkov not knowing this was the Russian Marshal Timoshenko's next target area, but the situation appeared frozen by inactivity. Bock was highly sceptical about any German offensive in this part of the southern sector, and during March it appeared the Russians might break through, but Bock decided to allow Paulus a free hand. However, Bock remained critical of Paulus's approach to the situation, and he felt the Sixth Army needed some stimulus. As such he organised the replacement of Paulus's Chief-of-Staff Heim in May, with the tougher Colonel Artur Schmidt who remained with Paulus to the bitter end. Schmidt was a resolute soldier but was different from Paulus in that he lacked manners, could be autocratic and overbearing, he had a limited conscience, and most who met him disliked him. He was, according to many accounts, to dominate Paulus who tended to act on whatever Schmidt advised. This underlined one of Paulus's weaknesses of allowing himself to be dictated to, despite the fact he held the senior position. As he had once been dominated by Reichenau and Halder, so Schmidt did the same, but never as effectively as Hitler. As such Paulus as a field commander never had the decisive impulse needed in decision making, which is the normal expectancy of a general in charge of an army. Even when many other commanders thought a breakout was necessary, Schmidt always said it would be an error, and Paulus listened to a man who was merely his immediate subordinate.

In April Hitler had issued Directive No. 41 for the summer campaign, it was complex and for many controversial, as he regarded the southern sector (Operation *Blau*) with the breakthrough to the Caucasus with its resources as incredibly important. In Paulus's sector there were a variety of minor and major bulges which caused considerable discussion. Even before Operation *Blau* had started Hitler dismissed Bock because he did not always agree with the Führer, especially over splitting forces in the drive south.

However, by May Russian tanks were only a dozen miles outside his area and Timoshenko had created a salient known as Barvenkovo which was to become a trap for the Russians. The historian Beevor described Paulus as 'a talented staff officer who had never commanded a formation, was taken aback by the severity of Timoshenko's attack on his Sixth Army'.[37] Timoshenko had managed to extend what was called the Isium bulge close to the German forces. Paulus had to accept that Halder's advice, with which Hitler for once agreed, was the best. The advice appeared correct which for some observers embedded in Paulus a trust of the High

Command, causing him to doubt his own judgements. Eventually the Russians had to withdraw, and Paulus with this small success at Kharkov became for a brief time the centre of Nazi propaganda, increasing his prestige. By the end of May an estimated '241,000 Red Army men went into captivity…few reserves were in hand to meet the Germans when they launched their own main strike in June'.[38] The battle ended on 29 May and Paulus received the Knight's Cross and moved his headquarters from Poltava to Kharkov. However, despite Hitler's belief that the Russians were on the point of collapse, they were becoming more powerful by the day, with Stalin, like Hitler, demanding from his military commanders a prompt victory. Stalin, unlike Hitler, had more resources. Paulus's son Ernst had taken part in this battle and was wounded, which at least helped him survive the war, while his other son Friedrich, as noted, was later killed at Anzio. Later, when speaking to his father Ernst felt he was not satisfied on the grounds that Paulus had not grasped the fact that the Russians had untold reserves. Paulus's popularity rose in the German propaganda machine, and he was inundated with letters of congratulations.

Hitler was obsessed with taking the massive city which bore his opponent's name, and Stalin was equally fixated with its defence. On 1 June 1942, a major Führer conference was held in Poltava with all the leading commanders, including Paulus, where Hitler made it abundantly clear that victory had to be soon because, in his opinion, the Red Army was bottled up. He totally ignored the vast area involved, the size of Russian manpower, and the over-stretched length of the German supply lines. Hitler was convinced the Russians had been beaten, although the Operation *Blau* plans had fallen into the hands of the enemy (known as the Reichel Affair), but they were, fortunately for the Germans, misread by the Russians who saw the proposed movement north being the main thrust. As he had on a similar incident earlier on the Belgium border (Mechelen when plans for *Fell Gelb* fell into Allied hands) before the invasion of the Low Countries, Hitler was furious, demanding court martials from the lowest to the highest ranks. In his diary Field Marshal von Bock heard that Paulus was suggesting that as the senior man he – Paulus – was the one who should be put on trial, but he told Paulus,

'Out of the question! Keep your eyes on your own plate and get on with the job.'[39] This was indicative of Paulus's humane attitudes and his high personal standards.

Despite the lack of resources and supplying what they had to their exhausted troops, Hitler was forever pressing for immediate victory. As such, the Sixth Army pushed on towards the Don and close to the large western turn in the Volga, where the two great rivers are at their closest point. During this summer of 1942 Paulus advanced towards the city of Stalingrad with some 250,000 men, five hundred tanks, 7,000 guns and over 25,000 horses. There was a halt because they ran out of fuel, it eventually arrived and the advance continued, but when less than forty miles from Stalingrad, they ran out of fuel again. Such were the problems with supplies he decided that once again re-fuelled he would only advance with the XIV Panzer corps. The Soviets attacked and Paulus had to call the other forces in. The closer and deeper they came into Stalingrad the greater the Russian resistance.

However, Hitler's belief that victory was at hand increased, and in Directive No. 45 he ordered the army forward to surround the Russians. Paulus had a victory at Kalach in early August gaining a crossing at the Don, and a fortnight later his army battled their way over. It was now that the order was given to march into Stalingrad, despite the fact that Paulus and others were concerned that the northern flank was not protected. The battle for Stalingrad was about to explode, and it is often depicted as one of the decisive battles of the war, it would cost untold lives, unbelievable suffering, and in his frustration, Hitler would sack many of his generals, even the most able. Stalin, meanwhile, had ordered three more armies to move in, and although more Russians were killed than Germans at this stage, it was clear that Stalin's reserves were formidable. As the months passed the statistics of deaths and wounded would reverse, it was estimated in December that more than 28,000 Germans died in a month, with at least 12,000 wounded. In October, the whole front was inundated with heavy rain which turned the roads into streams and muddy quagmires, but it would be even more treacherous when during mid-November it turned to snow and freezing conditions.

In his post-war account of events, Wilhelm Adam the senior ADC, frequently described Paulus's sense of horror over Hitler's dictates and views. The veracity of these insights must be treated with caution because Adam became an ardent anti-Nazi and pro-communist following his capture. He remained fond of Paulus, and he may have been acting as his shield during the post-war period. However, it is equally inconceivable that later in the unfolding drama of Stalingrad, Paulus and many others would have been puzzled, if not outraged by Hitler's orders, which they were expected to act upon without question. Paulus as a skilled staff officer and planner had already noted that the Russians were moving east and the German supply line would be too far stretched, and his flanks were not looking reliably defended.

Chapter Three

Stalingrad

The Horror of the Stalingrad Battle

In his detailed account of the battle for Stalingrad, David Glantz who studied the battle from the Russian perspective, referred to the two Soviet Operations of *Mars* (October 1942) and its companion *Uranus*, which was the Russian strategic counter-offensive, both named after the classical gods, and were planned by Marshal Zhukov. Glantz noted that the Soviets emerged the victors, and in Russia had their reputations enhanced to 'almost superhuman proportions, causing readers to forget the fact that, after all, these leaders were human beings who shared liberally the faults so obvious in every human'.[1] This was of course true for the Germans until they failed, and Paulus was denigrated in Nazi Germany and even post-war his reputation suffered. Paulus's opposite number on the Soviet side was General Chuikov who offered both stubborn resistance and then attack. Glantz's study provided a blow-by-blow account of the battle, but he mentions Paulus only about ten to twelve times in passing, and he only has one entry in the index. However, while the commanders played their battles from their headquarters, following instructions from their respective High Commands, the soldiers on both sides and the Stalingrad citizens suffered in their tens of thousands under the most appalling circumstances. Some of this must be explored to understand not only the nature of this war, but what Paulus was facing as an individual who had once had a reputation for caring for his soldiers.

The Eastern Front war in Russia is still regarded as one of the most bitter, cruel, and ferocious battle fronts of the Second World War, and Stalingrad was probably the most horrific clash of arms in Europe. To this day over 80 years later nearly everyone has heard of the battle of

Stalingrad, not just because of the ramifications of the Russian victory, but the sheer brutality of the conflict in the most appalling background of a Russian winter, with constant hand-to-hand fighting. The horrors are surveyed in this sub-section, as it was the responsibility of Hitler who demanded this version of Dante's Inferno, creating a scenario of suffering which should not be forgotten.

The German anti-war film entitled *Stalingrad* by Joseph Vilsmaier made in 1993, was popular because of its sense of realism. It followed a group of ordinary German soldiers and their battle against the Russians, the weather, and even against some of their own officers. The film was not based on specific events but the conditions under which men fought. Paulus's ADC Wilhelm Adam occasionally commented on the circumstances, indicating the film could almost be viewed as a documentary. Adam described the propaganda which convinced German soldiers they would be shot in the back of the neck if captured. There was a general acknowledgement that despite old popular German views, the Russian soldiers were good at fighting and were well led. Stalingrad was a massive complex, a city of over half a million residents, it had civilians, men, and women, who were prepared to assist and fight alongside the official troops. In the tractor factory, a centre of intense fighting, Russian civilians were still repairing their tanks and guns. Adam wrote that 'no soldier today speaks of Ivan in disparaging terms, which used to be quite normal'.[2] The Russians also deployed women in huge numbers, and the Russian General Vasily Chuikov recorded 'women soldiers proved themselves to be just as heroic in the days of fighting as men…serving on or near the front line, in their capacity as doctors carrying out operations, medical orderlies as young as fifteen carrying wounded men…'.[3] The Sixth Army was faced by dedicated Russians all taking in Stalin's 'Order 227' of no retreat, and utilising working groups and *Komsomol* youngsters (Soviet Young People's Association) using NKVD troops (not that different from the SS) to enforce the fighting.

Adam described how a unit could fight in a building clearing out the enemy at ground floor level, but who still occupied the floors above them. Civilians tried to survive in the sewers, and 'the chief foragers were children…German soldiers made use of Stalingrad orphans'.[4] The Luftwaffe's initial attack on Stalingrad had reduced it to ruins, described by a Russian 'Gefreiter [Lance Corporal] in the 389th Infantry Division…a mass of Stukas came over us, and after their attack, one could not believe that even a mouse was left alive'.[5] 'Stalingrad itself was reduced to rubble, first by a massive Luftwaffe raid and then by bitter street fighting', and outside the vast cold plains it was equally as bad with the weather and fighting making it one gigantic hellhole.[6] General Vasily Chuikov, commanding the 62nd Army, wrote 'The streets of the city are dead. There is not a single green twig on the trees; everything has perished in the flames.'[7] Men had to sleep in the open often freezing to death, and if surviving the night had next to no rations. 'Men no longer take cover from Russian shells', one soldier wrote. 'They haven't the strength to walk, run away and hide.'[8]

The promised supplies of food, fuel, ammunition did not happen, and men were starving and eating their horses. They were running out of ammunition, had hardly any fuel, and thousands froze to death not having the warm clothes or the camouflage of their opponents. There was a lack of medicine, and the hospitals soon became not only overcrowded, but men lay beside one another on floors just waiting to die. A pathologist, Dr Hans Girgensohn, who had flown into the cauldron (the encircled and trapped Germans), 'came to the alarming discovery…that soldiers were dying from hunger far more rapidly than they would do in other circumstances'.[9] Men froze to death even in hospital camp beds, had limbs sawn off and frozen fingers removed by sharp pliers. Another affliction the soldiers suffered from was their inability to bury their dead, especially 'in the closing stages…for the men had by this time become too exhausted to be able to dig graves in the hard, frost bound ground'.[10] Even in this century as new buildings and road works are constructed in Volgograd (Stalingrad's new name) skeletal remains of the conflict often come to light. There was terrible cruelty and barbarity committed by both sides, and no pity was shown. When the Russians liberated a small hamlet, a report claimed, 'our soldiers found in two buildings with bricked up

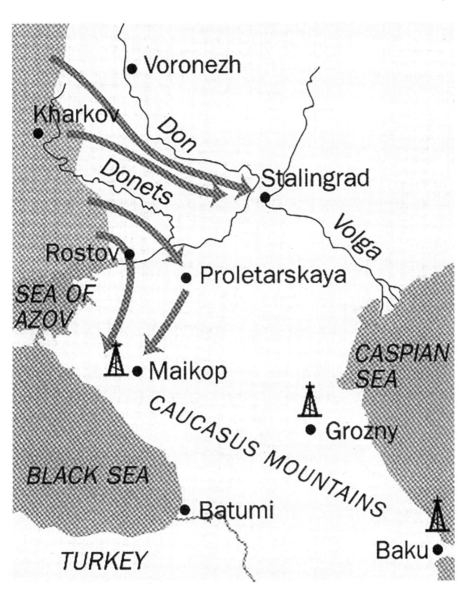

The Don and Volga dominate.

windows and doors, seventy-six Soviet prisoners, sixty of them dead from starvation, some bodies decomposed'.[11]

Both Adam and the film portray the reality of all this, especially the frenetic and disastrous struggles to try and get on the last planes leaving the encirclement, often known as the cauldron, in German *Kessel*. The casualty rate was appalling and there was no hope. Hell is often painted as red-hot and fiery; that was Stalingrad but with reverse temperatures, with men trying to sleep in snow with temperatures often well below 20 degrees, which even disabled what machinery they had left, and froze their guns.

Stalingrad, The Battle

It was Paulus (Sixth Army) along with General Hermann Hoth (4th Panzer), with Romanian and Italian armies who led the drive to Stalingrad which eventuated in the horrors described above.* Paulus's Sixth Army pushed down the north side of a corridor between the Don and the Donets (the largest tributary of the Don), but before it had reached the area of the River Don, Stalin had ordered the city to be placed on a war footing, knowing that if the Volga were crossed the country would be left in two parts.[12] The keeping of the defence along the Volga at Stalingrad was, as Stalin rightly saw, essential.

When the Luftwaffe commander Wolfram von Richthofen met Paulus for a meeting about supplies and support in August, he was able to explain the Luftwaffe plans, and gave various reports of what they were observing from their higher altitudes. It was noted even on 2 August 1942, that the Sixth Army was making slow progress because of stiff opposition and lack of supplies. Richthofen recalled Paulus telling him that his planes would do well by knocking out Russian tanks, and later in November when the disaster was becoming more apparent, he noted that Paulus and his staff were complaining of 'numerical inferiority, lack of training in this type of warfare, shortage of ammunition…they trotted out all the same old arguments…which are partly true', he added.[13]

In August, Richthofen noticed that Paulus was exhibiting signs of intense strain. Paulus, known for his ability as a staff officer was now in the combat frontline with its isolation and sense of loneliness, major responsibility and all the strains of that position. Paulus's nervous tic, on

---

* In the closing months of 1942, the Sixth Army had 260,000 German, Italian, Hungarian, and Romanian soldiers.

the left side of his face, had now become overactive when under strain. He was also suffering from persistent dysentery (which he developed in the Balkans) which was often known as the Russian sickness, with Richthofen describing Paulus as nervous. Being nervous in such a situation must be normal for any combat commander, but military tradition, especially the Prussian army, would expect any commander to exude confidence. It was not that Paulus was soft: when General von Wietersheim suggested at one time a partial retreat Paulus promptly sacked him, replacing him with General Hans-Valentin Hube. As the summer ended, it was clear that walking in and occupying Stalingrad was not going to be as easy as the battles fought in Western Europe or as straightforward as Hitler believed. It was called the battle for Stalingrad, but it covered a vast hinterland, including the two rivers of the Don and Volga, and Stalingrad itself was a large complex city. On 12 September, Paulus attended Hitler at his Werewolf headquarters with Halder present. Paulus asked that the left flank be extended along the river Don, which in terms of sound planning may have helped avoid the chances of encirclement by the enemy, which was becoming an increasing concern. Hitler was not interested as his obsession was taking Stalingrad, with the expectancy that Paulus could just walk in and occupy it under the swastika. Hitler could not be argued with, 'sweeping everything aside to repeat his conviction that the Red Army was beaten, and the resistance at Stalingrad could only be expected locally'.[14] Following his success in western Europe Hitler and many others believed he was a military genius. Others were terrified of him, some suffered from what had been called the 'commander bug' of feeling buoyed up after meeting him, and most obeyed orders. At this stage Paulus appeared to admire the Führer, thought Hitler knew what he was doing, and that he never broke promises. Paulus was deeply embedded with the sense of obedience to all orders from above. This feeling that Hitler could not be wrong, was bolstered a few days later (20 September) when the Russians appeared to have run out of ammunition, and the Germans were able to make slow progress through the city outskirts. By 27 September they occupied the southern area, but not the centre or the north, and critically the Russians constantly controlled their support ferries crossing the Volga. It had become a war of attrition with fighting hand to hand with thousands of casualties. During the entire battle there would be areas of street fighting, with industrial complexes becoming infamous for unending conflict, such as the battle around the Silos and the tractor factory. Paulus even chose a grain silo for the arm badge to commemorate the projected victory. Stalingrad stretched some five miles along the bank of the Volga, with the Russians increasing their forces, especially with their 62nd and 64th Infantry Divisions, yet Hitler intended to occupy this massive city and surround the area relying on what he was told or hoped, a place which he had never seen first-hand.

During the battle Goebbels had sent a propaganda radio team led by his man Hans Fritzsche. Naturally, they were not overly welcome in a difficult battle-zone which was not going well. Goebbels had sent this top radio broadcaster Fritzsche out of personal annoyance with this man. It was curious that Fritzsche would later be a defendant in the Nuremberg Trial probably as a replacement for the dead Goebbels, but he was one of the few who were acquitted. Ironically, during the court breaks at Nuremberg, it was Fritzsche who came to the defence of Paulus amongst the other defendants, pointing out that Paulus was a good commander, stating that 'the tragedy of the German people was right there. Paulus was caught between the devil and the deep blue sea', which was close to the truth.[15] Fritzsche supported Paulus to the hilt in the Nazi luncheon room, explaining how Paulus had used his meagre reserves to support hard-pressed troops in the north, stating that 'I knew what terrible despair he experienced at the time – and just imagine what a tormenting position he was in – to have this assignment to take 200,000 German souls into the jaws of hell – and then to wonder what the purpose of the whole thing was.'[16] Fritsch, despite being just a radio broadcaster who had been there, had gathered his own insights into the unfolding tragedy, and at Nuremberg was not unhappy about talking of his views. He was among the very few who did not hurl insults at Paulus or snarl about him at a social level.

It was not enough for Hitler that the Germans were now in Stalingrad, he wanted the task finished at once. He dismissed Halder as Chief of

Army Staff, replacing him with General Kurt Zeitzler, and had a row with Jodl who had visited and supported Field Marshal Wilhelm List in his request for a retreat. Such was Hitler's fury Paulus picked up the rumour he would be replacing Jodl, but eventually Hitler just sulked, leaving Paulus in the uncertain future of Stalingrad. According to a recorded conversation between Hitler and Keitel (referred to under the exploration of Keitel) Paulus may well have replaced Jodl had he won at Stalingrad. It was the final crunch-line in terms of the friction in High Command as they had simply become Hitler's rubber stamps. There is little doubt that Paulus missed his mentor Halder, who wrote to him (24 September 1942), 'Dear Paulus, A line to tell you that today I have resigned my appointment. Let me thank you, my dear Paulus, for your loyalty and friendship and wish you further great success as the leader you have proved yourself to be.'[17] Paulus responded four days later writing, 'I am most grateful, Sir, for the unwavering confidence you have always placed in me, for the kindly friendship you have so generously bestowed upon me and which I hope I shall also enjoy in the future.'[18]

The task in Stalingrad was gargantuan, and Paulus's only hope was when Hitler informed him that the Russians were running out of reserves and resources. Paulus treated the views of Hitler as if they were always factual and true. Paulus was on the front line, yet he always hoped that Hitler, safe in his faraway safe and warm headquarters, somehow knew more than he did. Some critics have questioned why Paulus was not more aggressive and pushed forward because he had, by then, the largest formation in the German army. It could be counter-argued that as a trained staff officer he needed better information, others that he cared for his soldiers, and for some observers it was that he was not experienced enough in a fighting command position. At first, by early October it appeared like a stalemate, there was a lull in the fighting, but Paulus was constantly pressurised by Hitler to finish the job. It was the same for his Soviet opponent General Vasily Chuikov, brought back from China, who was constantly harangued by Stalin. The Luftwaffe bombed Stalingrad, destroying much of the city, but although many of their pilots were experienced, they failed to establish air-superiority as the Russians could quickly replace downed aircraft and pilots. The bombing on 23 August 1942 had consisted of some 600 bombers and attacked Stalingrad all day, creating a day of terror. German aircraft bombed the city 2,000 times, there were 50 km of ruins, 40,000 people dead.[19]

On 25 October Paulus told Hitler that 'he expected to complete the capture of Stalingrad at the latest by 10 November', Hitler was naturally exhilarated.[20] Quite why Paulus said this is confusing, begging the question whether he really believe it at this time, or whether it was a hope that it would calm or placate his Führer. Paulus was under extreme pressure at ground level fighting a battle, while trying to oblige the High Command instructions. Doctor Flade, who had once served the Sixth Army sent him letters warning him to take care of 'his shattered health', and that he 'should obtain leave and have a complete rest'.[21]

Following Hitler's demands, Paulus launched a final assault, but his men were exhausted, and supplies were running short. On 11 November Paulus's soldiers had reached the Volga but on a short front, this divided the Russian forces, but the Germans failed to push the Russians into the river or access the other side. Paulus was often praised for his care of the men under his charge, and it was noted at this time he was concerned that some of his men deserved home-leave, as they had been involved in continuous conflict since June.[22] Paulus himself was also under heavy strain being warned again by his army doctor that he was heading for a breakdown.

His state of health and the weariness of his troops must have taken a severe blow when in November, it was realised that the Russians had launched a massive offensive (Operation *Uranus*) in which Paulus had found himself surrounded by the Soviet Army Group, with some critics wondering why Paulus did not immediately order a prompt evacuation. The news of the onslaught was brought to Paulus by General Karl Strecker of the infantry, who came to speak with him personally. It may have been that Intelligence was poor and Paulus and his staff had no idea about the numbers opposing them, but the criticism that Paulus was too passive has remained constant and probably justified in military terms. In the meantime, Göring gave a speech in Berlin claiming 'success was going to be announced at any moment and everyone knew about Russian winters'.[23] It was true enough that it was widely known that Russian winters could be dangerous, but not everyone had experienced them.

Paulus decided at one point to establish an observation post behind the Don, but High Command rejected his proposal claiming the Red Army was defeated.[24] The passivity of which Paulus was frequently criticised may have had much more to do with the ridiculous demands and reasonings of the High Command, safely ensconced hundreds of miles away. If the criticism of passivity had any validity, it was Paulus's acceptance of higher orders which were both damaging and downright misguided. Adam was told by a Colonel Elchlepp that 'all the generals avoided contradicting Hitler. All feared the hysterical outburst of this lofty dictator.'[25]

Both Paulus and General Artur Schmidt, his chief of staff, believed many of the problems they faced should be resolved by other commanders outside the encirclement. The attacks, as far as he was concerned, were to his rear and should be dealt with by commanders in those areas. The main debate which would emanate from the battle of Stalingrad would centre on who held the responsibility. Should the commander on the spot in an incoming disaster react according to his judgement, which for many is the reason for being made a commander, or rather seek and wait instructions from Higher Command. Opposition to the government of the day and its High Command begs many questions, there were matters of military rules of obedience, matters of caring for soldiers relying on their immediate commander; it was a militarily and politically complex situation for Paulus. What was needed at this time was a prompt response, but the much-criticised passivity of which he has often been accused, and with some reason, led to Paulus having to flee his headquarters at Golubinsky on 21 November because of incoming Russian tanks, and their files had to be burnt in the panic exit. Paulus and Schmidt flew to Nizhne-Chirskaya outside the closing cauldron and held a conference about the situation with General Hermann Hoth. Hitler heard of this and accused Paulus 'of abandoning his troops' and ordered him to return. 'Paulus was deeply aggrieved by this slur and Hoth had to calm him down.'[26]

The Cauldron

The first snow had started to fall a few days before (16 November) and this was the start of one of the harshest known eastern European winters, with German troops inadequately dressed for such extreme weather conditions. Goebbels had quickly organised a collection of winter clothes from the German public, including expensive fur coats and hats, much of it useless and not evaluated before it was sent.[27] The Soviet counteroffensive was effective as it was cleverly planned, and the Russians were better equipped with winter clothing in terms of disguise and sensible protection from the cold. When other commanders pleaded with Paulus to move out and escape, he reportedly replied 'I am no Reichenau', adding 'I must obey.'[28] On 19 November the Russians opened a powerful attack, which was successful in the sectors north and south of the city held by the Romanian troops, many of whom must have wondered why they were there in the first place. It was evident that the Soviet plan was to encircle the German army, making the situation drastic and demanding an immediate response. It was also a day of intense snowstorms, and the Luftwaffe was grounded by the weather. The Russians in this attack had many freshly built tanks of the famous T-34 type, 'Stalin's Organ' which was a rapidly firing missile launcher, and many more effective weapons than the Germans. The Soviets also made much of their newsreels of the battle and used it as excellent propaganda.

However, Paulus felt hamstrung by Hitler's demands, and although the Sixth Army was all part of Manstein's army formation, Paulus later wrote that he wished it had not been, because Hitler had his own radio officer, which meant he was constantly taking control. Manstein knew Paulus was hamstrung by Hitler's orders and demands, noting 'by the evening of 19 November at the latest, therefore, the OKH should have given the Sixth Army fresh orders allowing it freedom to manoeuvre'.[29] He added in his memoirs that 'the fact that it was a serious psychological error to put this request to Hitler at all is another matter'.[30] Manstein tried to understand the problem:

It is conceivable, of course, that such an action might have cost Paulus his head. Yet no one must think that it was any fear of what might happen to him personally that kept Paulus from taking things into his own hands and doing what he believed to be right. It is more likely to have been loyalty to Hitler which impelled him to try to get the army's break-out authorised, particularly as he was in direct touch with OKH by radio.[31]

As Manstein noted, when Paulus had missed the opportunity to break out at the best moment, Manstein questioned as to when would be the next opportunity as the pocket tightened. Had Paulus reacted at once on or after 19 November there was a possibility of some success even if it were only saving the bulk of his army.

The question became whether the Luftwaffe was in a position to help, and could the Supreme Command offer relief forces? Only Hitler had this authority. As Manstein had noted, the OKH should have given the Sixth Army fresh orders allowing it freedom. Hitler instructed Paulus to take command of General Hermann Hoth's troops to the south, and what was left of the Romanian corps. Paulus would have preferred to withdraw from the Volga to join Army Group B which was sheer common sense. Schmidt tried to explain the lack of supplies, especially fuel and ammunition, and although Göring then and later made promises, they did not have enough aircraft for the amounts required. It was clear to anyone involved with the Luftwaffe that dropping the necessary supplies of such a large amount into Stalingrad was simply impossible, with some 400,000 men on the ground needing basic resources. Göring was simply pandering to his master's wishes, and Zeitzler tried to convince Hitler of the logistical facts and 'called Göring a liar to his face', but Hitler refused to listen.[32] In his personal diary Richthofen (21 November 1942) noted that 'the Sixth Army expects to be supplied by the Air Fleet. We have done our utmost best to prove to them that this is not possible, since we have not sufficient transport aircraft available.'[33] Later Richthofen noted (25 November) that all our Jus [Junkers] employed today in flying in supplies. But we now have only thirty of them left…yesterday twenty-two were lost…today we were able to fly in only 75 tons, instead of the 300 tons as directed from above.'[34] His reference to 'From above', was Hitler's persistence to ensure supplies arrived in a difficult area. It was virtually impossible, because Hitler had insisted that they stood their ground in hopeless circumstances, in a vast remote area in terms of supply lines. It has also been noted that 'the entire Caucasian advance was hamstrung by Hitler's orders to divert available fuel and ammunition supplies to Paulus'.[35] On the other side of the great divide, it was no problem for the Russians, who successfully managed to get supplies across the Volga, usually at night when the Luftwaffe was not a threat. Paulus was entirely encircled, but Hitler gave the instruction to stay there. Göring's assurance to Hitler that he could supply Stalingrad with the necessary resources was a major factor in the enveloping disaster, it was almost a death sentence. By 23 November, the Soviets had all but closed the ring and trapped the Sixth Army.

Schmidt, by many accounts, appeared to have an overbearing influence on Paulus, with Adam and others feeling that Paulus never overruled his chief of staff. Some have regarded Paulus as a mere cypher in Schmidt's hands who took over many of the command responsibilities. This in some views made Paulus weak, always appearing as vacillating. On one occasion Paulus's daughter Olga's husband, called von Kutzschenbach, was a staff interpreter and met with Adam expressing his concerns over Schmidt's influence. He accused Schmidt of being 'overbearing and dogmatic', which he felt Paulus found repugnant and had led to some generals complaining about the way they were treated.[36] Much later when Adam flew back into the suicidal centre known as the cauldron, he met three elderly officers going there. He asked why, they explained it was on Schmidt's orders. Adam explored and thought their presence was unnecessary with which Paulus agreed. Schmidt, however, said they should stay, and Paulus promptly accepted Schmidt's ruling.[37]

Meanwhile, according to Manstein's recollection, he became aware of the radio message from Paulus to Hitler stating that the army should break out to the south-west, which would mean shifting some formations for such an operation, which Hitler had promptly declined. Manstein noted that 'evidently Paulus did everything possible, within the limits of Hitler's orders binding him to Stalingrad, to extract forces from those of his army fronts which were not so seriously threatened in the first instance'.[38] Post-war while being interviewed, Manstein admitted that it was impossible for Paulus to break out at this stage, stating that 'they would perish in the cold even if they had escaped the trap' which was all too true.[39] It was a time of personal conflict for Paulus, who had established a forward post west of Gumrak near a railway station. As a one-time staff officer, he knew resources were essential for survival, let alone fighting back; his historical hobby of studying Napoleon's war had warned him of Russian winters, but neither he nor Schmidt had realised that instant action was required rather than sitting and hoping for the best. Their only hope was in High Command and Hitler sending in supplies and organising outside help. They were both, especially Schmidt, believers in the Führer's word, who sent them a message of encouragement:

> The Sixth Army is temporarily surrounded by Russian forces. I know the Sixth Army and your commander-in-chief and have no doubt that in this difficult situation it will hold on bravely. The Sixth Army must know that I am doing everything to relieve them. I will issue my instructions in good time. Adolf Hitler.[40]

Hitler was demanding that Paulus stayed put as he was obsessed that Fortress Stalingrad was to be Hitler's post on the Volga. Göring had promised the necessary supplies in the full knowledge that it could not be achieved. Paulus had hoped that Manstein would take overall charge, but he was more bemused that Hitler suddenly divided the command between Paulus and General Walther Seydlitz-Kurzbach. Seydlitz had argued for a breakout from the south contravening Hitler's orders, later telling his subordinates they were free to decide for themselves, so Paulus relieved him of his command. Seydlitz was from Prussian nobility but was very much the soldier's man, highly trained and a natural leader with combat experience. Unlike Paulus he was a strong proponent that the field-commander had not only the right but the duty to make the final decisions within his area of combat.

In a recorded conversation between Keitel and Hitler, the former suggested that Seydlitz should replace Paulus, but Hitler ignored this comment and moved on to replacing other generals such as von Kluge and wanted to discuss von Manstein.[41] Whether it was Keitel's hope that Jodl would soon be replaced by Paulus, or he thought Paulus to be failing in Stalingrad is not clear. For Hitler, the important aspect of Paulus was that he constantly obeyed his orders, even though they made no sense and meant further deaths. It has been noted that 'Paulus showed little tactical skill in the Battle of Stalingrad, which he fought as a series of frontal attacks, in an area that allowed no room for manoeuvre and in which all the advantages of terrain and position accrued to the defence.'[42] However, it should be noted that such was the overwhelming strength of the Soviets, the nature of the terrain, the weather, long supply lines and lack of resources that probably the best field commanders would have been in serious trouble.

General Kurt Zeitzler, Chief of Staff to the Army, when discussing Stalingrad with Hitler in late November, said he could see no other alternative. Hitler's reply was 'Never. The army will remain in Stalingrad! I don't want to present the world with the spectacle of a German defeat at Stalin [*sic*]. We must hold the city, whatever the cost.'[43] 'Zeitzler did not lack courage in standing up to Hitler, but he had to fight his battle alone, for Keitel always backed Hitler.'[44] Many historians have often indicated that Stalingrad was important to Hitler because it was named after his hated opponent, and there may be some truth in this view, as there was in Stalin's own obsession with the city bearing his name. However, 'in reality, the city had real strategic importance', because the lower broader aspect of the Volga served as a protection from the German thrust, and if Stalingrad were left in Soviet hands, it would leave a resourceful area for cutting off German spearheads moving south to the Caucasus.[45] Hitler and Stalin both understood that the move by the Germans to the south, 'would deprive the Soviets of the oil and much of the food and industry they desperately needed to carry on the war'.[46] The war, especially after

America had become involved, was rapidly becoming a matter of supplies and oil was in high demand. The success of the so-called Blitzkrieg in the West was not working in Russia with its vast spaces, and the more astute could see, if not the turn of the tide, that Russia was going to prove difficult to overcome.

When the term 'Fortress Stalingrad' was first used by Hitler and German propaganda, the men fighting there thought it was somewhat ludicrous, almost a joke because the battle zone consisted of destroyed buildings and vast snow-swept areas, with nothing left which could be described as a fortress. Paulus was caught between his sense of obedience as a German officer, and his instincts for caring for his troops. When he was challenged by a senior Corps Commander, asking him if events could ever turn in their favour, Paulus replied, 'I am not sure that the Führer's ideas can actually be put into practice, but of course, I don't have a sufficiently clear command of the overall situation to appreciate the finer points of the Führer's plan.'[47] The general suggested he used his rights as commander to help his own men who relied on him, but Paulus would do nothing without a direct order from Hitler.

There was discussion amongst senior officers whether Paulus was right in his act of obedience. The commander General Seydlitz suggested they disobeyed the Führer and broke out of the tightening circle. Seydlitz never changed his mind that he was correct, concluding that Hitler was no military genius and was sending thousands of men to their deaths. Paulus would not listen, he was too Prussian to disobey senior orders, a dispute which would persist long after the war creating considerable heat. On 22 November Paulus and Schmidt flew into 'the cauldron', the centre of much fighting with the immense danger and probability of a tightening encirclement. The next day (23 November 1942) he sent a message to Army Headquarters:

My Führer, since receipt of your wireless signals of the 22 November, the situation has developed with extreme rapidity. In the west and south-west, we have not succeeded in completing our hedgehog position…enemy breaches are anticipated…ammunition and fuel are running short…a timely and adequate replenishment is not possible…my Army will be faced with imminent destruction…I must withdraw all the Divisions from Stalingrad…although my subordinate commanders, Generals Heitz, Strecker, Hube and Jaenecke, all agree with my views, I personally accept full responsibility for this grave communication.[48]

No one can claim having read this message that Paulus was not confronting Hitler with the facts, and not shirking his responsibility. However, trying to make Hitler change his mind was like pushing water uphill.

On 26 November, Manstein received a letter from Paulus which underlined the 'necessity of freedom of action in an extreme emergency', they were running out of fuel, food, and ammunition.[49] The letter had a deep sense of urgency which laid out the bare facts:

For the past thirty-six hours I have received no orders or information from a higher level…either I must remain in position on my western and northern fronts and very soon see the army rolled up from behind (in which case I should formally be complying with orders issued to me), or else I must make the only possible decision and turn with all my might on the enemy who was about to stab the army from behind. In the latter event, clearly, the eastern and northern fronts can no longer be held, and it can only be a matter of breaking through to the south-west…in this situation I should admittedly be doing justice to the situation but should also – for the second time – be guilty of disobeying an order…the airlift of today has brought only a fraction of the calculated minimum.'[50]

Manstein wondered that if this were the case, how would they ever break out? Manstein wanted to fly in and see for himself, but he was sensibly advised against such a risky move. His decision was not well received by Paulus and Adam.[51] Manstein sent a staff officer Major Hans-George Eismann who tried to reason and even persuade Paulus to breakout, but with no headway. Written communications were difficult, and there was no reliable phone link to harmonise actions making clear messages difficult. Manstein felt there had to be a stubborn defence to keep the army intact, then a breakthrough.

On 12 December Manstein of Army Group Don launched Operation *Winter Storm* as a rescue attempt, but it would fail, and Paulus's troops stayed in their fixed defensive positions. The chief of the Army General Staff again tried persuading Hitler to permit Paulus to break out, as General 'Hoth had fought his way to within 40 miles of Stalingrad but was now spent', only to be met with Hitler's unbelievable stubbornness.[52] Hoth had made some progress, but General Zhukov started Operation *Little Saturn* which forced him to stop. The real danger for Paulus was at the rear of his forces, rather than in the city from where a Russian breakthrough would occur. 'Zhukov and Vasilevski persuaded Stalin to bring in and train large quantities of fresh troops…the Soviet Union was already producing over 2,000 tanks a month to Germany's 500.'[53] The Russians also knew that the Romanians and Italians supporting Paulus were not the best of troops, mainly because they were poorly equipped, and speculatively, many of them did not want to be there, lacking the commitment of the Germans. Neither of these nationalities had the inbuilt soldierly discipline of the Germans, and it was not their war. Later, an 'Italian general asserted that 99 per cent of his fellow countrymen not merely expected to lose the war, but now fervently hoped to do so as swifty as possible'.[54] It was easy for the Germans to blame the Romanian, Italian, and Hungarian troops but they were fighting for their lives under appalling conditions, in a war their leaders had sent them to, with weapons of different makes and needing special ammunition to fit, with their essential resources running out.

On 7 December, Paulus in a letter to his wife explained that 'at the moment I've got a really difficult problem in my hands, but I hope to solve it soon', and on 18 December 'we will survive, there's another May to follow'.[55] None of which he could really believe possible, but like many of his soldiers' letters to their families, his letter was optimistic for their sake, and perhaps some hope for his situation, even if it were a mere dream. It is of course possible that he still hoped the supplies would arrive and that Manstein's wishful thinking would help, but every day made this less likely.

However, when Manstein had managed to push a relief column to within forty miles of the Stalingrad perimeter, he set up a possible crossing point at the Mishkova river. By 19 December, Hoth's forces after some bitter fighting established a bridgehead over the river, just about thirty miles from the besieging Russian forces, but here it had been forced to stop. It had been expected that Paulus's tanks could now break through and form a corridor, but they had insufficient fuel. Hitler regarded it as a way to keep Stalingrad in German hands, but the local commanders hoped it would supply an escape route. Paulus was not only short of tanks and lorries, but fuel was insufficient, and even if they managed to reach Hoth there was not enough fuel even for the tanks to retreat.

It was on 24 December, Christmas Eve, that Hoth was obliged to withdraw, not suffering the same obligation of staying put which bound Paulus. There had been hopes that Hoth would create a channel of escape, but Manstein's efforts to open a corridor had been blocked. Despite the intense pressure Hitler insisted that Paulus held firm, though it has been suggested that following Manstein's efforts Hitler may have given some form of 'conditional approval', but this does not sound likely.[56] Hitler had refused to listen, stating a retreat could only happen with the proviso he held Stalingrad which was not only a hopeless task, but it was evidently absurd and probably reflected the 'conditional approval' mentioned above. This suggestion was in effect no approval at all, because holding Stalingrad and being allowed to retreat was a contradiction in terms. There was 'no conceivable military purpose served by holding the German troops in their positions, but Hitler's personal prestige as a leader was now engaged, and in comparison, with the lives of the thousands of surviving men of the Sixth Army it was nothing'.[57] Paulus had received another message from Hitler instructing him to hold on, fulfilling the Sixth Army's historical mission on the Volga, with Paulus stating that 'my hands are tied in every way'.[58] In his memoirs Manstein claimed he gave the orders to Paulus to break out, but they were unclear, contained some reservations and Paulus was confused, and very angry when he read the memoirs post-war. Manstein had revealed in his memoirs that he did not feel correct in anticipating going against High Command Orders. At every level of command, the picture was one of total confusion.

As recompense and to offer encouragement, Hitler promoted Paulus to colonel-general, but meanwhile, the German troops, cold, starving, ill-equipped and running out of ammunition and fuel were being rapidly worn down by the constant attacks. Quite what Paulus's officers in the shell-holes and sewers thought is not difficult to imagine. This writer as a young boy played chess with an old German soldier who always insisted on sitting by a radiator. He had been wounded at Stalingrad and walked with a stick, and in his own words, considered himself one of the lucky ones by being flown out at the last minute. He explained that he could not cope with being cold because it brought back nightmares of Stalingrad, and explained they were like the walking dead, would die of hunger, or freeze to death or be shot, and told if captured they would be executed. He never knew what was happening above his paygrade, realised they were completely surrounded, but hoped the order for a breakout would eventually happen. Many at home knew what their soldiers were suffering as their letters revealed the situation, until the postal deliveries were blocked by Goebbels for fear that it spread unrest. In his diary of 17 December Goebbels had written 'in future, cards to relatives should no longer be delivered, because they offer an access door to Germany for Bolshevik propaganda'. It has been suggested that senior commanders hoped Paulus would defy Hitler and breakout, hoping it might trigger a reaction throughout the army.[59] It was a state of desperation, and Paulus managed a discussion with Manstein over a teleprinter, later claiming that if he had received enough information, he would have realised his impossible situation and may have reacted differently. The teleprinter discussion underlined the difficulties not only of reliable conversations, but the growing impossibility of escape from the tightening encirclement. It was agreed that the code-word *Thunderclap* had to be followed immediately by *Winter Tempest*. Operation *Hoth* which had been that general's attempt to open a corridor was code-named *Winter Storm/Tempest*, while *Thunderclap* was code for the Sixth Army breaking free to meet Hoth. In this strange conversation, Paulus made the situation abundantly clear. The essence was that Paulus was uncertain, horses had been eaten, it was too cold for survival, all resources were diminishing and not being replaced, and they were all suffering from total exhaustion. However, it was the precarious fuel position which was the main reason a breakout could not happen. Paulus's tanks on their fuel allotment could barely travel twenty miles. As a consequence of this teleprinter discussion, Manstein tried to convince Hitler on the phone, but again the dictator refused. On Christmas day itself the long bitter fighting at the Tractor factory ceased as the Germans were finally expelled. The Russians managed this by building piece by piece a howitzer inside the factory which had a devastating impact.

On 26 December, Paulus sent Manstein a painful message reporting 'bloody losses, cold, and inadequate supplies have recently made serious inroads on division's fighting strength, I must therefore report the following'.[60] He continued to explain that his army could beat off small attacks, but only while supplies lasted. Secondly, if the enemy concentrated its forces Paulus could not hold, and finally, he was no longer able to break out unless replenished with men and supplies. Therefore, he continued, relief is essential, pointing out that 70 tons had been flown in the day before, a miniscule amount, that bread supplies would runout the next day and 'fats' that evening, ending his message that 'Radical measures were now urgent'.[61] November had raised many alarms, but by December the inevitability of defeat was abundantly clear. Paulus had handcuffed himself by his obedience to Hitler's orders, but because of the shortage of supplies and sheer exhaustion, even a sudden change of mind for a breakout was now impossible. The Russians knew about the situation and were busy calling out in German, telling their opponents to give up the hopeless fight. The messages and pamphlets often originated from German communists who had fled the Nazi regime years before. Amongst the recognisable names was Walter Ulbricht, a former member of the German parliament for the communist party, and later a leading figure in East Germany. None of this was helped by what was commonly called 'latrine rumours' that the SS were about to break through.

Paulus wrote to his wife that 'Christmas naturally was not very joyful… at such a moment, festivities are better avoided…one should not, I believe, expect too much from luck.'[62] He also added his main burden that 'I am here under orders, and I intend to remain here to the end.'[63] He also sent a message to his men claiming the New Year will bring our release, the Führer has never gone back on his word. Hitler sent a message to Paulus and the Sixth Army:

In the name of the whole German people. I send you and your valiant army the heartiest good wishes for the New Year. The hardness of your perilous position is known to me. The heroic stand of your troops has my highest respect. You and your soldiers, however, should enter the New Year with the unshakeable confidence that I and the whole German Wehrmacht will do everything in our power to relieve the defenders of Stalingrad and that with your staunchness will come the most glorious feat in the history of German arms. Adolf Hitler.[64]

To which Paulus responded, 'Your confident words on the New Year were greeted here with great enthusiasm. We will justify your trust.' Paulus, being always polite, respectful, and diplomatic can be the only explanation as to the manner of his response, but under the circumstances there is also a hint of obsequious obedience.

As the New Year's Eve began any chance of an escape slipped away. The Russians crossed the Don, the Eighth Italian Army as anticipated fell, and the Russians pushed south. Manstein was in danger and had little choice but to withdraw Hoth's armour. Even had Paulus ignored orders and pressed the emergency exit button the chances of escape were minimal, and it would have meant leaving the wounded and sick.

By January 1943, the situation was clearly a victory for the Russians. On 7–8 January, the Russian General Konstantin Rokossovsky suggested a ceasefire, offering surrender terms with help for the wounded and food. The prisoners, he stated, would be allowed their badges, medals, and personal effects, pointing out the obvious that the Germans had lost. The alternative would be total destruction. Paulus asked Hitler for permission to accept the offer, which was instantly turned down, with the German High Command stating that it was out of the question, and Paulus did not reply to the Soviets. It would be another month before the fighting ceased, and during that time thousands died in combat, from starvation, injuries, and frozen to death. Being taken prisoner for an ordinary soldier was not a guarantee of survival, but it was a better option than fighting on in a lost cause. The blame for this should be laid firmly at the doors of the High Command, especially Hitler, but also Paulus's Prussian obsession of obeying even the most absurd orders. The unnecessary prolongation of death and suffering has been seen by some as a form of war crime. Not long after this occurred Paulus appealed to the troops, informing them that the Russian offer was mere propaganda, to undermine their morale. A few days after the rejection of surrender, on 10 January, the Russians attacked with shells and rockets with devastating results, and there was disturbing news that on the western defence side Russian tanks had broken through. The ground was so frozen it was impossible to dig trenches or any form of cover. There was also news that some junior officers and their men had gone over to the other side. At the end of the day on 10 January, Adam recorded a conversation he had with Paulus relating to their different viewpoints about fighting on, but they agreed the Sixth Army 'had to be sacrificed' if the war were to be continued.[65] Quite how they believed this reasoning is difficult to fathom, but this made it sound like a game of chess, with thousands of lives being treated as a strategic table game. It was noted that this Russian attack was the last straw for many of the fighting men: 'The men then tended to become apathetic and slack, and more and more of them, exhausted and dispirited, began to seek refuge in the cellars of Stalingrad. Many voices were raised against the pointlessness of carrying on the struggle, though an equal number sternly demanded that we should fight on.'[66]

In his biography Adam referred to some officers who asked to be flown out before it was too late. Adam described how some made varying excuses but were always turned down.[67] Later he claimed that even Schmidt had tried, but such was his long-term distaste for this man the veracity of his statements may hold some question marks.

Hitler, who admired General Hans-Valentin Hube, had him flown out to see what was happening. Hube was honest about the situation, but like many other commanders he was influenced by Hitler, who 'had declared that everything would be done to supply Sixth Army for a long time to come and had drawn his attention to the plan for relief at a later date'.[68] On his return Hube explained to Paulus that Hitler was adamant about not being defeated, which did not please many. By 12 January, the appalling winter weather stopped the airlift, and Paulus now a Colonel General was told the Russian attacks were intensifying. He ordered his men to fight to the last round, but no heavy weapons could be moved as they were frozen in, the Pitomnik airfield was closed as Russian tanks approached, and wounded men were trying to flee for their lives. This left only one landing site in the Stalingrad pocket near Gumrak. Paulus continued to plead for equipped troops to be flown into the pocket which was now rapidly closing. Hube having failed to convince Hitler, Paulus tried again with a Captain Winrich Behr who explained the situation as frankly as he dared, but Hitler who was paranoid about failure, refused. Fewer aircraft arrived, and fuel, food and essential supplies were almost finished, making any chance of escape impossible even if Paulus had ordered such a measure.

A few days later on 15 January, Hitler instructed the Luftwaffe Field Marshal Milch to increase the airlift, but Göring ordered him not to send planes inside the encirclement. The same day Hitler awarded Oak Leaves to Paulus's Knight's Cross. To men suffering the thought of death or imprisonment it must have seemed a strange action. Paulus made it clear that he was not leaving his men, and in a farewell letter to his wife he included his medals, wedding, and signet rings, which he had given to Captain Behr to take with him on his journey west, but the Gestapo expropriated the package and its contents. On 24–25 January, the last emergency airstrip was taken by the Soviets, who again made an offer for them to surrender. Paulus tried again, informing Hitler that they had no food or medicine with some 18,000 wounded men, no fuel or ammunition, the situation was desperate and there was no choice. Paulus had sent a message to General Zeitzler Chief-of Staff to the Army:

Fortress can be held for only a few days longer. Troops exhausted and weapons immobilised as a result of non-arrival of supplies... imminent loss of airfield will reduce supplies...heroism of men and officers nevertheless unbroken...shall give orders just before final break-up for all elements to fight through to the south-west...those who break through will cause confusion behind Russian lines... failure to move now will mean men will die of hunger and cold... suggest flying out a few men, officers and other ranks as specialists for use in future operations...appropriate order must be given soon as landing facilities unlikely to exist much longer. Please detail officers by name, obviously excluding myself.[69]

Manstein claimed that it showed the willingness to fight, but Hitler would not move, and he demanded that Paulus stood until death.

Such was the nature of the enclosing encirclement it was necessary for Paulus and his senior staff to find new headquarters. They found a place in some constructed bunkers called Hartmannstadt, which had once been the centre for an infantry division. Even as they approached their new quarters the sound of guns and bombs was closing in. There were discussions over whether specialists should be flown out to assist elsewhere, but few aircraft were landing, many were happy to drop their supplies hopefully near their own troops, to avoid the dangers of landing in what was virtually the centre of a battle. When the last airfield at Gumrak was overrun a few pilots managed to land at a make-do airstrip hurriedly prepared at Stalingradski, where General Jaenecke and a Colonel Selle escaped on 23 January.

Many took matters into their own hands, and on 25 January, news was received that Major General von Drebber had surrendered the 297th Infantry Division, undoubtedly because they had run out of food and ammunition. As they were reading this news a bomb blew in the windows of Paulus's headquarters, causing his head to bleed, it was not serious, but probably unsettled him. Drebber had written a letter to Paulus claiming the Red Army was treating them well, and that Goebbels was a liar about the claims that they would all have a bullet in the neck. Having read this they then heard that General von Hartmann had fallen, and the next day that General Stempel had committed suicide. On 26 January, disturbing news also reached them, namely that Seydlitz had informed his senior officers that if they wished to surrender it was their decision. To add to this overheating inferno, Paulus was informed that the wounded could not be treated because typhus was becoming widespread. They also had to move headquarters again to the cellars of a onetime grand department store, the largest in Stalingrad. The small cauldron was now in two parts with no telephone connections available. The Sixth Army remnants had become the sacrificial lamb and since then various rumours accumulated. Amongst them was the order to shoot any Russians appearing to discuss a truce or surrender, and food should be withheld from the sick and wounded and given only to the remaining frontline fighters. In his account Göerlitz raised these issues and denied them, and he was right to do so, as there is no convincing evidence that such orders were ever given.[70]

Paulus was understandably demoralised and suffering again from dysentery. It has been stated that Paulus was by now on the verge of physical and mental collapse, and probably not helped when Göring gave a broadcast, which was more like a funeral speech, comparing Stalingrad to the Spartans at Thermopylae. This broadcast was not well received in Stalingrad, and the next day Hitler created four new field marshals including Paulus. It was widely known that no German field marshal had ever surrendered, it was a clear message that Paulus should commit suicide. Paulus was a Roman Catholic which considered suicide sinful, and he told General Max Pfeffer that 'I am not shooting myself for this Bohemian corporal'.[71] It was later revealed that Hitler had a change of mind and decided to withdraw the promotion, but it was too late as it had been announced.[72] Some officers decided rather than surrender, they planned to walk or fight their way out, but they never made it and were soon captured, and many suicides were being reported. A few days later Paulus was told that Russian tanks were approaching the department store whose basement was his latest headquarters, with their guns aimed at their building. In Germany, Stalingrad held the headlines, and even in the last week of January the popular *Völkischer Beobachter* 'daily carried headlines about the heroic resistance in Stalingrad, which would be to the immortal honour of the Sixth Army'.[73] It was a difficult time for Goebbels trying to adjust the public views while Hitler raged.

According to the historian Liddell Hart:

> Stalingrad henceforth worked like a subtle poison in the minds of the German commanders everywhere, undermining their confidence in the strategy which they were called on to execute. Morally even more than materially, the disaster to that army at Stalingrad had an effect from which the German Army never recovered.[74]

How far this affected all generals is questionable, not least Liddell Hart's view that had Paulus surrendered earlier 'a much greater disaster might have overtaken the other German armies'.[75] The night before Paulus was taken prisoner, 30 January, he sent a telegram to Hitler on the anniversary of his assumption of power. It seems almost unbelievable that Paulus had the time or reason to concoct the following:

> On the anniversary of your seizure of power, the Sixth Army greets its Leader. The swastika flag is still flying over Stalingrad. May our struggle be an example for the present and coming generations that we should never capitulate even when we have lost hope. Then Germany will win. Hail my Leader. Paulus.[76]

It has been suggested that Paulus had turned against Hitler by refusing to kill himself, and there may be some truth in this, but it would take time for Paulus to convince himself and make his views public.

Capitulation

Paulus technically did not surrender but was captured, in so far that the time came when the Russians knocked at his door. His subordinate and friend Colonel Wilhelm Adam recalled it was still dark at 7.00 a.m. on 31 January, he woke to the door being knocked and was told the Russians were outside. They entered and informed Paulus and Adam they were now prisoners, leaving Adam no choice but to put his revolver on the table. It was a polite interchange, with the Russian explaining he would be back at nine but leaving Russian guards at the door. Despite German propaganda it appeared that the Russians were courteous in their approach, and although the ordinary captive German soldiers suffered, the Soviets treated the senior German officers with a degree of respect, which may well have been due to their organised propaganda. The Russians noted that 'Paulus was completely unnerved…a Jewish lieutenant called Zakhary Rayzman described Paulus having quivering lips'.[77] A Major General Ivan Burmakov described Paulus as a cornered animal living in unbelievable conditions.[78] These viewpoints are sustained by Russian photographs taken on the day when Paulus emerged from his bunker looking distraught, dirty, unshaven, with hints of illness or mental distress visible in his facial features.

The first thing that Adam noticed was the Russian soldiers were dressed in the best winter gear and looking well fed and fresh, whereas the German troops had ragged clothes and make-do civilian clothing to keep them warm, looking hungry and unshaven. Elsewhere many officers were removing their rank tabs, and many units surrendered once they had run out of ammunition. The last message Zeitzler had from Stalingrad read, 'the Russians are outside our bunker. This is our final transmission. Long live Germany,' while at the same time Göring was hunting hares on his estate. Göring had promised the supplies to the Sixth Army knowing that it could never be achieved, and alongside Hitler was responsible for the disastrous defeat. The precise figures of men who survived Stalingrad will never be known accurately, but it rocketed to unprecedented levels. It is generally accepted that between November 1942 and October 1943 the Russian front 'sustained well over a million and a half casualties (including the sick) of whom, close to 700,000 were permanently lost'.[79] The estimated losses often vary, but there is no doubt they were horrendous, 'and Hitler would not be able to mount an offensive on this scale again', giving much credence to the Russian claim they won the war.[80] In terms of those fighting at Stalingrad under Paulus, 'he was followed into captivity by 91,000 survivors of the quarter of a million with whom he had set out three months before. Half of the survivors perished within a week or two of capture. Only five per cent would outlast the Soviet camps and return home to Germany and Austria to tell the tale.'[81] The Soviet prison camps were similar to their Nazi counterparts for Russian prisoners, typhoid spread quickly, and up to two thirds had died within a few months, only about 5,000–6,000 ever made it home to Germany. This happened because military leaders accepted an oath to Hitler without question, even though it meant accepting absurd and immoral orders against their better judgement.

Meanwhile, Paulus was having his personal possessions searched for any object he might use for suicide, causing Schmidt to shout that a German field marshal would not kill himself with a pair of nail scissors, but Paulus calmed him down. The senior Russians knew that suicide was a possibility, and it would enrage Stalin. As they left Paulus was accompanied by Lieutenant Lev Bezyminsky of Red Army Intelligence. He was driven in his own car to Don Front headquarters outside Zavarykino about fifty miles from Stalingrad, and naturally the Russians kept his Mercedes. Schmidt travelled with Paulus while Adam followed in another car. Paulus wore a fur cap, in the uniform of a colonel-general, recently granted, but stated he was now a field marshal, but not explaining why.

Paulus told his interrogator Marshal Voronov, 'I didn't surrender. I was taken by surprise', which the Russians ignored. He refused to sign the surrender paper, telling the Russians that even if he did it would be seen as a forgery. He was told he would have to appear before journalists, but would not have to answer questions, they just needed photographs to show he was not dead. Paulus wondered whether a new version of the stab in the back theory would be developed, not communists and Jews, but this time general staff and aristocracy. On 2 February, the Luftwaffe flew over the battlegrounds and reported that all fighting had ceased. The Russians had taken some 91,000 plus PoWs with over twenty generals, of whom only one failed to return to Germany, whereas only a tiny minority of their soldiers survived the prison camps.* The Russians

---

* General Walter Karl Heitz died from cancer in a Moscow hospital in February 1944.

treated their high-ranking prisoners with care, the frost-bitten soldiers less so. General Shumilov asked Paulus if he had given permission for the northern sector to surrender which Paulus denied. It was almost, given Goebbels' propaganda about an instant bullet in the neck, a surprising and pleasant reception. Adam described his surprise and pleasure as they were allowed to wash with soap which he had not seen for a long time, as 'for days we had only been able to wash our faces and hands in thawed snow water, damply rubbed off'.[82] Shumilov asked what he could do for Paulus who replied would he be able to keep Major Adam with him, which was granted, thereby giving other generations a chance to understand what happened to Paulus during this time through Adam's somewhat biased pro-communist account in his biography.

Looking Back to Stalingrad

An interesting book entitled *The Discursive Construction of History* basically reviewed the way Stalingrad has been viewed over the years in various documentaries and international broadcasts.[83] It offers an interesting insight into the numerous ways the battle was regarded by future generations, and the different interpretations and views it has engendered. In the earlier explorations the emphasis is on a 'suddenly occurring natural phenomena which helps to conjure the impression of the forces being delivered up to an inescapable fate. This fatalistic viewpoint obscures the fact that the massive loss of life at Stalingrad was brought about by human decisions…in other words, the cause of the catastrophe is to be found in the war aims of the Nazi leadership and in a totally militarized National Socialist society.'[84] The study noted that in schoolbooks the causation of events is epitomised by 'Hitler', which to the modern era sounds some sense, but:

> There is little discussion of the questionable value of unconditional military obedience as a defining characteristic of the Nazi *Volksgemeinschaft* [National community]. The same is true of the role of General Field Marshal Paulus and his responsibility for the

hopeless position of the soldiers encircled at Stalingrad. He only comes into the frame after the defeat – as the distinguished co-founder of the anti-Nazi PoW movement 'Free Germany'.[85]

The writers of this exposition noted that there were three major questions often asked, the first about the military strategy of the Wehrmacht leadership; secondly, why the Sixth Army fought on; and finally the fate of the German soldiers. Throughout the documentaries some themes are always occurring. The German losses are frequently mentioned, but until later reviews, seldom were the Soviet casualties raised.[86] Other major themes were the excellent battle conduct and losses by Austrian soldiers, the nature of Paulus's character, Hitler's tactical errors, but seldom a mention of the Russians. In some of the documentary views 'the Soviet side is airbrushed out, as is the context of the war as a whole'.[87] The emphasis was often on the suffering of the German soldiers, partisan war was mentioned but there is no reference to the massacre of Jews.[88] When as mentioned in the main text that human remains were still found in the new Stalingrad, renamed Volgograd, one documentary observer assumed they were all German bones.[89] It was in 2000 a German television documentary was produced which interviewed an ex-Soviet soldier about the losses sustained by the Red Army. There was a growing tendency to look at Stalingrad from the point of view of the human suffering, many being seen as the victims of the Nazi regime.

Such were the views of popular documentary and academic analyses of Stalingrad, many still exposing human bigotry, but not avoiding the tragedy of so many deaths in appalling circumstances. Paulus's role was frequently raised with a variety of opinions, leaving the reader to adjudicate whether he was weak by being controlled by Hitler and others, whether he was too obedient, or a product of the Germanic and Nazi background. It remained a long-term debate as to whether Paulus was a hero or a traitor. After his capture, another view of Paulus came to light.

Chapter Four

In Soviet Hands

In Captivity

Paulus and his two senior officers left the area by car, then train, and the other senior officers were moved to a prisoner-of-war camp at Krasnogorsk near Moscow. They were bathed and deloused, and Paulus with Schmidt and Adam given their own room in a large log hut. They were looked after because Paulus was seen as a prize catch, but their soldiers died in droves. At one stage the Germans offered an exchange of Stalin's fighter pilot son for Paulus, but the Russian died in Sachsenhausen concentration camp.[1] Stalin was alienated from his son and may not have given this consideration.

In prison they had to become accustomed to an alien way of life, a mixture described by Adam as a mixture of stress and expectation. They had a library in the camp and the Russians were keen to convert their captives into anti-Nazis if not becoming communists, for use in the psychological war they were attempting against German forces and their public. In late April they were moved to Susdal (sometimes spelt Suzdal) some sort of old bishop's seat of power, where Adam was to share a room with Schmidt. Again, it was a matter of adjusting to their new circumstances, looked after because of their connection with Paulus. It was at Susdal that Adam met a professor of history, and he gradually started to think about the Nazi leadership and the values of Russian communism.

While in this new setting Paulus was told he would be meeting some Germans who wanted to speak with him. One would be Wilhelm Pieck, who like Ulbricht had once been a member of the German Reichstag.*

---

* He would later be chairman of the Socialist Unity Party from 1946 to 1950, and then president of the GDR between 1949 to 1960.

Pieck was well informed and communicative, telling Paulus the current disaster would never have happened had he and the German people not allowed themselves to be misled by Hitler. Paulus could only reply that he could not believe that the head of state would betray his people, and he was only doing his duty. There is little doubt that these questions started to have an effect on Paulus once he realised what was happening to his homeland of Germany.

This was the beginning of a tension which would stay with Paulus and many generals for the rest of their lives. The Prussian or Germanic tradition was that the military leaders stayed out of politics and obeyed the orders of their government. This was shared by many other countries including Britain, but it was severely deep-rooted in Germany. In Britain officers and soldiers swore allegiance to the Monarch and in America to the President. In Germany, the oath mentioned only Hitler's name, and was taken to a life and death situation. It is impossible to rule out the influence of morality from politics, and there were many amongst those who were fighting, who questioned themselves as to whether their politicians were morally corrupt. In the officer prison camps, especially amongst the senior generals, there would grow a deep division between the so-called non-political adherents who would never say a word against Hitler, resenting those who decided that the Nazi regime was evil, or had become morally misguided. After the war, many generals tried to distance themselves from Hitler, others, like Kesselring kept quiet on the issue. In the prison camps these divisions of opinion started and caused rifts, as the Russians tried to find those who would oppose the Nazi regime. Paulus remained stubborn during these months of early imprisonment, and although Adam's account may well be biased, it is not unreasonable that deep inside Paulus there were gathering doubts about the Nazi regime. The question Pieck raised was all too familiar, as to why Paulus had continued to obey senseless orders which led to the death of many thousands of soldiers. Paulus maintained his usual answer, with his only response being the continuous traditional argument, that soldiers do not become involved in politics. Before their time was finished Pieck asked if he might speak to Paulus alone, possibly detecting a man who was inwardly wavering. It transpired that Pieck intended to establish a national German committee prepared to challenge the Nazi regime, a proposal which at this stage simply horrified Paulus.

After about two months in Susdal they were on the move again. They were taken to their semi-permanent base Camp 48 at Voikovo, which had once been an inn with a spa, and was known as the castle. It was a camp intended for generals run by a Russian colonel who spoke German. Adam calculated there were some twenty-two German, six Romanian and three Italian generals, and they had a well-equipped library. Once again, even though the group was small there were divided opinions on the matter of politics. One group wanting to turn against Hitler's operational policies, the next wanting to turn against Hitler the leader, another group who would not budge from their oath to Hitler, and some, probably including Paulus who were uncertain as to where they stood.[2] This hesitant attitude by Paulus reflected the earliest criticisms of him as a young officer then later as a field marshal, namely that he was indecisive and needed time to work his way through a problem. These issues divided the camp, often with a sense of hostility between the groups.

It was at this stage the NKVD 'moved the implacable Schmidt away from Paulus, because he was seen as a bad influence'.[3] Schmidt was known to be a self-confident officer, making sure his views were voiced, which drew in supporters, but others disliked him. It has also been claimed he exercised too strong an influence on Paulus, especially as his health and mental fatigue increased. Schmidt's removal would have been a relief for Adam who never had time for Paulus's Chief of Staff. Schmidt spent much time in the Lubyanka and was tortured, by being kept awake day and night, mainly because he remained staunch in his anti-communist views, and he was not released until 1955, following the West German Chancellor Konrad Adenauer's visit to Moscow.

The political groupings continued to raise the temperature causing dissent within the group, and there were angry protests when a newspaper in German called *Free Germany* was circulated, with the news that in their old prison camp of Krasnogorsk, this paper and organisation had been founded by German emigrants with some officers and soldiers. It was also becoming abundantly clear at this stage that Germany was losing the war on all fronts. Paulus managed to stand apart, but his friend Adam eventually joined, having held back for a time probably because of his closeness to Paulus. It is not difficult to understand the friction created by these political divisions, with the Germanic sense of obedience and loyalty on the one hand, with the growing recognition of the reality of Nazism and its destructive demands on the other. It very much reached a head for many people when the full impact of the war was experienced, with Germany occupied and divided between the victors.

Their sometimes-difficult colleague Seydlitz left the camp, and then to Adam's surprise returned, but this time on a mission. He was discussing the founding of a league of German officers (*Bund Deutscher Offiziere*) and its first leader would be General Seydlitz himself. This movement's new development further increased the hostility between the different camps within the prison, with rowdy hostile meetings. However, by early September 1943 nearly a hundred had joined and they were gathered together in Moscow. It was ideal for Russian propaganda, as their intention was to encourage German soldiers to withdraw to the Reich boundaries. This involved broadcasts, letters home, pamphlets, and copies of the *Free Germany* newspaper. It was also intended to influence the German public, which by this time was suppressed not only by the Nazi regime but suffering the bombing and appalling news of casualties. However, one Berlin diarist heard the broadcast from Moscow, which was a brave act listening to it, and she noted that some of her friends were commenting 'That's what we should have done in Russia from the start.'[4]

Paulus refused to collaborate with his communist captors, still insisting he was captured and had not surrendered, though nobody listened or believed his version. Unlike ordinary troops he was not used in forced labour and starved to death, he was too important to the Soviets, a prestigious trophy, and they were keen to make the most of him, hoping he would denounce Hitler. He had good reason to co-operate because Hitler had badly let him and his men of the Sixth Army down. He had been consistently assured of reinforcements, fuel, ammunition, and every form of assistance which were all promises never fulfilled. He had been ordered to stand firm to the last man, and if he were the last man, Hitler had made him a last-minute Field Marshal, with the evident hint that he should therefore kill himself as the final act. Somehow, his sense of honour and obedience made him stubborn in the prison camp conflicts. Others started to join the dissenters but many of the resisting Germans would not budge. When after the Teheran conference the unconditional surrender terms became public it worried some officers, mainly because it implied the enslavement of the Germans with the loss of their country; not all believed this possible, but again it increased the hostility between the groups of senior officers.

It was probably the 20 July plot against Hitler's life which gave Paulus a moment to re-think his traditional views. The news of this plot implied there were military men deeply unhappy about the way Hitler was conducting the war with the dangers of imminent defeat. 'Then came news that his old comrades Witzleben and Hoepner had been in the front rank of insurgents, and he soon heard that they had been executed by strangulation. He was acquainted with Claus von Stauffenberg, who had served under him in the Organisational Section of OKH', and clearly his sense of loyalty had been challenged too far.[5] According to the journalist and historian William Shirer, Paulus had been approached by the plotters while he was encircled at Stalingrad. They had assumed he was bitterly disappointed with Hitler's outrageous orders, and they sent a personal appeal from General Beck which was flown into their headquarters by a Luftwaffe officer. According to Shirer, Paulus responded by sending 'a flood of radio messages of devotion to his Führer' and kept this to himself.[6] Paulus probably now felt that he was not alone, as he now knew that colleagues and men whom he had respected had decided that some form of action had to be taken against the Führer, who had let the military and the country down, and was now leading Germany into the abyss of defeat, with an uncertain future. Paulus, all too typically, had not made a sudden decision, but the enormity of Nazi evil was slowly being exposed forcing him to question himself, the Nazi regime, and the past.

To the delight of his Soviet captors, they now had a field marshal to be the leading figurehead joining the *Bund Deutscher Offiziere*, Federation of German Officers, and he soon became an outspoken critic of the Nazi regime, joining the Soviet sponsored National Committee for a Free Germany (NKFD). The aim was for the committee to function as a propaganda unit aimed at the German forces. They had their own newspaper and radio station, sent leaflets to PoWs, and some were even attached to frontline units to talk with captured comrades. It amounted to a form of psychological warfare and some, known as Seydlitz troops, were dressed in German uniforms, and sent to the front to spread confusion. For his part Paulus, as early as 8 August 1944, spoke on the *Free Germany* radio. During this broadcast address he referred to the pointless sacrifices made under Hitler, and the need for the people to disassociate themselves from the Nazi regime and rid themselves of the dictator.[7] He was the leading proponent not just because of his rank, but he and his Sixth Army had been the ideal example of a 'pointless sacrifice'. It was an appeal to the Wehrmacht and German people, which could have little effect until Hitler and his henchmen were either dead or incarcerated and the results of the war experienced by total occupation.

Before his capture and for a time afterwards, Paulus had remained loyal to Hitler and the corrupt machine. He had once thought Hitler was brilliant and the OKW to be first class in judging military strategy. He had constantly held hopes in Hitler's absurd promises that supplies were coming, and the Russians were finished at Stalingrad. In the days of his early success, he had had a letter from Stauffenberg, a prominent figure in the 20 July Plot. Stauffenberg had written (12 July 1942) that it must be good for Paulus to be surrounded by men prepared to give their lives without complaint, 'while the leaders and those who should set an example quarrel and quibble about their own prestige or haven't the courage to speak their minds on a question which affects the lives of thousands of their fellow men'.[8] According to the historian Beevor, 'Paulus either did not notice, or more likely he deliberately ignored, the coded message.'[9] It is, however, curious that the journalist Pierre Galante noted that 'Paulus had already associated himself, to some degree at least, with the military conspiracy against Hitler', though little mention of this is made elsewhere, indicating how little is known about Paulus's personal views.[10] The 20 July Plot and possibly news about how his family had been treated had opened his eyes. He must have realised by joining the NFKD he was becoming part of the Soviet propaganda, especially as he was the highest-ranking German officer to be part of this anti-Nazi machine. He recognised his rank was important to the Soviets, so he asked to meet members of the Soviet Central Committee to ask about Germany's future, wondering if at Hitler's death Germany would be totally destroyed. He was given the assurances he needed and never seemed to doubt them. It was his age-old problem of trusting his perceived superiors and seemingly accepting all he was told.

He gave various propaganda speeches, and immediately this added to the Nazi hatred of him, and his family at home were in trouble. This Nazi reaction must have increased his sense of anger and sorrow. His son Friedrich had been killed at Anzio, but his other son Ernst arrested, and Paulus's wife was told that she would be left alone if she renounced her name. She refused and was placed in a camp. This had all been under the *Sippenhaft* decree, which had been an old Germanic policy that a family of a criminal shared the blame. This long forgotten medieval law had been reinstituted by the Nazi regime after the 20 July Plot, and further underlined their warped sense of morality and justice.

After the War

During the Nuremberg trial the Russians swiftly utilised their captive and he stood as a witness for the prosecution. They flew him in without prior warning, and his sudden appearance created both shock for some and startled others, including the defendants and the court personnel. Curiously, a Russian, Lieutenant Colonel Fyodor Karpovich Parparov, who was working on the details of the Nazi background (later published in English) organised and made Paulus ready for the Nuremberg Trial to ensure he was well-prepared. There had been rumours that some elements amongst the Allies thought the Russians should be reproached for not trying Paulus and Seydlitz, but it was agreed there had to be sound evidence of crimes against humanity. To Paulus's credit there was no evidence, and it was known that he had blocked Hitler's orders regarding political commissars and Jews within his sector.[11] While at Nuremberg, he was asked by a journalist how the German prisoners were faring. He said they were treated well, only thinking of himself and other senior officers, seen by the Soviets as key trophies. He probably had no idea that of his 91,000 plus captured troops at Stalingrad, nearly half had died on the forced march to Siberian prison camps, and many more died while in their long captivity. No precise figures are available, but those who survived captivity were few in number. It could be argued that Paulus was blind to the circumstances of his men, or more probably blinded by his captors and the pictures they drew for Paulus, informing him that they were being treated the same as him. This may not have been his fault as he would have been ignorant of such information, but he was too often unrealistic in always trusting seniors, even the policies of the tyrants Hitler and Stalin. When the question of ordinary soldier prisoners was raised in the trial proceedings the Russians, who feared this subject, objected to the question being raised.

During the trial, the Russian prosecutor General Rudenko questioned him about the attack on Russia, and he blamed the High Command mentioning Keitel, Jodl and Göring. Paulus's appearance at the trial came as a shock to everyone, especially as the defence had challenged a deposition by General Warlimont on the grounds he should appear as a witness. The Russians had suddenly produced Paulus unexpectedly, almost like a bombshell, when they announced that Paulus was there and ready everyone was shocked, having no idea he was even in Germany.[12]

He revealed nothing startling, just a series of statements about the Nazi plans for occupying Russia, all well-rehearsed before his appearance. He could not be doubted on this issue as he had been part of the planning process from an early stage. 'But Paulus's testimony cut the defendants to the quick' because he was a prisoner of war and not a war criminal, even though he had been a member of the General Staff.[13] According to the American prosecutor Telford Taylor, 'Paulus presented his testimony, in a measured and highly professional way, his evidence was not sensationally new…but a witness can convey meaning beyond the bare reading of documents'.[14] According to Taylor he also added some stings by being there in person, and by naming Keitel, Jodl and Göring for being mainly responsible, agreeing with the question that *Barbarossa* had been on the planning table for a long time. Paulus also bore witness that Hitler's decision to 'destroy Yugoslavia postponed the beginning of *Barbarossa* by about five weeks', endorsed by others that this decision proved costly.[15] The implication being that Hitler was not the military genius he and many others assumed.

During the trial some of the defendants' counsels made use of Paulus's appearance. When Dr Otto Nelte was defending Field Marshal Keitel's argument of obeying orders he stated that:

> Keitel says, it was the unconditional duty of the soldier to do his duty obediently to the bitter end, true to his military oath. This concept is false when it is exaggerated to the extent of leading to crime. It must be remembered, however, that a soldier is accustomed to measure by other standards in war. When all high-ranking officers, including Field Marshal Paulus, represent the same point of view, the honesty of their convictions cannot be denied, although it may not be understood.[16]

Keitel himself declared 'It is a shame for him [Paulus] to be testifying against us', while men like Jodl simply exploded noisily with anger.[17] Keitel during the lunch break claimed that Paulus should not have accepted his promotions and his decorations and not kept sending messages of loyalty to the Führer,[18] perhaps not knowing that Paulus had not turned against Hitler after his capture but months later, whereas Keitel himself had done the same, especially in his private thoughts expressed during cell conversations.

Paulus then had to face a barrage of questions from nine defence counsels, and at one point he was forced to admit that it had taken time for him to realise some of the orders he obeyed had been criminal. The three-hour session was not easy for him, appearing disturbed by the questioning, and he was seen to be trembling. Naturally, his appearance for the defence angered many of the military defendants, who described him as a traitor. He had to face Dr Otto Nelte who questioned him about the criminal nature of the attack on Russia, to which Paulus replied that 'he saw nothing unusual in basing the fate of a people and a nation on power politics and thought he was doing his duty to the fatherland', and he believed that many of the other defendants thought the same way as he did.[19] He was by this answer assisting some of the other military defendants, probably inadvertently.

When the prison psychologist sat at lunch with Jodl, Keitel, and Dönitz, they discussed whether Paulus had been under pressure to give evidence, or simply to preserve his own existence. The psychologist Gilbert queried whether Paulus had decided that Hitler was destroying Germany, with Keitel becoming angry stating he should have taken that position before he was captured. Jodl pointed out that Paulus had sworn the Hitler oath, with Dönitz adding Paulus had cost thousands of lives, by the undermining of morale with the Soviet broadcasts of *Free Germany*. After lunch in the courtroom the defendants of the military group shouted their anger, with Göring asking if Paulus had applied for Russian citizenship, all accompanied by shouts of traitor. Some others made more sympathetic comments about Paulus, and it was clear that the hatred emanated from the military with their inbuilt Prussian views.[20] Many wondered how Paulus would cope as he left the dock looking emotionally drained, but he was soon spotted sharing a cigarette and laughing with some Russian officers.

After the trial Paulus spent a few days in Dresden, which after the bombing was in a state of appalling destruction, a stark reminder of the power of bombing and its effects on civilians. During the post-war period Paulus was at Tomilino near Moscow and given a dacha and garden. Adam was allowed to catch up with his old leader and friend, both happy at the reunion. As far as Stalin was concerned, Paulus was a valuable commodity. It was there they were told they would be released back into Germany, but it would take a long time and had to wait for Stalin's death, despite various pleas on Paulus's behalf.

His captivity during this period was relatively luxurious, and it has been claimed 'he had a dacha with his own cook, and from time to time was allowed to see theatrical performances in Moscow...while thousands of his former soldiers were dying in Russian prison camps...he continued to curry favour and, in 1947, asked to be allowed to settle in the Soviet occupation zone.'[21] There were, of course, other views as to why Paulus stayed with the Soviets, one being the hope that communism would bring some form of peace, another he was aware that he would be criticised in the West. In East Germany he was promised a villa, offered his own Opel car, would be able to read western newspapers and his two remaining children would be allowed to visit him.

Paulus was one of the first to be released into East Germany, then the German Democratic Republic (created on 7 October 1949) giving an arranged press conference in Berlin which Western journalists attended. He had been released after over ten years in captivity, albeit not in a Siberian prison camp. He arrived at Frankfurt-an-der-Oder railway station on 26 October 1953 late morning. He was welcomed by the Minister of the Interior, and he spoke about General Heinz Guderian who had recently died, and then took time to criticise the political leaders for bringing destruction upon Germany. Paulus further endorsed these views pointing out that in both world wars, one started by the German Empire the other by the Nazi regime, both had demanded the impossible from the German military. He may well have developed deep feelings for this viewpoint, as he must have been conscious of the enormous ramifications for post-war Germany, now divided into sectors by the occupying allied forces. His exit speech from Russia included the lines that 'I do not want to leave the Soviet Union without saying to the Soviet people that in blind obedience I once came to their country as an enemy, but I now take my leave of this country as a friend.'[22]

His faithful servant Adam was there and went with him to his new home in Dresden. Paulus was by now part of the Soviet propaganda, and he criticised the Americans for an aggressive foreign policy, while pleading for some form of appeasement between Germany and France. He underlined the danger of power politics, claiming that a rich country can bend the will of its neighbours, again seen as criticising America. The Soviets needed a German field marshal to make their own viewpoints clear. He also agreed with the criticisms levelled against the West German Chancellor Konrad Adenauer, who was always seeking support from America. Circumstances had left Paulus on the communist side of the German border during the initial stages of the Cold War, and by this time sympathetic to their cause, having reached the conclusion that Nazism had destroyed Germany. He may not have been a dedicated communist, but it was clear that he felt the arrangement with Soviet Russia would ensure some level of peace for Germany. He may have had little choice but to settle in East Germany, but he also knew that his presence in the West would be uncomfortable amongst many of his one-time colleagues, and the death of his wife reduced the reasons to go to West Germany.

The friction between those generals who had turned against Hitler and those who protested continued unabated. The political generals, namely those who claimed they obeyed orders of the Nazi regime, governed by the dictates of Hitler, mainly found refuge in West Germany. Paulus was especially annoyed by the publication of von Manstein's book, *Lost Victory* because, as he explained to Adam, Manstein seemed to lay the blame on Hitler and Paulus. It was the start of many post-war tensions as military commanders wrote their memoirs, trying to distance themselves from the regime which they had all served. According to Adam, Paulus started to write his own account of the war on the Volga but was either too busy or not well enough to manage his own account.

Paulus lived comfortably in Dresden from 1953 to 1956 in what was regarded as an exclusive social area, working as the civilian chief of the East German Military History Research Institute, gave lectures on the battle for Stalingrad, though some claim he was also an Inspector of the People's Police, possibly both roles.[23] Undoubtedly, like so many he was observed by the Stasi and he had, as most commanders, a lonely life which became more so in East Germany. He was no longer surrounded by family and friends, and his surviving son Ernst was allowed to visit him a few times. However, it was apparent he did not approve of his father's conversion to communism, whatever the reasons. It was unlikely that Paulus was a committed communist but had to appear as such on the surface. From the moment he was given command of the Sixth Army, life had given him little joy. He was bereft of family and genuine friends, and life concluded for him when he fell ill in late 1956. He was suffering from a form of organic cerebral sclerosis which led to paralysis of the muscles, though his mind remained stable and active. He died on the 1 February 1957, aged 66 years of age, and 14 years and one day after his capture at Stalingrad. He had asked for his cremated remains to be interred at Baden-Baden with his wife who had died in 1949, having never seen her husband since he left for the Eastern Front.

Chapter Five

Divided Opinions

The Nazi Regime

The impact of the Nazi regime and Hitler had at one time seemed to unify the Germans after the defeat of the First World War and the humiliation of the Versailles Treaty. However, as the war unfolded, and global tragedy ensued, Nazism divided Germany. At first the opposition was deeply secret out of sheer fear, it was guided by men like General Beck, but blossomed as the war drew to an end amongst the devastation and revelation of the crimes against humanity. This overall pattern of division was reflected within the military as well. Wearing Nazi symbols and insignia, and the personal oath of allegiance to Hitler had ended the pretence that the army was not political. Paulus later said, 'The generals followed Hitler in these circumstances, and as a result they became completely involved in the consequences of his policies and conduct of the war.'[1] It has been claimed that 'when Hitler came to power, Paulus felt the self-made aristocratic disdain for the upstart corporal...however, he remained unswervingly faithful to the dictates of his soldier's conscience: "This is an order from the Führer, and I must obey it."'[2] Hitler was the political leader who many commanders believed had to be obeyed because he was the legitimate government. He had also taken control over the armed forces, mainly because even the most senior men were scared to disagree with him with the exception of a few like Beck who had resigned. The political orders to kill Soviet Commissars, annihilate Jews, slaughter other innocents, had bewildered many men and officers. However, the Prussian tradition of obeying all orders was deep, and bolstered by the underlying sense of fear, and for some senior officers the need to avoid removal from their positions.

In the campaign in Russia, it was Hitler who took the initiative, not the generals, reversing their decisions, refusing to listen to them, and insisting on fighting to the last man. At Nuremberg Manstein claimed this caused the army's opposition to Hitler. On the other hand, as the historian Bullock noted, it seemed 'to illustrate the docility with which the generals submitted to treatment'.[3]

There is little doubt that Hitler had many personal psychological issues, obsessive, and what is often called the condition of being a 'control freak', though one of gigantic proportions with many ramifications. When Zeitzler had passed on Paulus's request to break out from the Stalingrad cauldron, 'Hitler went red with rage…pushed his spectacles across the table, something that always presaged an outbreak of fury and roared that Paulus should not dare come to me with such things.'[4] Even passing on a critical message to Hitler could be damaging for the messenger. When Seydlitz radioed that he could no longer take responsibility for his corps, Hitler threw a fit shouting 'reject responsibility – that is cowardice. I will not freely give up Stalingrad, even if the whole Sixth Army perishes in the act'.[5] Halder once recorded the Führer's 'intolerable language used about other people's mistakes when they are merely carrying out an order which he himself has issued'.[6] Most of the commanders obeyed either because of the Hitler oath, fooled by propaganda, a sense of fear, not ruining their career prospects, or believing in Hitler's genius, without recognising his evident fallibility and incompetence. There is no question that Hitler mesmerised his generals, he convinced them the Russians were about to attack even though their own military intelligence told them otherwise. He seemed to cast a hypnotic spell over them and even after the war some thought he was correct in assuming Russia would attack. Later this view would be almost encouraged by some because of the Cold War exigencies of the day. Paulus never aired this view and according to the American William Shirer, 'Paulus seems to have been more honest.'[7]

Nevertheless, Paulus followed the pattern of most Nazi commanders bred within the old Prussian/Germanic tradition of obedience. Like many others, and perhaps understandably, Hitler's reversal of the Versailles Treaty and recovering German land on the basis of irredentist nationalism and without bloodshed was widely applauded, and the fall of Poland and France made him for some a heroic if not a military genius. Paulus's messages to the Führer seem to endorse this, at times even admiring the dictator, respecting his views and decisions.

His aide de camp Wilhelm Adam's biography has to be read with care, but it appears from his and other accounts that during the closing days for the battle of Stalingrad, Paulus started to accrue doubts about Hitler's decisions. He had remained a stubborn Prussian even in the early days of Russian captivity until the 20 July Plot to kill Hitler, which told him that others whom he respected thought the same way. His background, military training, social influences had made him almost robotic in terms of obeying orders, and it took the loss of hundreds of thousands of men's lives to force him to question himself. It would be trite to say he should have listened to his wife, but he was caught up in the Nazi web which was easy to criticise once it had collapsed. The influence of Nazism was all pervasive and for Paulus to speak out even in captivity took its own form of courage.

Views of Contemporaries

Views by contemporaries can be interesting, but in Paulus's case there is always the hidden agenda that he turned against Hitler, or that his not having a major field command hampered him, and naturally he should have reacted to his military instinct and not wait for Hitler to make the decision. These were the major thrusts of the overall criticisms which have plagued his reputation, namely a traitor to Hitler who governed Germany, and his lack of aptitude in a field command.

As noted above the views of Paulus and many other generals changed during the war, especially when it became evident that Germany could not win, and more so when the atrocities of the massacres, camps, and Holocaust emerged. Some held that Hitler's behaviour relieved them from the oath while others held it to be unbreakable. The Prussian/Germanic military tradition was a powerful factor. In Trent Park, a British holding house for captured German generals, they were bugged for their private conversations. Generals Lüdwig Crüwell and Wilhelm Ritter von Thoma were known to be perpetually quarrelling. However, they found a moment of agreement over Paulus, with Crüwell saying 'I would have put a bullet through my head. So, I am bitterly disappointed.' Thoma concurred and said 'It was a dreadful thing that so many generals have been captured at Stalingrad'.[8] Thoma added that 'It's impossible for the commander to go on living in such circumstances…because I know Paulus, it must have been his nerves, and everything completely shattered. But it is unsoldierly, and it upsets me as a soldier.'[9] It was the expectation that commanders would set the example to their men and fight to the death, though both these generals were safely imprisoned. It was the same militaristic tradition that held such a psychological hold over Paulus, not disobeying Hitler leading to many thousands of deaths.

When Field Marshal Milch expressed his views, saying that 'had he been in General von (*sic*) Paulus' position at Stalingrad, he would have abandoned the city even against Hitler's orders'. According to the historian Heiber, Goebbels was there when this was said, and 'instead of striking down the impious one with his thunder, he debated the point with him'.[10] Some were more sympathetic to Paulus's plight. Rommel, in a letter to his wife, described how the battle in North Africa was turning against him with the lack of supplies. He also added 'Paulus is perhaps even worse off than I am. He has a more inhuman enemy. We can only hope that God does not desert us altogether.'[11] It was of course known that Rommel had his own doubts about the Nazi command and their strategy, whose orders Paulus once had the duty of conveying to him.

Manstein wrote that:

It is easy to criticise the attitude of the future Field Marshal Paulus in those vital days. Certainly, there was more to it than 'blind obedience' to Hitler, for there can be no question that Paulus had grave conscientious doubts as to whether he should mount an operation which must inevitably lead – in direct contravention of the wish clearly expressed by Hitler – to the surrender of Stalingrad to the enemy.[12]

When post-war Manstein was questioned during the trials he was asked what he thought about Paulus. He replied that he 'was a very clever man though perhaps not a very strong character...my criticism of Paulus is that he should not have asked Hitler. He should have done it on his own hook...that is why I say Paulus was not a very strong character, because to make a decision like that during war takes a strong personality.'[13]

Before the Stalingrad battle, and before the political criticisms started Paulus was highly regarded. '[General]Heusinger, who first met Friedrich [Paulus] in 1927, remembers him as "an intelligent man, an engaging personality, and an officer who had already embraced the creed of absolute obedience"'.[14] Files from the Bundesarchiv, the so-called *General Kartei* have a comment by Reichenau, that Paulus was an upright, honourable person, clever, clear, commander and staff officer, and one from von Bock (5 April 1942) that Paulus has commanded the Sixth Army for the first time since three months ago. More and more a decent man and a valorous soldier, very deliberate. First things first he must prove himself as an army commander before he can be considered for any other employment in the superior class.

It was evident that Paulus was regarded highly by most, especially by Halder and Reichenau, but his decisions at Stalingrad have proved divisive in the memory banks. Admired as a competent staff officer when a planner, used in military diplomatic missions, and at first an acclaimed hero in his first battles around Kharkov to the Don, it was the disaster at Stalingrad that has, perhaps unfairly, coloured the views of many of his contemporaries.

Views of Historians

Most history books are more curious about the battle than the commanding figures, mainly because the battle, which was rapidly publicised worldwide, clearly sent the message that the German military could be defeated, and Stalingrad was a highly significant victory. It is often noted that it was a critical battle because it had been directed by the so-called military genius and undefeated Hitler, who the defeat proved, was otherwise. It was also regarded as an indicator of Russian strength and manpower. Post-war there were many debates about the battle, not only amongst the Germans who had participated, but the Soviet historians. The latter argued that those Germans who claimed Hitler could have saved the day by allowing a withdrawal were wrong. They argued, probably correctly, that the Russians had such resources and workforce at hand, that even a retreat in November could have been destroyed.

Many Germans quarrelled amongst themselves, not least von Manstein tending to blame Paulus and *vice versa*. The question was whether Stalingrad could have been supplied, and Göring's usual bluster and self-assurance gave Hitler the belief it could happen. However, the weather, the Russians sending up the same rockets as the Germans to identify safe landing places for the Luftwaffe pilots thus endangering them, and with the few available aircraft, made the relief-operation of supplies, for the more level-headed analysts, an obvious impossibility.

Some historians are more sympathetic to Paulus than others, Henri Michel writing 'in these circumstances what else could Paulus do but obey?'[15] It was this question of Paulus standing by his Prussian tradition of obedience or defying Hitler which has surfaced as time has passed. Henri Michel, however, pointed out that Paulus was an 'experienced tactician… and he cancelled the orders for the execution of the Red Army's political commissars and the systematic extermination of the Jews'.[16] With the same line of thought Beevor wrote that 'although Paulus's rather aloof manner made him appear cold, he was more sensitive than many generals to the well-being of his soldiers' and cancelled Reichenau's order against Jews and partisans, but noted that on reaching Stalingrad Paulus issued similar orders.[17] No other historian or available evidence appears to state that Paulus issued such orders, although it is conceivable that his Chief of Staff Schmidt may have done, but it makes it crystal clear that Paulus remains one of the least studied field marshals. There is also a clear indicator from people's views that at least Paulus was more civilised than many of his contemporary commanders.

Richard Humble, an historian who worked on the military efforts of Hitler's generals, described Paulus as 'the dull-witted Paulus continued to batter his way forward into the city at a cost which any Allied general would have been familiar with on the Western Front in the First World War'.[18] He later added that 'Paulus compounded his ignorance by sacking his two Panzer corps commanders, Wietersheim and Schwedler, for protesting that it was madness to keep tanks stuck up at the forward edge of a stationary front where all they could do was get knocked out by shellfire.'[19] Herein was the suggestion that in doing this Paulus was behaving in the same way to his subordinates as Hitler dictated to him. Humble was harsh in his critical views of Paulus as a military commander, referring to the whole Stalingrad disaster as Paulus's fault: 'Paulus shilly-shallied, egged on by his Chief of Staff, General Artur Schmidt, who echoed the theme that the Sixth Army would still be in position by Easter if it were properly supplied.'[20]

The historian Kenneth Macksey also noted that:

There is very little doubt that if Paulus had been allowed to break out immediately after 23 November or had the courage to disobey Hitler's ludicrous command…the crisis would have been solved. But neither the weaker-willed Paulus nor his other four corps commanders had the moral courage to disobey.[21] [However, at least General Seydlitz had urged him otherwise.]

Whether Macksey was correct that Paulus's breakout would have succeeded given the size of Russian opposition begs a few questions. Richard Evans wrote that as a German commander, Paulus 'was in some ways less than ideally suited for the job of taking the city…he had spent almost most of his entire career, including the years of the First World War, in staff posts, and had almost no combat experience'.[22] Max Hastings in his usual straightforward way wrote that when Manstein's efforts to open a corridor suggesting Paulus should defy Hitler and break out to join him, Paulus refused 'condemning 200,000 men to death or captivity'.[23]

Some claim Paulus had no choice but to obey, which given the facts of the Nazi regime control makes some sense, others that Paulus was more humane than most which must not be lost in the history of this man.

Most tend to think he should have disobeyed Hitler and escaped when he might have succeeded in November, after that any attempt would probably have been disastrous. The historian Andrew Roberts argued that Paulus was not the only one in this dilemma. Manstein had thought Paulus was right to withdraw, as Kluge had protested at the central thrust on Moscow, and Bock had not supported Hitler's strategy in *Barbarossa*, but, as Andrew Roberts wrote:

> The fact that they rarely spoke up simply shows that when dealing with Hitler the generals, for all their Iron Crosses and Knight's Crosses, were generally as cowardly as so many others in Nazi Germany. They were also aspirational professionals who knew that gainsaying the Führer was not a good way to secure promotion.[24]

Historians are just as divided over Paulus as were his contemporaries, and there is no black and white answer, neither in the historical analysis, or moral judgement, as Paulus argued that a sudden withdrawal was not only highly risky for his soldiers, but it might have created dangers for comrades in other areas.

Final Thoughts

When the Japanese watched film shots and heard about Stalingrad, they knew Hitler was going to lose the war, and at the same time were horrified that Paulus had survived. The Stalingrad victory was highly significant, as it seemed to indicate that with this major defeat coupled with the success in the North African theatre, the fear of Nazi domination lessened as it was only a matter of time before they lost the war they had provoked. However, it was the defeat at Kursk in the summer of 1943 which 'in Germans and Soviet eyes, constituted the politico-psychological turning point of the whole war'.[25]

As for Paulus, his capture, imprisonment, and turning against Hitler's regime was of little interest at the time, but his change of attitude towards Nazism has since provoked considerable debate and interest. He was a humane type of person, socially well-balanced, pleasant, not a Nazi monster, happily married, yet he obeyed and even respected Hitler, until it eventually dawned on him that Germany was being led to destruction. He had been respected as a staff officer and knowledgeable in planning matters, and although he was long aware of the stretched supply lines to Stalingrad, he accepted Hitler's absurd orders, and it took a long time for him to think twice about his Führer's military ability and overall intentions. Hitler never trusted his generals, and when Paulus refused suicide, this deepened Hitler's suspicions about the military commanders. Many generals in post-war memoirs hinted that they may have won the war had Hitler let them get on with the job, and they may well have carried out their war tasks better than Hitler managed. There were many attempts on Hitler's life, and perhaps it was best for the Allies he stayed in power to direct the military, rather than give the professional German commanders control.

Some of the military commanders were convicted of war crimes, but there was no evidence that Paulus fell within this category. The crunch-line in any discussion about Paulus tends to revolve around his decision to obey Hitler. By doing this he lost many of his soldiers and the surrender of the Sixth Army. The fact remains that it was Hitler who gave the directions, even against the advice of his own senior staff in his headquarters, but whether Paulus should have obeyed him like a Pavlov's dog is a question which will never go away. The cause of the Nazi hold over Germans and the military had started with the adoration of Hitler's early successes, but the conditioning of responsive behaviour came increasingly to rest on a sense of fear. This was true for many ordinary everyday members of the public, and it was equally true of military commanders wanting promotion rather than dismissal or even fear of retribution as some had suffered. Hitler's presence and influence dominated German life, and continued to do so for imprisoned generals in the prison camps even though he was invisible.

As is well-known the military were conditioned to obeying orders and to do otherwise was often regarded as a cardinal sin, and Paulus had been imbued with this sense of blind obedience. It has been claimed that when Hitler made him a field marshal, in effect instructing him to commit suicide, this opened Paulus's eyes to the danger of Nazi leadership. However, his aide de camp Adam in his own record implies that because of the gross nature of the orders sent from High Command, Paulus was already accumulating doubts about Hitler and his management, but Paulus remained unbelievably stubborn until news of the 20 July Plot.

Paulus's own expressed post-war views offer some insights:

I believe that by prolonging to its utmost our resistance in Stalingrad I was serving the best interests of the German people, for, if the eastern theatre of war collapsed, I saw no possible prospect of a peace by political negotiation. To have stepped on my own responsibility out of the general framework, to have acted deliberately against the orders given to me would have entailed the acceptance of a sequence of responsibilities: at the outset, by breaking out, I should have been responsible for the fate of my neighbours; later, by prematurely giving up the fight, for that of the southern sector and with it the whole of the eastern front; and that would have meant – or so it seemed – that I should have been responsible to the German people for the loss of the war.[26]

He later added the pertinent line that 'The responsibility – *vis à vis* the officers and men of the Sixth Army and the German people – for having obeyed orders and resisted till we could do no more and collapsed is mine and mine alone.'[27] He always accepted responsibility for his actions not only in Stalingrad but many other times.

It feels impossible not to have some sympathy for Paulus caught up in the period of Nazi influence with its dangerous tentacles, and he was trained in the sense of obedience. The Nuremberg trial would define illegal and immoral orders, especially those which created war crimes and crimes against humanity. This brief biography demonstrated that Paulus rescinded the Commissar Orders and killing civilians and Jews in his sector, as ordered by Hitler, and carried out by Reichenau. Paulus was not known or condemned for personal misconduct in this dreadful sphere of activity. If Paulus were guilty of anything it was for obeying ridiculous and absurd orders and not having the sense to disobey, a common fault all too characteristic of humanity in general, and especially in the military.

Paulus was a product of his background, an inexperienced field commander, too dependent on the advice of others and hamstrung by his sense of obedience to Hitler whom he regarded as the country's rightful leader. All the criticisms levelled at Paulus tend to have some relevance, but it must not be forgotten that he was fighting against overwhelming odds without the resources, and above all he was not a war criminal, and he had deliberately disobeyed Hitler in stopping the killing of political commissars and Jews within his sector.

Field Marshal Erich Von Manstein

The Military Mind

Chapter One

Introduction

Generals often try and impress others with an image of themselves from the professional perspective, one which epitomises their skills and capabilities, thereby advancing their careers. This was the case with Erich von Manstein, whose strategic skills were never matched by a career which remained tied to the battlefield, but he never made it to the high-level command.

Manstein, above all, had a good reputation for developing a military doctrine which put him at the same level of other well-known German strategists. In 1989 the Office for Military History Research of the Bundeswehr, the German armed forces, published a small book titled *Operational Thinking of Clausewitz, Moltke, Schlieffen and Manstein*.[1] The title revealed the thinking about Manstein, who is placed at the same level of other top military minds, each representing a particular era, in Manstein's case the age of mechanised warfare. The book analyses the different military theories related to the wars fought between France and Germany from the nineteenth century, focusing on the famous idea of the Schlieffen Plan, namely, the drive through Belgium to outflank French defences. Manstein's contribution to the evolution of the plan has often been considered crucial, and it can certainly be stated that it largely contributed to the German victory against France in 1940. This earned Manstein his reputation, but at the same time it contributed to shape his military career. Manstein was considered for the Army Staff, but this never developed into an actual appointment. He would remain a commander who enforced his theories on the battlefield, and it is difficult to estimate to what extent this influenced the course of the war.

Natural Born Soldier

Many have found von Manstein's complete name puzzling, which was Erich von Lewinski *genannt* (named) von Manstein. This relates to the story of his birth which was somewhat curious. Erich was the tenth child of Major Eduard von Lewinski and of Helene von Sperling. Helene's sister, Hedwig, was married to Major Georg von Manstein and the couple were childless. Some years before Erich's birth, the two families, clearly united by strong ties, decided that if Helene von Lewinski had a tenth child and he was a boy, the von Manstein family would have him as his guardian. This is why Erich, who was born in Berlin on 24 November 1887, received his complex name. At the moment of his adoption, according to the regulations of the time, he was registered as 'von Lewinski named von Manstein', the name he was known by. Apart from the oddity of the circumstances, probably better suited to the twenty-first rather than the nineteenth century, Manstein's birth also shows a curious peculiarity. He was born into a military family and was adopted by another military family. He might have been seeking in the army career what he probably missed in his youth, namely a proper or normal family, but it is difficult to think of Erich von Manstein choosing anything other than a military career.

Coming from a family related to at least five Prussian generals, one of which had commanded an army corps during the war against France, Erich hardly knew anything else than the military life. After attending the Strasbourg Lycée, aged 13 he went to the Cadet School at Plön, in the Schleswig-Holstein region, also serving at the same time in the Corps of Pages of Kaiser Wilhelm, which Erich seem to have thoroughly enjoyed. In 1902 he joined the High Cadet Prussian Academy at Gross Lichterfelde, near Berlin, which was the primary training centre for Prussian officers. This paved his way to an army career, and after attending the Royal Military Academy at the Engers Castle near Koblenz, on 6 March 1906 he received his commission as Ensign, or officer cadet, in the 3rd Guards Regiment of Foot, an elite unit and Field Marshal von Hindenburg's own regiment. He was commissioned as a Second Lieutenant on 27 January 1907, and in 1913 von Manstein was sent to attend the War Academy course at Berlin, to be trained as a staff officer. He never completed the course because of the outbreak of the Great War, but after his promotion to First Lieutenant on 19 June 1914 he became the regimental 'aide' (same as the aide de camp) of the 2nd Guards Reserve Regiment with which he served in Belgium before the unit was transferred to the Eastern Front, in East Prussia. In October 1914, von Manstein took part in the German advance towards Warsaw and the subsequent Russian counterattack, during the withdrawal which followed von Manstein was wounded and hospitalised for six months. He returned to the front in 1915, serving at first as a junior staff officer in Poland, then in Serbia. The latter earned him the Iron Cross first class, and a subsequent transfer to the Western Front, where von Manstein fought at Verdun and on the Somme. He was promoted Captain on 24 July 1915, and on 19 August von Manstein became an aide to the staff of the 12th Army until, on 22 January 1916, he was given a junior staff position in the headquarters of the 11th Army. This was followed in July by another appointment as a staff officer, this time with the 1st Army command. The major step forward was his appointment, in 1917, as operation officer to the staff of the 4th Cavalry Division fighting in Courland, which was followed in May 1918 by the appointment as operations officer with the staff of the 213th Assault Reserve Division, also fighting on the Western Front. The appointments as a staff and operations officer for somebody without the necessary training was unusual, but also disclosed the esteem with which von Manstein was held.[2] The interesting point is that von Manstein, unlike other officers who were to command troops during the Second World War, never held a troop command during the entire First World War (which also accounted for the lack of awards and decorations) and mainly served as a staff officer in second rate units.

Undoubtedly it was von Manstein's background and his reliable reputation during the war as a staff officer which prevented him from being discharged after the war. In 1919 von Manstein, still serving, faced without any problems the transition to the Reichswehr, the Weimar's Republic 100,000 strong army. In 1919 von Manstein joined the staff of General von Lossberg, the commander of Germany's Eastern Border

Defence, which was one of the focal points for the reconstruction of the army following the defeat. Von Lossberg came to be a mentor for von Manstein who, having secured some stability, took another step forward.

On leave to Silesia in January 1920, von Manstein met Jutta Sybille von Loesch, the daughter of a wealthy aristocratic couple. A mere three days after meeting her for the first time, von Manstein proposed to her. The two were married on 10 June 1920. In April 1921, the couple had a daughter, Gisela, and in October von Manstein was given his first command: the 6th company of Infantry Regiment 5 at Angermünde, near Berlin. In December, his first son, Gero, was also born. This may have been a difficult period for Germany, but von Manstein's career, as well as his personal life, were on the rise. Between 1923 and 1927 he served as a staff officer in various military districts, or area commands, at Königsberg, Stettin and Dresden. On 1 February 1927 he was promoted to major, and on 1 October, he took the position as staff officer with the Infantry Training School IV at Dresden. Despite his lack of training and experience as a unit commander, von Manstein was noted, and he was selected for higher appointments. On 1 September 1929 he went to the Truppenamt, the equivalent of the army general staff, serving in the T1 section, the covert operations and planning office quietly working as the former general staff had once done. His task was to develop mobilisation plans and studies on the development of new weapons, which apparently, he did to everybody's satisfaction, because, on 1 April 1932, he was promoted Lieutenant Colonel. Manstein clearly enjoyed his work, and his family life also proved to be happy as indicated by the birth of his third son, Rüdiger. More importantly, von Manstein proved he could assert himself despite his different background. When Colonel Wilhelm Keitel, the future chief of the Wehrmacht High Command, proposed a secret mobilisation plan based on the creation of 'shadow divisions' without armament and troops, von Manstein dismissed the plan as nonsensical, and instead suggested organising the existing units in such a way that they could be rapidly expanded creating new units three times the size of the original ones. Manstein's plan was accepted, setting the roots for the swift transition from the Reichswehr to the Wehrmacht. In 1931 and 1932 von Manstein was part of the group of selected officers who were sent to the Soviet Union, as part of the newly developed military cooperation with Germany. He visited the tank-training establishment at Kazan, and other military installations in cities he would visit again but under very different circumstances, especially Moscow, Kiev, and Kharkov. Apparently, he was neither impressed by the Russians nor by the development of the new weapons, the tanks, and in October 1932 he was given command of the II Jäger (light infantry) battalion of the 4th Prussian Infantry Regiment at Kolberg. He thoroughly enjoyed the new assignment, which he later described as one of the happiest periods of his military career, but it must be recalled that he was no longer serving with the army staff at a time when other officers, such as Lutz and Guderian were developing the German Panzer arm with its doctrine and usefulness.

Following his promotion to Colonel on 1 December 1933, von Manstein's career was again in the ascendancy. On 1 February 1934 he was made chief of staff of the military district III Wehrkreis, under General Erwin von Witzleben. This paved the way to his return to the new general staff, which was created following Hitler's rise to power, with the denunciation of the Treaty of Versailles which led to the creation of the Wehrmacht. On 1 July 1935 von Manstein became head of the operations branch at the Army General Staff, promoted Major General on 1 October 1936, just before being appointed *Oberquartiermeister I* (commander of the operations department) of the general staff under the new Chief of Army Staff, General Ludwig Beck. Manstein's first and foremost task was to draft a plan for war against France or Czechoslovakia, this was to produce the *Case Red* plan aimed at defending the Ruhr industrial region while starting the construction of fortifications along the border. However, eventually von Manstein's lack of background, experience as a commander, and little familiarity with the new armoured warfare came to the surface, and he clashed with General Lutz. The issue was a matter of doctrine, or rather over independent new branches of the army. Lutz and Guderian, his chief of staff, were pressing for the creation of an independent Panzer arm provoking Lutz's reaction to Manstein, seeing such newcomers as mere technicians. Manstein's approach to the matter indicated that he was still imbued with his background as an infantry officer. His suggestion was to create an assault artillery to provide fire support to the infantry units, this new speciality was to become part of the artillery. Even though von Manstein's proposal eventually led to the creation of the *Sturmgeschütz* (assault gun) units, his suggestions indicated how far distant his approach was from the new concept of armoured warfare developed by Lutz and Guderian. The fact that the two eventually succeeded in their aim of creating an independent Panzer arm was due to Hitler's support, and it may well have undermined both Beck's and von Manstein's positions, had it not been for a series of favourable events. Following a request, von Manstein drafted a plan (*Winter Exercise*) aimed at militarily occupying the de-militarised German region of Rhineland. The plan was eventually carried through, resulting in a political triumph for Hitler who took notice of the officer who had prepared the event. The next step was all but unavoidable. Hitler having decided on seizing Czechoslovakia, in June 1937 von Manstein was part of the team which developed the *Case Green* plan for the occupation of that country, along with the Special *Plan Otto* intended for a swift seizure and annexation of Austria. In 1938 von Manstein experienced his first fall from grace as he became involved, albeit only indirectly, in the clash between the army and Hitler. The minister of war and the commander in chief of the army, Generals Blomberg and Fritsch, were forced to resign following a series of trumped-up scandals, allowing Hitler to reorganise Germany's military leadership. The ministry of war was disbanded, its place taken by the Wehrmacht High Command (Oberkommando der Wehrmacht, OKW) which was to be led by Wilhelm Keitel. The army staff was not reorganised, but changes took place. General von Brauchitsch took over as new commander in chief of the army, with General Halder as new *Oberquartiermeister I*. This meant that von Manstein lost his position, and on 4 February 1938, he was given the command of the 18th Infantry Division at Leignitz. At the end of September 1938, he had first hand dealings with the crisis which followed Hitler's decision to seize Czechoslovakia, because his division became part of General von Leeb's 12th Army which was to attack the country head-on, breaking through a rather formidable belt of fortifications built along the border. This was the time in which von Manstein's *Case Green* plan was to be utilised against Czechoslovakia, but the September 1938 Munich agreement prevented immediate war. Von Manstein's career development depended at this point more on the political developments in Germany than on his own merits. Promoted Lieutenant General on 1 April 1939, on 18 August he became chief of staff to General von Rundstedt, the Commander in Chief East then, shortly before the outbreak of the war, commander of the Army Group South.[3]

Chapter Two

Staff Officer and War

His appointment as chief of staff to von Rundstedt's Army Group South, pleased von Manstein, who appreciated von Rundstedt, and he had as his operations officer Colonel Günther Blumentritt, one of his few close friends. Together, the two developed the plans against Poland which became effective at 4.45 on 1 September 1939, when Germany attacked Poland. Manstein did not criticise Hitler's decision to attack Poland, and this transpires from his memoirs, with the campaign providing him with a first-hand opportunity to observe the development of the newly armoured warfare on the battlefield. He managed this from the headquarters, some 80 kilometres away from the frontline, keeping in touch with the subordinate armies by telephone. The co-ordination worked well, and the Polish resistance was soon broken. On 23 October, von Rundstedt's command was moved to the west, facing the Belgian border, and was re-designated Army Group A. Its task was now to prepare for the attack in the west, and this is where von Manstein's name made its place in history. The central feature at this time was that Hitler had hoped to keep the war against Poland isolated, without either a French or British intervention. Their declaration of war against Germany took him by surprise, and this reaction moved him to a resolute decision, namely, to attack in the west as soon as possible, even during the winter. The problem was the absence of a plan, which was worked out only on 19 October 1939. It envisaged three main drives which, moving across Belgium and the southern Netherlands, were to converge on Brussels and from there advance to the coast at Dunkirk. The plan was neither original nor brilliant, and already on 29 October it was redrafted, this time envisaging two armoured drives, the northern one aimed at the coast towards Bruges, the second to the south moving across Belgium towards Charleroi. There were continuous postponements due to severe weather and the unsatisfactory plans led to yet another revision, which was prepared by 30 January 1940. This time the new plan moved back to the three armoured drives across Belgium, but without taking the Channel coast into account. The aim was to break through the Belgian defences and advance to the north and to the south of Brussels, again towards Charleroi, while a third drive moved from the south to reach and break through the French defences at Sedan. Manstein criticised the plan which, in his opinion, could achieve no decisive result, and was too weak in its southern prong. This led him to suggest a further revision, which was the absolute achievement of a brilliant military mind. Manstein's plan focused on a single main thrust across the Ardennes, aimed at breaking through the enemy defences along the Meuse, between Sedan and Namur, with the aim of reaching the coast at Abbeville, and thereby encircling any enemy force in Belgium and Flanders. The idea was bold and innovative, and this was typical of von Manstein.[1]

The precise circumstances of the events which followed vary from account to account. According to some, Hitler's military aide General Schmundt noticed von Manstein during a table exercise (a form of wargame) and arranged a meeting. Others claim that von Manstein had the chance of talking to Hitler of his plan during a dinner held on 17 February 1940, for the generals in command along the western front. Further developments are also unclear. General Halder, who opposed Manstein and was not convinced by the plan, eventually adopted it, and turned the suggestion into a proper war plan. Hitler, who undoubtedly had the opportunity to discuss the matter with von Manstein in depth, eventually developed it as well, making it his own. The consequence was the third, and final revision, of the *sickle cut* plan known as *Case Yellow*. It was submitted on 24 February 1940, providing the basic plans which was all put into action from 10 May as the German army attacked across Belgium and Holland. As von Manstein had predicted, the plan was a complete surprise for the enemy which expected a repetition of the 1914 plan by von Schlieffen, which envisaged a turn to the south with a subsequent advance towards Paris. In just ten days the German armoured drive advanced across the Meuse and through Belgium and northern France, reached the Channel coast encircling the bulk of the enemy forces, which were cleverly evacuated by sea at Dunkirk. Many German generals made their name because of this brilliant victory, especially Guderian and Rommel, but not von Manstein. Once again, he experienced the customary switch between staff appointments and field commands which had characterised his early career, and on 15 February 1940, he was given command of the XXXVIII Army Corps at Liegnitz, some 700 kilometres away from the battlefield. Eventually, the corps joined the second echelon of troops and, after moving by train and marching across Belgium, the XXXVIII Army Corps was re-deployed to Amiens by 27 May, taking over a 50-kilometre stretch of the front held by General Kluge's 4th Army. Manstein's task was to hold the two small bridgeheads the German troops had created on the Somme at Abbeville and at Amiens. Manstein, as soon as he reached the front, suggested they should be expanded and prepared a plan, but von Kluge ordered him to remain on the defensive since more troops were on their way. It was not until 5 June, when the second part of the campaign in the West started, the *Case Red* plan, that von Manstein's troops moved in to attack the enemy. With two divisions in the lead, von Manstein's troops succeeded in breaking through the French defences and pushed them back, starting to pursue them after two days of combat which saw the enemy defeated and in retreat. By 9 June, the XXXVIII Army Corps had reached the Seine River, establishing a bridgehead which was soon crossed enabling the corps to advance towards the Loire River, which was reached on the 19 June. Despite the fact that his troops had never engaged the enemy in any major combat, von Manstein's command of the XXXVIII Army Corps was not unnoticed, especially because it advanced in just 17 days for some 480 kilometres while moving almost entirely on foot. The achievement was rewarded, and von Manstein's role in the defeat of France was recognised, and on 1 June 1940 he was promoted to full generalship, and was awarded on 19 July 1940 the Knight's Cross of the Iron Cross.

Unlike many others, von Manstein remained in command of the same unit, this time preparing for the invasion of Britain. His XXXVIII Army Corps was moved to the Boulogne area as part of the planned operation *Sealion*, which in the case of Manstein's corps, foresaw the landing in the Bexhill area. The corps prepared for the landing, some 380 barges were put at disposal for training and experience, but as is now well-known, the conditions for Operation *Sealion* never materialised and the invasion plan was shelved then put aside. Manstein's view of the plan agreed with the high command, which considered the invasion risky, while knowing that it was the only possible solution to defeat Britain. The only result achieved by von Manstein and his men, was once the invasion was postponed indefinitely, they had time to visit Paris, go on leave, or do nothing.

Since the summer of 1940, the plans to attack the Soviet Union were being prepared by the Army Staff, supervised by General Paulus. These plans were further developed from the end of 1940, and despite von Manstein's skills and capabilities, General Halder made sure that he was not involved in their development. Unaware of what was being prepared, in February 1941 von Manstein left the XXXVIII Army Corps to take command of the motorised LVI Army Corps, which was being formed at Bad Salzuflen. On 30 March, von Manstein, and some 250 other German commanders, realised what was being prepared as the entire group was briefed on the plan to attack the Soviet Union. Manstein, in particular, would become part of Field Marshal's von Leeb Army Group North, forming the motorised spear of the offensive towards Leningrad, along with General Reinhardt's motorised XLI Army Corps. Manstein had under his command the 8th Panzer, the 3rd motorised Infantry and the 290th Infantry divisions, which indicated again that he would not be part of the main drive against the proposed enemy. The main effort against the Soviet Union would be in the centre, where both Kleist and Guderian's Panzer Groups had been deployed. The advance towards Leningrad was, albeit important, secondary to the main effort, and the composition of the LVI Army Corps made it clear that it was not capable of fast deep advances, which characterised the early stages of the campaign using the fully mechanised units. Amongst others, von Manstein was informed of the Commissar Order, which required the liquidation of all the captured Soviet political officers. In late May, von Manstein's corps started being re-deployed near Tilsit, and he moved his headquarters close to the border with the Soviet Union less than a week before the attack, which started on 22 June 1941. His task, as outlined by von Leeb, was to break through the Soviet defences and advance swiftly across the Baltic states towards the Dvina River, encircling and destroying any Soviet units in his path. The first aim was the push across the Dvina River in Latvia, reach Estonia and from Luga move towards Leningrad. Von Manstein was not to complete the task he had been given.[2]

The Eastern Front, 1941

Deployed at the centre of the Army Group North area, Manstein's LVI Army Corps succeeded in advancing across southern Lithuania, exploiting a gap created by the other corps' advance, and stretching along a single road, some 320 kilometres were covered in about four days. On 26 June, von Manstein's leading units, helped by a group of German special troops, the Brandenburger, which for the occasion had camouflaged themselves wearing Soviet uniforms, seized the bridge on the Dvina River at Daugavpils intact. This was a remarkable achievement, even though von Manstein's corps was in a precarious situation being some 100 km from the rest of the German forces. This compelled von Manstein to expand the bridgehead and try to slow down his pace of advance while waiting for the XLI Corps to reach the Dvina, even though the Red Army started to react and focused against Manstein's spearhead. Further advance was hampered by the terrain, the area being full of swamps, and by some confusion reigning amongst the German commanders. Manstein argued with his superior von Leeb and with his colleague General Hoepner about the direction the LVI Corps should take, and eventually it was decided that von Manstein was to advance towards Novgorod. This was a critical moment because the Soviet resistance was becoming stronger, and it was only on 10–11 July the corps' spearheads seized Opochka, but soon faced a series of counterattacks. Von Manstein lost no time and continued to advance between Opochka and Novgorod, despite the many difficulties. His troops were confined to a single road, and the neighbouring German units still remained some 80–100 km behind. Having recognised the threat posed by von Manstein's troops, aiming at cutting the Moscow-Leningrad rail line, on 14–18 July the Red Army launched a strong counterattack which isolated the 8th Panzer Division, LVI Corps' spearhead, which had to be rescued by two other divisions. The 8th Panzer Division lost about half of its tanks in the battle and was subordinated to another command, while von Manstein was given the 3rd Motorised Infantry Division *Totenkopf*, a Waffen SS unit for a replacement. The pace of advance slowed down, and after starting his attack on 24 July von Manstein, facing a determined Soviet resistance, had to move back to the starting positions preparing to attack again on 2 August.

Weather delayed the start of Army Group North's offensive towards Leningrad, which started on 8 August. Manstein's LVI Corps' attack started two days later, facing determined Soviet resistance. At this point Hitler's intervention added confusion to the situation, as he ordered switching the main axis of the German offensive towards Leningrad, against General Halder's view, who was focused on the advance towards Moscow. As von Manstein recalled, the clash between Hitler and Halder hindered the necessary collaboration on the battlefield, which resulted in a serious setback which undermined the possibilities of success in the German campaign. Once again, von Manstein was to act in support of the main action and not be part of it, as his LVI Corps advance towards Novgorod caused General Hoepner to turn to Reinhardt's Corps for a direct attack against Leningrad. The determined Soviet resistance met by the LVI Corps, which took six weeks to advance to the Luga River, eventually delayed Reinhardt's advance, while the Red Army launched a massive counterattack at Staraya Russa. This spread panic amongst the German commanders and even Hitler, and von Manstein was asked to intervene to stabilise the situation. With the 3rd Waffen SS Division in the lead, the LVI Corps marched for about 200 km striking at the enemy forces, stabilising the front. Reinforced by the newly arrived LVII Army

Corps, the Army Group North resumed its offensive on 12 September and reached Demyansk four days later, only to be halted by the lack of supplies. At this point, the main axis of the German attack against the Soviet Union was being switched once again, this time against Moscow. This also marked the end of von Manstein's command with the Army Group North and his first rise on the step upwards, as he was given command of an army.

On 17 September 1941, von Manstein took over command of the 11th Army, which was part of von Rundstedt's Army Group South. The appointment followed the accidental death of the former commander, General Schobert, who had died in an airplane crash. As the forces for the attack against Moscow were being regrouped, the Army Group South was given a double task: to advance across the Dnieper River towards Kharkov and to seize the peninsula of Crimea. Rundstedt gave von Manstein the task of crossing the Dnieper and seizing Crimea, which the latter thought could be done at the same time. For the task, von Manstein had at his disposal three German army corps, for a total of nine divisions, plus the attached 3rd Romanian Army. Manstein's task was not easy, and it was made even more difficult by the fact that he was replacing a very popular commander, von Manstein never having such a reputation. The task of seizing Crimea was difficult, the access to the peninsula being defended by a massive moat dug all along the narrow isthmus at Perekop which was known as the Tartar Ditch. Trying to accomplish all the tasks at the same time, von Manstein split his forces and sent the XLIX Mountain and the XXX Corps to advance towards Melitopol and the Dnieper, while the LIV Corps was sent to attack Crimea, Manstein making it clear from the beginning that the forces at his disposal were not enough to seize the entire peninsula. The attack against Perekop started on 24 September, the moat being crossed two days later when the first Soviet defensive belt was broken through. By mid-October the German advance had approached the end of the isthmus bottleneck, the intense fighting was made harder by persistent rains which hampered their movements. In the meantime, the advance towards Kharkov continued, with the bridgehead along the Dnieper having been established, and von Rundstedt ordering Manstein on 25 September, to advance all along the southern coast of the Sea of Azov. By 3 October, the Soviet forces were retreating, and von Manstein's forces started making gains which led to the encirclement of the enemy forces at Melitopol, with the capture of some 106,000 Soviet prisoners of war. As soon as von Manstein had achieved this success, attention was turned again to Crimea following the arrival of the much-needed reinforcements, bringing the total to six German and two Romanian divisions. The attack to invade Crimea's mainland started on 18 October, the German advance being quickly halted on the eastern wing, which prompted von Manstein to switch the main axis of advance to the western wing just as the weather conditions worsened, again making necessary supplies difficult. One of his commanders complained on 25 October that supplies and weather had made his corps ineffective, but von Manstein sharply replied he would not hear of such a thing and that troops could not be finished by such situations. Eventually, on 26 October the Soviet resistance broke, enabling the German forces to pour into the peninsula, at first from the western wing then all along the front. By the end of October, the entire northern part of Crimea had been seized, and the Soviet forces split in two: one army headed for the Strait of Kertsch, the other towards the Sebastopol fortress. By 2 November, von Manstein's forces had reached the Alma River, to the north of Sebastopol, which was approached by the 18th. On the eastern flank, Feodosia was within range and eventually seized on 3 November, the German advance driving towards Kertsch, with the aim of preventing the remnants of the Red Army from escaping to the Kuban. Manstein's 11th Army succeeded in the task, and by 18 November the entire Crimea was in German hands, the victory resulting in the capture of some 100,000 Soviet prisoners of war. Only the fortress of Sebastopol resisted, preventing von Manstein from crossing the Sea of Azov and landing in the Taman peninsula.

Sebastopol, the most important position in Crimea, was defended by a series of lines made of a total of some 3,000 bunkers, connected by anti-tank ditches and trenches, whose approaches were protected by some 140,000 mines and by wide barbed wire obstacles. The first defensive line stood 15 kilometres from Sebastopol's harbour, the second one eight kilometres with the last three defence lines being between one and three kilometres away from the harbour. The Soviet Coastal Army, defending the fortress, had six infantry divisions and one mountain brigade at disposal, while von Manstein deployed his LVI Corps to attack from the north and the north-east and the XXX Corps to attack from the south. The attack, planned to start at the end of November, was delayed again by heavy rains which afflicted supplies and the soldiers' conditions, it was also weakened by strong partisan activity in the rear areas. Without mechanised and armoured support, lacking heavy siege artillery and short of supplies, von Manstein's 11th Army nevertheless attacked the fortress on 17 December 1941, the six German divisions managing to gain some ground at the cost of some 8,500 casualties. All this, and the Soviet landing from Kubat at Kertsch and Feodosia on 26 December, compelled von Manstein to call the attack off. The time for glory had not come yet.[3]

The Victor on the Battlefield

On 5 December 1941, the Red Army counterattacked all along the Eastern Front, making the Wehrmacht face its first setback since the beginning of the war, with Hitler taking command of the army. The removal of Field Marshal von Brauchitsch had been in the air for some time, but the step eventually marked the beginning of a crisis which saw Hitler becoming more and more distrustful of his military commanders, with some exceptions such as von Manstein. His 11th Army had done well facing a difficult situation, with the Red Army in Crimea starting an offensive leading to the re-conquest of the Kertsch peninsula, Feodosia falling on 29 December, which was only halted in early January 1942, with the Soviet forces having broken out into the Crimean mainland. A serious situation was created by the withdrawal of the XXXXII Army Corps at Kertsch, which was carried through in blatant disregard of Hitler's typical 'hold fast' order. Manstein opened an enquiry into the losses suffered by the 46th Infantry Division, which was reduced in strength and effectiveness despite the lack of contact with the enemy. He was only the first one, Field Marshal von Reichenau, the new commander of Army Group South, following suit, reaching the conclusion that the division had lost its honour and therefore no promotion or award would be bestowed on its members until this had been recovered. Hitler asked von Manstein to counterattack at once. Facing a precarious situation, von Manstein decided to remain on the defensive at Sebastopol, which could not be taken without reinforcements and adequate supplies, and by taking troops from there to employ them to counterattack at Kertsch. The German troops started moving towards Feodosia just as the Red Army attempted another landing in the area, which this time was repulsed due to the intervention of the coastal artillery. With the situation under control, von Manstein decided to attack Feodosia on 11 January 1942, the weather suddenly changing and freezing conditions over the entire area. Eventually, on 15 January the German counterattack started with three German and two Romanian divisions, which broke through the Soviet defences. A last counterattack was needed to throw them off the Kertsch peninsula, but the tank battalion initially put at von Manstein's disposal was recalled because it was needed elsewhere, just as the frozen water on the Strait of Kertsch enabled the Red Army to move reinforcements and tanks to Crimea. The attack was halted, waiting for a more suitable time.

Even though Manstein managed to hold the line and prevent a Soviet offensive into the Crimea, he made a serious mistake. He had been sent the 22nd Panzer Division as a reinforcement, but he used it to attack a solid and well-prepared enemy defence line. The result was the loss of 32 tanks, without any achievement. Manstein, whose experience of armoured warfare was limited, learnt a lesson and decided that, in the future, a tank attack against enemy prepared positions could not be carried out unless supported by pioneers, infantry and artillery. The Panzer Division was no longer the instrument of warfare which, until then, had seemed capable of overcoming any difficulty on its path. This lesson would be of use in the future. By March 1942, the situation on the Eastern Front was stabilised, and Hitler could look forward to the next offensive. The aim this time was to drive into the Caucasus, in order to seize the Soviet sources of oil and use them for the German war effort. Amongst others,

Crimea had to be seized in its entirety in order to clear the peninsula from enemy forces and be able to move into the Kuban. This meant that Sebastopol had to be attacked and seized. On 5 April Hitler issued a specific directive, ordering von Manstein to eliminate the enemy forces from the Kertsch area, and then attack and seize Sebastopol. Manstein met Hitler at his headquarters at Rastenburg, with the meeting clarifying the situation. Strong air support was needed in order to accomplish the mission of driving the Soviets out of Crimea, and Hitler agreed putting at von Manstein's disposal the elite VIII Flying Corps, with the reminder that because it was also needed elsewhere, the actual attack was to adhere strictly to a rigid timetable.

Manstein and his staff started worked on the plan at once, naming it *Bustard Hunt*. The forces available to von Manstein were the same as those he faced on the Soviet winter counter-offensive, which were five German infantry divisions, the 22nd Panzer Division, and two Romanian divisions, all facing 19 Soviet divisions supported by four tank brigades. The only advantage was that, by early May, the VIII Flying Corps brought some 400 aircraft into Crimea, thus altering the balance of forces in the area making air supremacy possible. Manstein's plan aimed at taking the enemy by surprise with an attack in a swampy, unsuitable terrain where an infantry division was to break through the enemy defences, paving the way for the subsequent advance of the 22nd Panzer Division, which could then manoeuvre and attack the enemy in its rear areas.

Operation *Bustard Hunt* started on 9 May with an initial German success, due to the air support disrupting the Soviet commands. The ensuing chaos was such that the German advance succeeded in reaching the Marfovka airfield, where 35 fighter bombers were destroyed on the ground ensuring German air superiority in the area. In the afternoon Manstein committed the 22nd Panzer Division whose advance, initially slowed down by rain and the ensuing muddy roads, was supported by the Luftwaffe which destroyed the bulk of the Soviet tanks gathered together to counterattack. On 10 May the 22nd Panzer, followed by three infantry Divisions, reached the northern coast of the Crimean Peninsula and the Sea of Azov effectively closing the trap on the Soviet forces in the central area of Crimea, which surrendered the next day. This paved the way for the advance towards Feodosia and Kertsch, which were only defended by a uniformed NKVD division, a police unit intended for rear area security. Facing the enemy armour, the Soviet troops opted for withdrawal and eventually for the evacuation from Crimea, which called for the intervention of the VIII Flying Corps. The Luftwaffe brought havoc to the troops trying to cross the strait into Kuban by attacking and sinking several boats between 10 and 12 May, while Kertsch was heavily bombed. The city was then seized on the 15th, as the last Soviet troops attempted to cross the strait, with relatively small groups still attempting to reach the Kuban in the following days. Manstein had achieved his first real success inflicting on the enemy the loss of some 147,000 men out of the 250,000 initially deployed, at the cost of 7,588 casualties and minimal losses of tanks and heavy weapons: altogether, 12 tanks, three assault and twelve artillery guns. The time had come for the final assault against the fortress of Sebastopol. For this purpose, the German army assembled a unique array of heavy and super-heavy artillery which started arriving in Crimea in May, including the super-heavy 800 mm gun 'Dora' which, however, only had 48 rounds available in its stocks. Once again, the Luftwaffe would provide the crucial fire support needed to break the enemy defences.

The bombardment of Sebastopol started on 2 June, lasting for the next four days. By then the heavy artillery had fired a total of 42,595 rounds, or about 2,540 tons of ammunition, while the Luftwaffe had dropped 2,264 tons of bombs. The effect left much to be desired, as most of the Soviet defences were not harmed and the losses suffered were relatively light, which certainly contributed to the decision to bring further reinforcements to Sebastopol by sea. This was a successful accomplishment, which vastly improved the morale of the defenders. After the first week of June, the Luftwaffe focused on attacking the enemy shipping in the Black Sea in an attempt to isolate the fortress and preventing it from receiving reinforcements and supplies. The German attack started on 7 June on the northern part of Sebastopol's outer defence line, followed on the same day by a second attack on the southern side, near Balaklava.

The first attack was partly successful, and it managed to break through the enemy positions leading to the seizure of some important hilltops on the Karnyschly ravine. The second attack met strong resistance and was repulsed with heavy losses. Obviously, the Germans focused on the northern part of the fortress, advancing towards the Severnaya Bay, and seizing the Mekerenzivy mountain position between 8 and 9 June. After a failed Soviet attempt to counterattack in the north, in the southern area a massive counterattack between 11 and 13 June led to the seizure of Fort Kuppe and of Kamary. This first success was followed on the 13th by the seizure of Fort Stalin in the north. As the German prongs started to close in, the resistance stiffened, as the flank of the northern prong shifted to the west and approached the sea, seizing the Neuhaus heights. In the south the advance towards Sebastopol was slow and by 21 June had not yet reached the Sapun heights. It was only on 17 June the German assault regained momentum as the northern prong launched a massive attack which brought into German hands the entire northern coastal fortifications, exposing Fort Konstantinovka and the northern part of Sebastopol. The seizure of the northern part of the Severnaya Bay was completed by 22 June, forcing the Soviet troops to retreat into the Martynovski ravine only to be defeated by a German attack. The pincer closed on 28–29 June with a double attack, in the north an amphibious assault took the German troops across the Severnaya Bay to the east of Sebastopol, just as the attack from the south successfully seized the Sapun heights after heavy fighting. The link up between the two arms came on 29 June, with the fall of Inkerman. Now the fall of Sebastopol was only a matter of time. The city, attacked on 1 July, fell in three days with the Soviets only managing to evacuate by sea the commander and his staff. The last resistance in Crimea ended on 4 July as the westernmost tip of the peninsula was seized. The losses had been heavy, 35,000 German and Romanian casualties against the 113,000 Soviet ones, but the seizure of Sebastopol, which came at the same time as the seizure of Tobruk in North Africa, provided the Germans with the success they needed. Manstein, like Rommel, had his reward and on 1 July he was promoted

Field Marshal, as was Rommel, but they were the last promotions marking the peak of the German victories before the fall.[4]

After the seizure of Sebastopol von Manstein enjoyed a period of rest, which was followed by the order to join with the 11th Army headquarters of the Army Group North, to take part in the siege of Leningrad. The logic was obvious, Hitler believing that since von Manstein had succeeded in seizing Sebastopol, he also had a good chance of seizing the Baltic capital. Manstein arrived on the Leningrad front on 27 August 1942, only to discover there were neither the troops nor the equipment and supplies needed to seize the city. A Soviet attack, threatening to open a corridor and relieve the city from its siege, made everybody face reality. The attack was eventually repulsed, heavy losses were suffered on both sides even though the siege was not lifted, and the plans to attack Leningrad were postponed for the time being. The attack never took place, and von Manstein was soon moved to another part of the Eastern Front. On 19 November, a Soviet offensive in the south started, threatening to encircle the German 6th Army at Stalingrad. The situation was critical, and as always, Hitler resorted to whom he considered to be his best commander on the Eastern Front to try and restore order. On 20 November Hitler made von Manstein commander of the newly formed Army Group Don, which included the 6th Army, the 4th Panzer, and the Romanian Fourth Army. It would take about a week before von Manstein actually took over command, part of the staff coming from that of the 11th Army. The appointment created a trio which, with hindsight, had fateful consequences. Hitler, who commanded from far away, was convinced that the tactics he had forced on the army during the Soviet 1941 winter offensive were the key to success, and persisted in a rigid defence denying any withdrawal, which in this case, was the consequence that he and Germany were staking everything on Stalingrad. Manstein, a military professional ruled by rationale, was as much an egotist as Hitler, and undeniably aimed at making his position within the army structure stronger. This he may have achieved if only the success he had at Sebastopol was followed by a victory on the battlefield, this time achieved due to his favourite method of warfare, namely manoeuvre and movement. It is worth noting, just a few months before von Manstein had been considered as a possible replacement for General Halder as Chief of the Army Staff. The step never took place, probably because of von Manstein's lack of friends at the top end of the Army Staff. It is highly likely that this was von Manstein's real ambition, the idea of becoming Hitler's 'Ludendorff' style commander, which he knew he could achieve due to the fact that Hitler had relied on him and had his confidence. The two may have made a good match had it not been for the third party involved, General Paulus who was a professional soldier as well, but better suited to work as a staff officer than as a field commander. The results of this combination would be disastrous, as noted in the above study of Paulus.

On 21 November, as Hitler promised von Manstein generous reinforcements totalling twelve divisions, four of which were Panzer (in fact only two infantry divisions were immediately available, the rest not until early December), Hitler ordered Paulus to hold his positions regardless of the possibility of a temporary encirclement. In fact, there was nothing new in German troops being encircled and resisting the enemy long enough to be relieved, and several small and relatively large pockets (such as Demjansk) had this experience in the winter of 1941–42. The sheer size of the encircled forces should have been enough to permit their survival until a counteroffensive materialised, and on 22 November, Paulus informed Hitler that, while in the need to create a front to the west and the south of the perimeter, if enough supplies could be brought in by air a hedgehog defence could be formed. In Hitler's view, as he explained to von Manstein in a message sent on 26 November, Stalingrad could not be surrendered since it represented the most remarkable achievement of that year, and also because re-taking it in 1943 would require an even greater number of forces. However, a defence perimeter could not be formed, thus endangering the entire army at Stalingrad, a breakout attempt would have been needed, and Paulus asked to be granted the necessary powers to make such a decision. There was no reply from Hitler, and while the many commanders inside the pocket started to state their own views, von Manstein sent his own appreciation of the situation. Even though he believed that a breakout represented the safest course of action, he did not support it stating that a relief operation could be started early in December, should the promised reinforcements be made available. There was some logic in this reasoning, the relief attempt being necessary in order to link up with the forces encircled at Stalingrad in order to ensure their safe evacuation, but it is now clear that von Manstein underestimated the situation, especially the Soviet capabilities. This explained why, when Paulus sent him a letter asking to be given full freedom of initiative, von Manstein failed to reply. Soon, he started preparing his own plan to relieve Stalingrad and restore the situation. The plan, known as Operation *Wintergewitter* (Operation *Winter Storm*) was based on an attack to be launched with two newly arrived Panzer Divisions to strike, along with another army corps, towards the Stalingrad pocket linking up with the 6th Army which was to attack from the inside breaking out of the pocket. It is not clear whether the operation actually aimed at re-establishing a link with the 6th Army in order to enable supplies, or if Manstein considered from the beginning that it should be evacuated with the subsequent abandonment of Stalingrad. Either way, time was of the essence and Manstein wanted the operation to start by 8 December. The Soviet attacks around Stalingrad and the belated arrival of the Panzer Division, first delayed then reduced the actual size of *Wintergewitter*, which now relied almost exclusively on the two Panzer Divisions. The attack, started on 12 December, initially made timely progress, but soon faced the Soviet reaction which slowed the advance. Some advance was made but, since Hitler limited the number of divisions to be made available to support the operation, because of his concerns for other sectors of the front, the attack could not be sustained. On 21 December, the staff of the 6th Army raised for the first time the possibility of a breakout from the pocket followed by an evacuation, since the situation was worsening by the day. This could have been the last possibility to save at least part of the forces encircled at Stalingrad, but the three commanders involved were unable to decide. Paulus considered the evacuation an act of desperation which had to be avoided unless absolutely necessary; von Manstein, who informed Hitler about these decisions, had become aware that the relief operation had failed, but he did not take a position on the matter. Hitler, in his headquarters, appeared to everyone as someone who could not make up his mind. It was, however, too late. The Red Army, concerned about the German moves, had started an offensive to the north of Stalingrad on 16 December, which gained momentum in about a week, threatening Manstein's left wing. The time had come to call the relief attack off and abandon the 6th Army to its fate.

The new Soviet offensive smashed the German front, at first by breaking through the weak Italian forces deployed along the Don River. Left without mobile reserves, von Manstein had no other option than withdraw along with the rest of the German army deployed in southern Russia. By the beginning of January 1943, it became clear that the Soviet offensive had large scale aims, as it pointed towards Rostov. The seizure of this city, close to the Sea of Azov, would have encircled all the German forces to the east. The Soviet breakthrough along the portion of front held by Romanian troops completed the crisis, and the German withdrawal started, albeit slowly. By mid-January, the bulk of the German forces had been pushed back towards Rostov, apart from two armies which were now fighting on the Taman peninsula. At the end of the month a line was created along the Donetz River, soon to be broken through by the advancing Soviet forces which, in the meantime, were also advancing north towards Kharkov. Only on 24 January, Hitler authorised moving the forces away from the southern part of the front to try and restore the situation, which worsened on 1 February following the start of yet another Soviet offensive. It did not take long to realise that the Soviet aims were much grander than anticipated. The new offensive towards Kharkov clearly echoed the German Blitzkrieg style of warfare, as it aimed at swinging to the south and surrounding all the German forces once the coast of the Sea of Azov had been reached. The moment was critical, and von Manstein turned it into an opportunity to achieve his greatest success. On 23 January, the Red Army crossed the Donetz River threatening Manstein's left flank, revealing that their main effort was against his Army Group Don which they threatened to encircle. Meanwhile, Manstein showered Hitler and his headquarters with messages and reports portraying the reality of the situation. Eventually, on 27 January, Hitler had the entire First Panzer

Army moved and put under Manstein's command, while the newly formed SS Panzer Corps was being deployed on the left wing of Army Group Don's front. Nevertheless, at the beginning of February the situation faced by Manstein was still critical after the Soviet troops managed to break through the thin German front and create a 60-odd kilometres gap, which they utilised for their enveloping movement. Hitler's idea to use the SS Panzer Corps to counterattack on the northern flank of the Soviet advance, at Kharkov, was dismissed by Manstein who believed the corps not to be strong enough to deliver a decisive blow. Instead, Manstein asked that all the remaining mechanised and motorised forces still left in the Kuban be put under his command, and to withdraw to the west of Rostov, effectively leaving only the 17th Army in the Kuban bridgehead and abandoning the remaining positions in the Caucasus for good.

In facing this crisis, Hitler seemed incapable of making decisions and eventually relied on von Manstein. On 6 February 1943 he was ordered to attend the Führer's headquarters at Rastenburg at once, which he managed due to a special aircraft put at his disposal. Once there, Manstein suggested that Hitler relinquished command of the army and appoint a qualified professional, which could have been himself of course, but Hitler replied with an evasive explanation. Another speech of the same kind followed once the situation at the front started to be examined. The result of the four hours meeting was that Hitler authorised Manstein to pull back to the Mius River, which might not have been much, but in a way meant granting to the field commander the full authority to deal with the situation. The German withdrawal started in an orderly fashion two days later, enabling von Manstein to regroup his forces, to the north of his Army Group Don's right wing, just as the SS Panzer Corps was compelled to abandon any project for a counterattack. The Soviet pressure and an unexpected uprising in Kharkov compelled the corps to abandon the city on 14 February. It was yet another hard blow to Hitler's prestige after Stalingrad, but von Manstein soon made it good. At the end of February his Army Group, which had been renamed South, was still facing a critical situation with the Red Army, who had achieved a huge breakthrough in the Kharkov area which aimed at Poltava and to the south, with the spearheading Soviet troops aiming at Dnjepropetrovks. As Hitler arrived on 17 February at Manstein's headquarters at Zaporozhye, the situation was described as 'hair raising'. The fact that Soviet tanks were reported as less than 50 kilometres from the top headquarters, and noted by Hitler himself, proved this to be correct. Hitler, while still seeking a counteroffensive, effectively put Manstein in charge as he ordered that all the troops that could be evacuated from the Kuban peninsula bridgehead, should be put under von Manstein's command. On the next day, some 100,000 men were airlifted from the area and put at Army Group South's disposal. At last, with his force reorganised and taking advantage of the fact that the Red Army had outstretched its resources, von Manstein unleashed the German counterattack. It started on 20 February with the SS Panzer Corps striking in the south, towards Pavlovgrad and the Soviet thrust aiming at Dnjepropetrovsk. Joined by the XLVIII Panzer Corps from the south on the next day, the attack penetrated deeply into the Soviet rear areas just as, on 23–24 February, the XL Panzer Corps also attacked in the east. In a matter of days, the Soviet advance started to crumble. Between 25 and 26 February the SS and the XLVIII Panzer Corps cut off the spearhead of the Soviet offensive aimed at Dnjepropetrovsk encircling many enemy forces. This step was followed by the swift redeployment of von Manstein's forces to the northern end of his deployment, the SS Panzer Korps halting a Soviet attempt to advance to the south of Kharkov. The last blow came in that area, and after regrouping, on 6 March the SS and the XLVIII Panzer Corps started to advance north, at first avoiding Kharkov and aiming to the north instead, at Belgorod. Supported by a northern prong, the German attack compelled the Soviet forces to withdraw, and the third battle of Kharkov was fought between 10 and 14 March with the Germans seizing the city again, the counteroffensive had effectively eliminated the Soviet threat. By 23 March the Army Group South had been able to repel all the Soviet advances, destroying many of the enemy forces and restoring a line running all along the Donetz River up to Belgorod.[5] The disaster had been avoided and turned into a victory, due to von Manstein.

Chapter Three

Turning Point

The successful recovery of the situation on the southern part of the Eastern Front in the winter of 1943, was von Manstein's crowning triumph. Not only had he succeeded in restoring the situation, but he did so despite Hitler's interference, thereby effectively making himself the true military leader on the Eastern Front. However, it did not appear that Hitler considered him for the Chief of Army Staff position, which von Manstein had effectively requested. Instead, it would seem that Hitler still preferred to divide, rule, and conquer with his own military staff, as he resurrected the formerly retired General Heinz Guderian by giving him the important position of General Inspector of the Panzer Troops.

As the troops on both sides rested and recovered, the Germans started to plan their next move and a new clash at the top started to take shape. Hitler, who did not want to surrender the initiative, looked at the Soviet bulge at Kursk and asked for an offensive which could crush it, destroying a good deal of the Soviet forces in doing so. It did not take long before a heated debate was started between Hitler, von Manstein and Guderian. Hitler's 15 April directives for Operation *Zitadelle* (Citadel), the planned offensive against the Kursk salient, revealed the still precarious situation on the Eastern Front, and of Hitler's awareness of staking everything on one card. The local commanders, which included primarily von Manstein, were advised to prepare for the offensive, and to bring it to a swift conclusion while paying attention to the other sectors of the front, where Hitler feared the Red Army could release its own counteroffensive. Manstein did not raise objections, even though he was not keen on *Zitadelle*, but problems came from the northern prong of the offensive which was not ready to attack within the scheduled date, forcing the first postponement.

Reconnaissance soon spotted Soviet troop movements, which clearly revealed that surprise could not be achieved at Kursk. In order to have a firsthand evaluation of the situation, on 3 May Hitler summoned to Munich the commanders of Army Group North and South, von Kluge and von Manstein, along with General Model, the commander of the 9th Army whose reports had raised some issues. Amongst those attending was General Guderian, whose role as General Inspector of the Panzer Troops had given him a prominent role in the whole affair. The discussion focused at first on Model's report, which described the Soviet fortifications all along the front, and the difficulties likely to be encountered in the attempt to break through them. The German tanks available had been outmatched by the Soviet anti-tank weapons, and this required more time to bring new ones to the front, which was Guderian's task. As the new delay started to appear, von Manstein and von Kluge started to make their objections clear, because they believed that any further delay would only give advantage to the enemy, and not the German forces. On his turn to speak, Manstein said that Operation *Zitadelle* had chances of success, but only if executed in May and not postponed too long. Waiting to be able to deploy a large number of the new tanks, which included the 'Panther' and the 'Ferdinand' self-propelled gun, was in fact more a danger than an advantage, because von Manstein realised that the imminent collapse of the Axis forces in North Africa would open the way for an Allied invasion somewhere in the European side of the Mediterranean. This would have required an immediate reaction, along with the need to take forces from the Eastern Front to repel the enemy invasion. Several others of those attending the conference objected to Operation *Zitadelle* being conducted at all, as it presented more dangers than opportunities. In a private conversation with Model, Hitler made it clear that *Zitadelle* would be carried out and there would be no postponement.

In recent years, a good deal of attention has been paid to Operation *Zitadelle* and the battle of Kursk, which naturally involved von Manstein. Several issues have been raised, questioning whether the battle should be considered a 'turning point' in the Second World War, and the real number of losses suffered by the German forces, which due to the available documents, are much less than usually reported in the books dealing with the history of the battle.* For this study the most relevant issues relating to von Manstein and his role in the battle are two, first the change in the German way of war, and secondly, the question whether *Zitadelle* should have been avoided. In 1943 the developments on the Eastern Front had created a new situation, which altered once and for all the way the Germans were waging war. The idea of Kursk as a 'turning point' is in fact more related to by observers than the actual battle, which (albeit a must for the military history buffer) only had limited importance. Between 1939 and 1942 Germany had fought relying on the Blitzkrieg concept, which was defeating superior enemy forces relying on speed, manoeuvre, and surprise, along with a combination of innovation and concentrated firepower (the Panzer Division supported by the Luftwaffe breaking through across the Ardennes). The battle of Kursk, which was fought at an unprecedented level of preparation and relying to a considerable extent on the new tanks, marked the end of this kind of warfare. After this battle the Germans were fighting mainly on the defensive, and relying, as much as possible, on firepower and technical superiority. The Blitzkrieg style of warfare had already seen its end in 1942, during the German offensive towards the Caucasus and Stalingrad. On this occasion, unlike the 1941 Operation *Barbarossa*, the Soviet withdrawals prevented the Germans from encircling the enemy forces taking large numbers of prisoners, thereby making the German advances a 'drive into nothing'. Only von Manstein's March 1943 counteroffensive, which led to the stabilisation of the Eastern Front, had resembled the old style 'Blitzkrieg' concept of waging war, as it had relied on speed, manoeuvre, and surprise. His most remarkable achievements provided a striking contrast with the July 1943 failure at Kursk, and it offers one of the reasons why the battle

---

* This issue arises because the figures for tank losses usually reported in the various accounts of the battle were not drawn from the German sources, easily available in both the German and the American archives, but in the post-war account made by a Russian general who over-inflated them for clear propaganda purpose. The influence of Soviet history writing, and possibly of the Soviet Union in general, concerning the accounts written in the Western countries after the war is an issue which should be analysed in depth, and considered whenever approaching the war on the Eastern Front.

is considered a turning point. The issue being, as some historians have debated, whether it would have been better for the Germans to avoid *Zitadelle* by seeking an alternative.

Setting aside speculations on this specific matter, it could be argued whether von Manstein actually opposed *Zitadelle*, and whether he might have prevented the catastrophe. His opposition to the plan is well known, and his view was shared by a good many other generals at the top. The answer has to remain speculative, whether at the time, von Manstein's opposition to the *Zitadelle* plan was such that he may or may not have considered abandoning the operation. The most critical issue was that it seems that von Manstein, despite his opposition to the plan, was offered no real choice. An alternative came from the Wehrmacht High Command which, on 18 June, suggested abandoning the attack plan by using the available forces to create a group of reserves, which could be used to face whatever crisis emerged, either in the east or the west. On that same day Hitler made it clear that he was determined to carry out Operation *Zitadelle*. The reasons, outlined in a subsequent order of the day, were clear: to obtain a success on the battlefield that could booster the morale of the German people, and also important, recover the image of Germany with her allies who had started to doubt they were on the winning side.

The battle of Kursk started on 5 July and, as the American historian Earl F. Ziemke noted, it was not foredoomed to failure from its onset, however, von Manstein certainly had a role to play in its eventual failure. As the historian Robert Forczyk pointed out, von Manstein had to take a risk and concentrate almost ninety per cent of his available tanks on a very narrow sector of the front, about 50 kilometres wide, leaving the rest with only minimal resources available to deal with possible Soviet counter-offensives. Manstein had taken a similar risk in 1942, in this case relying on the fact that the advancing Soviet forces were spread thinly on the battlefield. This no longer applied to the 1943 Eastern Front, and the Red Army in general, but von Manstein had not realised that the enemy he was facing had greatly evolved in the last months of war, and they had become a much more capable combat force than previously.

After just two days of fighting, it became clear that Kursk would not be a battle of speed and manoeuvre, but a conflict of attrition which suited the Soviet capabilities much better. Manstein fuelled the battle by sending in reinforcements, but to no avail. On 12 July, the battle of Prokhorovka was fought, to become famous in history as the greatest tank battle of the war, and even though the Germans won it they eventually realised that the attack could no longer be carried out. The day after this, Hitler summoned von Manstein and von Kluge to his headquarters in Rastenburg, announcing his decision to suspend *Zitadelle*. Manstein insisted on continuing the offensive, as he claimed that victory on the southern front was within reach. However, he ignored that in the north, Model's army had failed to come close to breaking through the enemy defences, thus nullifying any chances of an encirclement in the salient. Furthermore, as the Wehrmacht High Command and even Manstein himself had predicted, the Allies had landed in Sicily, and it was clear that Italy would soon become another critical front. As the battle of Kursk came to its end, it is only speculation as to what von Manstein's real attitude was towards *Zitadelle*.[1] After an openly critical attitude towards the plan, he failed to carry his ideas through and rather opted to follow Hitler's orders and directives. Also, von Manstein's incorrect appreciation of the situation during the 13 July meeting with Hitler, is suggestive that he was driven more by personal ambition than by the ideals of command. It is possible to argue that von Manstein fell victim to his own success on the battlefield, and trying to pursue another major victory, made a series of fatally incorrect decisions with regard to the entire *Zitadelle* plan.

Manstein's hope that the elimination of the Kursk salient might provide his armies with some breathing space soon proved illusory. Already, by 17 July, the Soviets attacked across the Donetz and the Mius River, established bridgeheads that the Germans were unable to eliminate. Immediately the German forces north of Kursk faced several Soviet penetrations along their front, the only reassuring point being the creation of a defence line (*Position Hagen*) to the west. It is worth noting that Hitler, as the situation in the central sector of the Eastern Front became critical, decided to rely more on General Model than on

Manstein. This proved to be a wise decision for once, since on this occasion von Manstein greatly underestimated his opponent and made several miscalculations. The Soviet attacks transpired to be a diversion for the main offensive, which was in the Belgorod-Kharkov area, which caught von Manstein off-side as he had concentrated all the available armour in the south. The Soviet main offensive started on 3 August, taking von Manstein by surprise and creating a huge gap in the German defences, which were smashed one after another. Facing a new Soviet offensive in the Kharkov area, von Manstein, acting against Hitler's orders, ordered the evacuation of the city, and even though he managed to concentrate his troops in such a way to slow the Soviet pace of advance, the Germans had no other option but start withdrawing all along the front. Meeting von Manstein on 27 August, Hitler faced a new crisis on the Eastern Front (at the time he had a crisis in Italy), which led to a confrontation between the two. Hitler insisted on a rigid defence prohibiting any further withdrawal, while von Manstein pressed for a flexible defence which, relying on local withdrawals, Manstein assumed would enable him to find the same success he had achieved in the winter. Namely, to concentrate the available forces to deliver a 'backhand blow' against the enemy drives and cut them off, thereby eliminating the threat of further advances. By mid-September the German front had been pushed back to the Dessna River in the central area of the front, and halfway between the July line and the river Dnepr, the crisis leading to yet another confrontation between von Manstein and Hitler. During another meeting held on 8 September von Manstein asked for the authorisation to withdraw to the Dnepr line, but he faced Hitler's expected refusal. Even the request to evacuate the Kuban bridgehead in order to spare the forces trapped there failed to meet von Manstein's satisfaction. Eventually, Hitler agreed to evacuate the bridgehead but did not allow the forces to be put at von Manstein's disposal, they would rather be employed to defend Crimea. It was only on 15 September that Hitler eventually allowed von Manstein to withdraw to the Dnepr line, which he did with three rather than four armies. The fourth one, the rebuilt (in name only) 6th Army was transferred from Manstein's to Kleist's command. A sign that Hitler was losing faith in von

Manstein's capabilities, not that much longer after Manstein's elevation. By early October, the Dnepr line granted to the Army Group South a temporary stabilisation of the situation.

On 3 September, Manstein and Kluge arrived at Hitler's headquarters, this time determined to ask for radical changes. The entire German strategy had to be revised and re-considered, and changes at the top were needed as well. They both considered a unified, militarily competent command necessary, which in von Manstein's view, needed radical measures. This meant stripping all other fronts of their forces in order to throw everything into the Eastern Front to re-stabilise the situation. The real aim of this bizarre strategy was to eliminate the existing dualism in command, which saw the Wehrmacht High Command dealing with the Western Front, and the Army Staff with the Eastern Front. Whether von Manstein saw himself as the ideal leader of the unified command is not possible to say. The real issue at stake was Hitler's personal position of power within the armed forces, which the creation of a unified command may well have undermined. Even though it is arguable that von Manstein's (and von Kluge's) step had meaning and some undoubted merit, it was clear that it was presented in a rather clumsy way which gave its approval little chance of success. Manstein's undoubted naivety was aggravated by the fact that, on this occasion, Hitler made him no concessions at all on matters regarding the situation at the front. The eventual decision to authorise the withdrawal on the Dnepr line shows that Hitler, if dealt with in a more appropriate way, could be persuaded to make certain decisions. The whole episode suggested that von Manstein was facing a critical time in his career, as he realised there would be no more victories to win and started to face defeat. His reaction was not different from those of many other German commanders on every front, which was to demand more reinforcements, knowing they would not be made available. This was not the kind of situation that von Manstein was going to face well, assuming any sound general would feel the same.

Dismissal

In ideal conditions the Dnepr River line could have represented a formidable obstacle, if not impossible it would be extremely difficult for the Red Army to break through. However, in September 1943, the conditions for the German defenders were anything but ideal, and in a way von Manstein's contribution made matters worse. As the Army Group South withdrew to the new defence line, the German soldiers believed they would be deploying along a well-prepared defence line or some kind of 'East Wall'. As they crossed the Dnepr, they discovered that nothing of this kind existed, and morale collapsed as a consequence. It soon became clear that the new defence line was not ideal, the German troops were thinly spread along some 200 kilometres front manned by an average of 60 men per kilometre, with the natural bending eastwards of the river in its southern end providing a natural position to attack. To make things worse, the Red Army gave no respite, and matching the same pattern as the Germans in the earlier years of the war, exploited the momentum attacking as soon as the Dnepr was reached. On 1 October, the bridgehead the German troops had maintained at Zaporozhye, east of the river, was attacked and penetrated, the Soviet wedge was quickly eliminated by a counterattack. This bought a week of respite, but the local commander asked von Manstein for permission to abandon the bridgehead. Hitler refused, and on 10 October the Soviets attacked the bridgehead and were repulsed for a second time. Only at this point von Manstein intervened, making it clear that holding the bridgehead cost too many troops, and on 14 October, asked for permission to evacuate. Hitler reacted by summoning Field Marshal von Kleist, whose Army Group A had its northern flank in the Zaporozhye region, asking him to investigate the situation and see if his forces could take over the positions in the bridgehead. Kleist was asked not to inform von Manstein, who Hitler believed was just trying to avoid facing a task with which he could not cope. Before any step could be taken, on 9 October, the Red Army attacked the Army Group A positions just to the north of the Sea of Azov, quickly achieving a breakthrough. As Hitler's attention focused on the matter of the evacuation of the Crimea, he had a suggestion from Manstein which might resolve the situation. This proposal was the use of freshly arriving units to attack the Red Army breakthrough, and just as Manstein managed in the winter of 1943, to cut them off, thereby destroying them. The proposal appealed to Hitler, but a crisis ensued before it could be enforced. On 15 October, the Red Army started a massive offensive at the very centre of the Army Group South line on the Dnepr, exploiting a small bridgehead which was soon expanded.

In facing this situation, von Manstein realised that the tide had turned in the East, and after abandoning his counterattack plans, suggested a major withdrawal with the Army Group A back to the Bug River. He knew that Hitler would hardly agree to such a plan. To make things worse, von Manstein was fooled by a Soviet feint and reacted slowly, thus enabling the advancing enemy to turn the initial success into a major breakthrough. By the end of October, the flanks of Army Group South and Army Group A had been penetrated, the Soviets advancing to Krivoi Rog in the north and all along the Crimean coast in the south. It was clear that a pincer movement was being developed, but the easternmost German positions were still holding at Zoporozhye. Reinforcements were sent and a counterattack launched, but even though it was successful it failed to repeat the success von Manstein had enjoyed in the past. Ordered by Hitler to recapture Kiev, von Manstein had to face the fact that the German forces were no longer strong enough to repeat the same successes, and after a series of setbacks, on 23 December he called off the counteroffensive.

Developments on all fronts and the dire situation of the German armed forces needed a new approach or mentality, which required commanders to be able, first and foremost, to withstand a crisis and react on the spot by relying on their forces in hand. This policy or attitude did not suit many of the commanders who had been in charge during the victorious Blitzkrieg years, and a new generation started to appear. On 25 December, despite the appalling weather and von Manstein's forecast, the Red Army attacked the Army Group South front again, threatening a new enveloping manoeuvre. Manstein's suggested withdrawals may have been sound from a strategic point of view, but politically speaking they could have disastrous consequences. Withdrawing further meant abandoning the Crimea, which Hitler feared could be seized and used as an instrument of pressure to induce Turkey against Germany. The two points of view clashed, and Hitler arrived at the point of claiming that von Manstein was not interested in such matters, because he would not want to take the blame. Manstein asked for reinforcements, but rather than the six he asked for, he was only given two divisions. He made it clear to Hitler that half measures could not help, and Hitler responded sharply. Manstein reacted by pointing out that without the necessary troops, a counterattack in the same style he had carried out before would be impossible. Hitler exploded saying that von Manstein was just trying to make himself look good by making pompous suggestions for counteroperations, while in reality he was just running away, probably because he was losing his nerve since his headquarters were coming too close to the front. Regardless of any truth in Hitler's remarks, which was von Manstein's clear reluctance to deal with the new situation and that counter-manoeuvres of the past were no longer possible, it was clear that he was no longer one of Hitler's favourite commanders. Eventually, the unavoidable withdrawal occurred, and the southernmost portion of the Dnepr River bend was abandoned. On 4 January 1944, Hitler summoned von Manstein to his headquarters for a first-hand report, during which von Manstein made it clear that no other option could be considered, and as he had done in the past, returned to the idea that a commander in chief for the entire Eastern Front should be appointed. Now Hitler had to face one of his favourite commanders who had ignored his orders, and it was clear that von Manstein was now threatening his own position of power within the army. At the end Hitler cut the meeting off abruptly, showing he no longer trusted von Manstein as in the past.

It is curious that, in January 1944, von Manstein succeeded in achieving his last remarkable success at the front despite the strained conditions. On 24 January he started Operation *Vatutin*, a counterattack aimed at destroying the Soviet spearhead approaching his headquarters. On the next day, a Soviet attack started encircling the bulk of two German army corps at Korsun. As he did at Stalingrad, von Manstein abandoned his attack and started a relief attempt by switching his forces, the attack starting on 1 February. Again, as at Stalingrad, the Soviet countermove stopped the German relief attempt forcing the encircled forces to break out from the pocket and linking up with the relieving forces. Manstein's attempt started on the night of 16–17 February, the breakthrough succeeded in linking up with the relieving force thus enabling the evacuation of the pocket. About two-thirds of the German encircled forces managed to escape the trap, even though there was a high cost of leaving behind all the heavy weapons and equipment. It raises the interesting question of what might have happened at Stalingrad if Paulus been persuaded or been forced to break out from the pocket: Korsun may provide the answer.

More critically, the losses suffered during the battle for the Korsun pocket had exhausted all the mobile reserves available to von Manstein, which were now irreplaceable. From that moment any counterattacks or counter-manoeuvres would be impossible to carry out. Manstein had to realise this soon, as on 4 March, the Red Army started another offensive, which by the 28th, led to the encirclement of the entire 1st Panzer Army at Kamenets-Podolsky. On that same day General Model was summoned to Hitler's headquarters and informed that he was going to replace von Manstein in command of the Army Group South. Manstein's dismissal was announced two days later, as he was summoned to Hitler's headquarters and informed of this while being awarded the swords to his Knight's Cross. About two weeks later, following von Manstein's original plan, the German forces trapped in the new pocket managed to break out.[2]

Manstein was never considered for another command, and he spent the last years of the war in a form of retirement, albeit without cutting himself entirely off from the army and the latest developments in Germany. Manstein never gave up hope of being recalled by Hitler for some other command, but this never happened, and he spent the years to the end of the war with his family in Dresden. The most important event relating the army to von Manstein was his involvement, indirectly and mainly based on his knowledge of what was going on, with the attempt to assassinate Hitler. In 1943 three leading members of the resistance group planning to assassinate Hitler, Tresckow, Stauffenberg and Gersdorff, approached von Manstein on three different occasions in order to draft him into the resistance and the plot. Manstein refused, and his argument for doing that was simply that Prussian Field Marshals do not mutiny. However, he took care not to burn the bridges with the group and left a door open. Needless to say, he never thought of denouncing his comrades or to reveal their plan even though, after the war, a relative of von Tresckow accused him of having denounced the general as a conspirator. Most importantly for von Manstein, despite his connections with the conspirators (which included two senior members of the Army Group South staff) and of his knowledge of the assassination plan he never came under suspicion, and even though Himmler and Göring never trusted him, he was never involved in the post 20 July arrests and 'clean ups'. Manstein's attitude towards the resistance and the planned coup is unclear, and he failed to mention the 20 July events in his book of memoirs, making only a few passing comments regarding some of those involved. Facing the ever-growing accusations, after the war, of having betrayed von Tresckow and the conspirators, von Manstein made his point clear. Hitler's regime was a totalitarian dictatorship and as such it could only be brought down by a putsch, still this kind of behaviour did not belong to the German military traditions and, in Manstein's view, the only way the military could have opposed Hitler was that the entire Wehrmacht decided to stand against him with the support of the German people. As Manstein pointed out, these conditions never existed, not even in the very last stage of the war. He also took care to add that no German military leader enjoyed such a standing with the German people to be able to overthrow Hitler and take his place, which made any attempt at a putsch void of any chance of success. Manstein named no names, but his reference to Rommel is quite clear, even though the latter did not initiate nor carried on with a putsch attempt. As von Manstein admitted, during the war the German soldiers had to face two options. One to serve the Nazis who were known for their terror and perversion of justice, but also a regime which had rescued Germany in her most difficult moment or face the possibility of a civil war which would have torn Germany apart, and possibly may have led the way to a victory for Bolshevism. All these issues, incidentally, would also have meant the disintegration of the Wehrmacht. Quite clearly, von Manstein never considered the possibility of a radical change in the German structure of power, and when confronted with the possibility of a putsch, he simply stood and waited for the events to happen with the aim of intervening at the right moment to save the situation. It could be added that such a view was quite delusional, and von Manstein never fully grasped the extent of the plot and its possible consequences.[3]

On 29 January 1945, von Manstein called at the Reich's chancellery, where Hitler had transferred himself after the forced abandonment of his headquarters at Rastenburg. Manstein intended to have his former aide Stahlberg with him, but Hitler refused to meet the Field Marshal. It is not known what Manstein wanted to say to Hitler, but one can imagine that Hitler was not in the mood to talk to him at this stage of the war. As the Red Army approached, von Manstein left Berlin and sought refuge at Weissenhaus, near Hamburg, where he asked Stahlberg to contact Field Marshal Montgomery. It is not difficult to imagine his disappointment when he was simply informed to stay at home and wait for developments.

Post-war

On 5 May 1945, von Manstein was taken prisoner while at the Hotel Atlantic, and on 26 August was taken to Britain to join the other generals in a special prisoner of war camp before being sent to Nuremberg. Since an agreement existed between the Allies and the Soviets on the exchange of prisoners of war, those who had fought on the Eastern Front were to be surrendered to the Soviet Union, it is easily concluded that von Manstein was clearly too precious for the Allies to be handed over. He escaped this fate, but not his post-war trial. At first, von Manstein simply provided the defence team of the Nuremberg and of the German Generals Trials with his expertise, which must have convinced him he would not have to face the same fate. His naive attitude, the same kind of behaviour adopted by practically all the defendants, worked against him. Manstein claimed that the armed forces were not involved in war crimes, which were the sole responsibility of the SS which acted independently, and for that reason carried out the war crimes without the Wehrmacht being either involved or having knowledge of the events. Unfortunately for him, as he was cross-examined by the American prosecutor Telford Taylor, he was obliged to face his own 20 November 1941 order. This stated that 'The Jewish-Bolshevist system has to be exterminated for all times.' Taylor's examination exposed von Manstein as a liar, and this made his testimony a complete failure which did not save his former colleagues from being found guilty. Worse still, the fact exposed von Manstein's involvement in war crimes, with the result that he found himself facing trial as well. The evolving political situation soon made the trial more political than judiciary. Its openings were delayed by the British Commander in occupied Germany, Sir Sholto Douglas who informed the Foreign Office that the Americans were likely to use evidence of a dubious nature. Consequently, the request to have an American tribunal to put von Manstein on trial was refused, and he ended up by facing a British tribunal despite the Soviet request, made in 1948, to turn him over along with von Rundstedt to face trial in the Soviet Union. This was not considered an option, and on 5 July 1948 the decision was made to put von Manstein on trial by a British tribunal. This produced protests in both Germany and Britain, as von Manstein's reputation appeared to make him the least suitable German general to face trial. The argument was raised that his dismissal by Hitler made him, along with other factors, not one of the generals involved with the regime to the last, unlike others such as Kesselring. However, as it transpired with the latter, strong support came from Britain with Churchill, Montgomery, and Liddell Hart making contributions to a defence fund which, along with the funds raised in Germany, collected some 50,000 Marks, at the time a large sum of money. The trial, which started in Hamburg, at the Curio House, on 23 August 1949, was considered at first a mere formality, expected to end with an acquittal. Manstein was also personally convinced of this, especially as the British had refused to hand him over to the Soviets. This attitude may well have tempted him to lower his guard, which with his naivety, contributed to his disaster. After a favourable beginning, on 8 September, the prosecution produced a series of undeniable documents, illustrating von Manstein's actual involvement with war crimes. These included his 20 November 1941 order of the day, mentioned above, which asked his soldiers to have an understanding for the harsh punishment reserved for Jews, along with evidence that von Manstein had ordered the shooting of the 15,000 Jews of Simferopol before Christmas 1941, when in command of the 11th Army. To make things worse, the former commander of the SS *Einsatzgruppe* D, the 'action group' active in the northern part of the Eastern Front, testified of having coordinated 'special actions' with the staff of von Manstein's 11th Army. Manstein's defence was particularly poor, as he could not understand the evidence being submitted, nor did he consider his actions to be war crimes at all. This was particularly true when his involvement in the Commissar Order was proved, the order which asked that all the captured Soviet Political Commissars were to be executed on the spot and not taken prisoner. Manstein had in fact ordered the execution of the Soviet political officers during the advance towards Leningrad. His argument was weak as he argued that they were not protected by the international law, despite the fact that they wore regular uniforms and were part of the Red Army. The most incredible result of the trial was establishing that von Manstein was a liar, especially when he claimed of having never heard of the execution of Jews. As the trial continued, von Manstein fell prey to an increasing state of confusion, especially when his defence team tried to appeal to the anti-Semitic feelings in the court. The popular reaction was immediate. The German press, once fully supportive of von Manstein, avoided reporting these developments at the trial, apart from a single newspaper which remained under British control.

The final sentencing was nothing like von Manstein and his supporters had foreseen. He was found guilty of the following charges: having neglected his duty as a military commander which required him to see that prisoners of war would receive humanitarian treatment, which resulted (albeit indirectly) in the death of 7,993 prisoners. He was accused of implementing an order which required that any escaped Russian prisoners of war were to be treated as guerrillas, and to have ordered that prisoners of war would be engaged in works that endangered their lives, as prohibited by the Geneva convention. Finally, he was accused of having permitted the execution of the Commissar Order and having tolerated (albeit without a direct involvement) the execution of Jews by the *Einsatzgruppe*, having deported Soviet citizens and utilising the scorched earth policy in the Soviet Union. All this was more than enough to destroy the myth of the field commander who claimed he knew nothing of what the SS were doing. Sentenced to 18 years, von Manstein saw the sentence being customarily reduced to 12. He never served the sentence. After a leave for medical reasons in 1952, he was released in May 1953 for 'good conduct in prison'. This was all part of the Cold War complexities, and as with Kesselring the British deemed their release as important to keep the German people onside in Western interests.

After his release von Manstein attempted once again to play a role within the military, as he had once been involved in the reorganisation of the German Army, the Bundeswehr. The success of his 1955 book of memoirs, *Verlorene Siege* (Lost Victories), was followed in 1958 by *Einem Soldatenleben* (A Soldier's Life), which gained him a role as a consultant within the newly created Bundeswehr. Between November 1955 and June 1956, he wrote memoranda on the military organisation, which resulted in the adoption of some of his suggestions, with the creation of brigade sized units. However, his conviction as a war criminal had cast a shadow on the professional soldier, and the cooperation was soon ended. As it transpired, von Manstein had had his day, and his operational concepts, based on manoeuvre, had become irrelevant at a time when the German army was almost exclusively focused on defence. He and his wife lived out their retirement in various places, eventually in a house near Munich, where von Manstein became involved mainly with the Veteran associations. Nevertheless, the Bundeswehr celebrated in grandiose style his 80th birthday. The death of his wife in March 1966 left von Manstein alone and ill. He died of a stroke on 10 June 1973 aged 85 and was buried with full military honours.[4]

Chapter Four

Manstein in the Contemporary Views

The most famous, and most used reference for an inside view of the German army until 1942 is the war diary of the Chief of Staff, General Franz Halder. Manstein is cited in this work for the first time in the 24 September 1939 entry, as he reported about masses of refugees streaming towards the German lines, and his own order to shoot during the night, because had the civilian population been allowed to leave, it would have become impossible to starve the city out, and the local garrison could exploit the opportunity for street fighting. As such this order, albeit indirectly, portrays the image of von Manstein as a professional soldier who looked at the problems from all angles, but at the same time displayed a ruthless commander without a shred of sensibility towards the suffering of the civilian population. However, in Halder's diary von Manstein is more conspicuous by his absence. Halder makes no mention of him in relation to the planning for *Case Yellow*, the attack plan in the West, and his name only crops up in reference to future appointments. Clearly Halder did not hold von Manstein in high esteem, and it is more than likely that he considered his role in the planning for *Case Yellow* as nothing more than mere interference. For the rest of the diary, Halder merely recorded von Manstein's corps advance into the Soviet Union as he did on 20 August, when the corps was supposed to have made great gains, before recording eight days later that it was making satisfactory strides. Even the fall of Sebastopol and von Manstein's promotion to field marshal are merely noted, and only on 6 July, Halder recorded a meeting with Manstein to discuss his future employment in the Caucasus and on matters of personnel regarding the general staff.[1] Halder's removal in September 1942 from the position of chief of the army staff prevents us from having a complete view, but the overall impression is that the top notches at the German army staff saw Manstein as a mere field commander who could achieve local successes, but not as a potential general staff officer.

The diary of Hitler's army aide, Major Gerhard Engel, gives us a different view of von Manstein and of his role in the development of the *Case Yellow* plan. On 4 February 1940, Engel recorded that Hitler's chief military aide, Colonel Rudolf Schmundt, returned from a war games session held at Koblenz greatly impressed by Manstein. He explained that Manstein,

> Had expressed great reservations with regard to the proposed Army Staff operational plan. Schmundt was very excited and told me that, whilst with Manstein, he had ascertained that his plan contained the same opinion regarding the best concentration of forces, albeit in a significantly more precise form, as that continually advocated by the Führer.[2]

On 19 February, in recording the meeting between Hitler and Manstein, Engel noted Hitler's 'overjoy' at Manstein's ideas, resulting in Hitler's comment that 'The man is not to my liking, but he knows something about how to get things done.' This view was expressed while Hitler was describing Halder's and other people's concepts at the army staff, as 'army cadet ideas.'[3] Manstein's name resurfaces on 22 November 1941, as Hitler was considering replacing the commander in chief of the army Field Marshal von Brauchitsch. As Engel asked him if he were considering people like Manstein or Kesselring to replace him, Hitler simply clammed up and refused to answer. On 6 December, Hitler seemed to be taking von Manstein into account for the position, having discarded Kesselring who was replaced in the list by von Kluge. Nothing happened, and von Manstein's name resurfaced on 26 November 1942 as Hitler was facing the Stalingrad crisis. Discussing his assessment of the situation, the conclusion was that Manstein had great ideas from the operational point of view of warfare, but that these ideas, in view of the overall situation, were nothing more than a grey theory. Hitler's personal dissatisfaction with Manstein turned into rage as he, on 18 December, reported he was unable to plug the gap in the vacuum left by the retreating Italian army. The 6 February 1943 meeting was described as 'dour, icy talk'. Manstein had asked for changes at the top, meaning the army high command, along with the creation of a commander in chief for the Eastern Front and the creation of a Chief of Staff for the Wehrmacht High Command. Engel's impression was that Manstein was trying to remove Keitel, trying to achieve a greater freedom of manoeuvre for the army groups at the front, which he considered to be essential in order to react to the situation as assessed on the spot.

Nevertheless, von Manstein relied more on his skills and capabilities, rather than on his almost non-existent people skills, as demonstrated by the fact that Hitler relied on him in 1940, albeit without liking him, and that their relationship deteriorated sharply after the Stalingrad disaster. On 11 March 1943, Goebbels noted in his diary that Hitler appeared unaware of Manstein's stunned reaction to their meeting, and this was because the latter was himself unable to understand Hitler's attitude, regarding his aim to restore the situation on the battlefield. As the German front pulled back, Goebbels noted how Manstein, amongst others, had taken a more humane attitude towards the population, an attitude he had not hitherto associated with him. This was in a way related to von Manstein's appeal and subsequent fear, spreading within Hitler's headquarters in February-March 1944, that the field marshals could join forces together to present Hitler with a united front, compelling him to make those changes at the top, which von Manstein had asked for months before. Hitler's definitive comment on von Manstein was recorded by Goebbels on 18 April 1944, as the field marshal was removed from his command. Goebbels summarised it this way: Hitler was not so much against von Manstein, as Goebbels previously supposed. He did not consider him to be a gifted army commander, or somebody who could inspire and lead the soldiers on the battlefront, but rather as a clever tactician who could be useful once again in the future should Germany return to the offensive.[4] Analysing the relationship between Hitler and von Manstein, the historian Benoit Lemay acknowledged its strictly professional nature. This was not marred by a snobbish attitude on von Manstein's side towards the 'jumped up' corporal clashing with the professional Prussian soldier. Manstein never faced Hitler's bursts of rage, and Hitler only made his critical comments on the field marshal to third parties. Manstein recognised in Hitler the actual leader and commander in chief, and the latter acknowledged von Manstein's professionalism even though he never went so far as to admire him, or even to recognise his stature as a field commander. Most importantly, with his Prussian military background, and not dabbling in politics, his subordination to Hitler and to the various aspects of the Third Reich, including the most gruesome ones, made it clear that von Manstein was not the kind of man who could have doubts of any kind about his leaders. The most striking remark about von Manstein was his attitude in a time of crisis, which he seemed unable to understand or at least was not fully able to grasp in its entirety. His strategic and operational concepts worked well under favourable circumstances, as if they could be tested in a laboratory. However, he was not able to deal with pressure, and he tended to indulge in pursuing ideal changes and counter-manoeuvres without being able to realise they had become impossible.

After meeting him on 13 July 1943 along with Field Marshal von Kluge, Rommel remarked to von Manstein's aide Stahlberg: 'Your Field Marshal is a strategic genius. I admire him. But he is an illusionist.' This remark could well be the result of the fact that, at that time, Rommel had lost all his illusions, but still described the man and the commander as best as one could.[5]

Manstein and the Historians

An aspect of von Manstein's career in the Second World War is that he, unlike other commanders such as Rommel and Guderian, never rose to the level of becoming an instrument of propaganda. Manstein could be a genius, he could win on the battlefield, but he had some kind of irksome personality which prevented him from becoming a troops' leader and a 'star' in the generals' firmament. Manstein's public moment of glory came with the seizure of Sebastopol, but this seems to have been an isolated moment in history never to be repeated. Nor did Manstein appear to have been seeking publicity, an attitude which was certainly far distant from his professional Prussian-style military mentality. The fact that, after the war, he rose to become some sort of a German military hero and became one of the few German generals to appeal to the wider public, is a matter entirely unrelated to his actual achievements and more related to his political post-war assets.

For the first example, Manstein is usually associated with events he did not take part in, but with which he was simply involved in an indirect way. The first was, of course, his involvement with the final plans for Operation *Yellow*. The second was the defeat at Stalingrad, which was a matter involving only Paulus. Much less known, at least from a popular point of view, is that the literature on the Holocaust devoted much space to him, much more than other German generals and commanders. Manstein came to the public attention mainly because of British historians, most notably the well-known historian Basil Liddell Hart. Other works followed, always putting von Manstein within the framework of a series of German military commanders, such as the book by Albert Seaton on the German Army, and the book, edited by Correlli Barnett, on the German commanders. These books greatly relied on the success of von Manstein's own memoirs, *Lost Victories*, and unavoidably portray him as the professional soldier who tried in vain to persuade Hitler to make the necessary changes, which could have made the situation on the Eastern Front turn in Germany's favour. This was the same kind of image that von Manstein gave of himself, more or less willingly, to the Americans who interrogated him, along with some other of his colleagues after the war, as a prisoner of war. The idea is very simple, and von Manstein was merely part of this portrait of the events. Hitler was, eventually, the sole person responsible for the German defeat in the East, as he refused to listen to his generals and make the necessary changes which they had asked for in vain. This image became extremely popular in history terms, and is still widely used, making the professional soldier to be seen as the one who might have changed events, but was prevented from doing so by the ruthless and incapable jumped-up corporal. Needless to state, this image was purposely built by the German generals starting at the time of their captivity in order to shake off any responsibility for the defeat, which was attributed to Hitler's nonsensical orders, while supporting their own image as solid professionals. This view has not been challenged as it should, with the result that the myth of von Manstein as the professional soldier who was prevented from winning by Hitler's orders, still survives today.

Most importantly, von Manstein's processing of himself and its final outcome have been largely forgotten, and until not that long ago he was still largely regarded by the German military as a genius whose operational way of thinking was put at the same level of that of other generals who constitute German military history. Only recently has von Manstein's image started to be portrayed in a more accurate, multi-faceted way mainly due to the works of historians such as Benoit Lemay and of Robert Forczyk, to mention the better publications. They took the advantage of putting the Field Marshal in context, highlighting his undoubted successes and skills, while noting his failures and the complex nature of his character. This was accomplished without ignoring the detail of von Manstein's attitude towards the military and the Third Reich, which appeared to match the ideal 'obeying orders' kind of soldier who cannot understand being put on trial for doing what he was ordered to do.[6]

Final Comments

The problem with analysing von Manstein is the multi-faceted nature of his character, and the role he had during the war, especially on the Eastern Front. Manstein comes across as a rigid, professional Prussian military officer best suited to military theory rather than commanding in the field, despite his successes. However, counting the victories, they are much less than one would initially think. First, it is almost impossible to say if, and to what extent, von Manstein influenced the final version of the *Case Yellow* plan. Both the army staff and, above all, Hitler had been revising the previous plans concluding that a more concentrated blow had to be delivered, and it had been long recognised that the Ardennes was the most suitable area. The influence von Manstein had on the final planning seems to have been limited to technical details and a more professional view of the entire matter, but he did not take part in the actual planning, and as is known, he did not take part in the combats in the area. One may genuinely question which one was the best commander, a von Manstein capable of planning the 'sickle cut' move, which altered the original von Schlieffen's plan in such an effective way to bring the entire Western Front to crumble, or the field commander such as Heinz Guderian, who put the plan into effect, making the German victory possible due to the decisions he made on the battlefield, once having appreciated the situation on the spot. Also, von Manstein's major success, the seizure of Sebastopol, was more the result of a well-planned siege and attack, than the result of decisive conduct of warfare on the battlefront. In this way, von Manstein differed from Erwin Rommel, who seized (at about the same time) Tobruk due to a victory achieved on the battlefield against a superior enemy. Manstein's most remarkable success appears as a mere victory achieved against a pinned down enemy, which could not hope for reinforcements or a change of circumstances.

This was more or less the same situation the Germans faced in 1944–45. It is somewhat ironic that von Manstein's main achievement, the stabilisation of the situation on the Eastern Front in the winter of 1942–43, was to influence in a negative way his subsequent decisions. This achievement was without doubt, quite spectacular and certainly more important than both the planning for *Case Yellow* or the seizure of Sebastopol. The Eastern stabilisation demonstrated that von Manstein was more than capable of putting his own theories and planning into effect on the battlefield. Writing and talking of attacking the enemy at its weakest spot, which were usually the rear areas, and at the critical moment when its advance is losing momentum and is closing to its own exhaustion is one thing, evaluating the situation first hand and enforcing one's own theories by putting them into practice is a different kettle of fish. It is worth noting that even Basil Liddell Hart seemed to note how von Manstein's greatest achievement was in fact the theoretical one, his role in the *Case Yellow* planning actually overshadowing the successes on the battlefield.[7]

Manstein proved capable of winning a battle when he had the necessary resources available, but he proved unable to recognise the situation when facing the fact that his plans could no longer be enforced because of the lack of resources. As a commander defending against an enemy constantly on the offensive, as Forczyk noted, he proved not as successful and not as capable as other German commanders, such as Kesselring or Model. Facing defeat, von Manstein also made his Prussian attitude come to surface, as he attempted in every possible way to deflect the blame from himself on somebody else. He failed to support and to protect his subordinate commanders, and his repeated appeals to Hitler for changes at the top had the taste of attempting to have other people blamed for the situation. He was definitely ambitious, but probably not as much as others, who attempted to climb the greasy pole of the military career no matter what. He certainly aimed at having a decisive influence on the entire Eastern Front, but this appeared more the consequence of a great deal of personal self-esteem rather than sheer ambition. He was clearly not an easy man to work with, and Hitler was not the only one who found it hard to have to deal with him. General von Choltitz, who was to acquire fame for having surrendered Paris, was at Sebastopol under his command, and he noted how von Manstein lacked the 'guts' for leading the troops on the battlefield. He may have had a strong theoretical mind, but von Manstein lacked the personality and the charisma to impose himself on his subordinates, and to assert himself on the battlefield as a natural leader.

Furthermore, his personality outside of the military world seems to have been quite limited by sheer lack of interest. He never displayed any particular interest towards politics, and his attitude towards the Nazi regime seems to have been dictated by the situation rather than by any personal view. His initial distaste towards Hitler was common amongst the German military, such as the enthusiasm that characterised the army following the German victory in the West in 1940. The blind obedience which followed, including the Commissar Order and the attitude towards the Jews, was probably the result of both a desire to obey orders no matter what they demanded, and also partly to a personal lack of interest towards the civilians and anybody who was not part of the professional army. Again, as noted by Forczyk, von Manstein never actually criticised Hitler's politics or decisions regarding the Soviet Commissars, the civilian population, or the Jews, but he only criticised his interference with the field command of the armies on the battlefield. The most obvious conclusion is that von Manstein may have been a brilliant theoretician, a good field commander but also a man who could not recognise his own limitations, and who indulged in blaming others in order to defend himself. He was also a person who at times had problems in grasping the reality for other people who were not in the world he knew. In addition to this, the fact remains that his fame is mainly due to the post-war portrait that the British historians made of him. It is easy to conclude that he was hardly 'Hitler's best Field Marshal' as some have concluded perhaps too rashly.

Final Observations

Once established in political power, Hitler with his future plans forecast in his book *Mein Kampf*, his autobiographical manifesto, he then turned towards the military for total control. From the early 1930s he realised the need to attract the traditional Prussian based military to his so-called ideals. Despised as he is now, it is known that he had the ability to enthral and captivate at all levels of society. At times it was claimed he had a hypnotic effect on those whom he met, even the top army leaders who always purported to have nothing to do with politics. These military commanders tended to be right-wing, and often alibied themselves by claiming that they only served the legitimate government of the day. Field Marshal Kesselring tended to hold firm to this belief to his death in 1960. This attitude provided them with a form of justification for serving an evidently corrupt and evil regime, putting military targets ahead of any sense of morality. Hitler virtually wooed them to himself with his undeniable charismatic persona until they became obedient to his policies, which once would have enraged many of them. Having done this, Hitler achieved what he needed, to be in total control. Keitel never disobeyed his master, and it was further demonstrated when Hitler demanded total command over every move Paulus made in the Stalingrad battle. Hitler had successfully evolved the traditional army establishment on side, later introducing innovations when the tide of war turned against the regime, but that is a subject for the next book. When Manstein disagreed and challenged Hitler, albeit one of Hitler's favourite commanders, he was dismissed on the spot.

Many of these commanders with their sense of high social status were at first bemused if not concerned about Hitler's rise to power in 1933. Keitel, as noted, was uncertain about the dictator, but as his wife noted he soon became enthused by Hitler, whereas Paulus's wife never trusted him, and Paulus later stated he had some initial qualms. It is claimed that Manstein with his Prussian background felt a distaste for the new man, though career motivation soon changed his views.

The main advantage for Hitler of enlisting men from the traditional Prussian background was their sense of loyalty and obedience, confirming this with the Oath of Obedience to Adolf Hitler personally by using his name. Keitel was the extreme example, unquestioning of Hitler's demands and subservient to his master's voice. He encouraged and often obliged others to react the same way, and treated obedience even to an evil dictator as his holy crusade. Paulus was equally obedient even though he knew that it would lead to the loss of his army at Stalingrad, and the only thing Paulus refused was the hint to kill himself. He only changed his mind about Hitler in captivity probably initiated by the machinations of the 20 July Plot. Manstein, although obedient much of the time was one commander who occasionally ignored Hitler's orders and even challenged him, only to be retired.

These commanders were enthusiastic with Hitler's ideas for restoring German power and undoing the perceived humiliation of the Versailles Treaty, and Paulus and most of the top commanders from the earliest stages recalled this as a major factor for his enthusiasm for the dictator. There is little doubt that nearly all serving military men and many civilians in the early days, wanted the Versailles Treaty crushed to restore Germany's perceived greatness. There was only a change of mind as the war brought total devastation on Germany.

These field marshals were only human, and undoubtedly career men looking for any opportunity to rise to the top which Hitler provided. Keitel, when given money by Hitler, claimed it was embarrassing (post-war) but his home farm grew during the early war years, and time and time again fought to retain his position and endear himself to *'mein Führer'*. Even as Paulus watched his army torn apart in the final stages of Stalingrad, he found time in the very last days to send a congratulatory message to Hitler on the anniversary of his seizing power. Manstein out of these selected cases was probably the most career-minded, and in the post-war years strived to be recognised in the new West Germany.

These senior military figures undoubtedly knew about the Holocaust and massacres, many tried to deny it post-war, or were evasive. Keitel had signed many orders and must have known their various outcomes, but its consequences only dawned on him at Nuremberg when he saw the evidence on film and heard the witnesses. He was not by nature an evil man, but it became clear to him that his sense of loyalty, obedience, and career hopes had been monumentally misdirected. Paulus was equally aware as he witnessed it first hand, but he was known for stopping it when he could and was never prosecuted. Manstein always put military success as his only goal, and not only carried out Hitler's morally obscene orders, but he instigated the killing of innocent people. Such was his behaviour during the war years it was surprising he was freed from prison so early (probably influenced by the Cold War) and even more surprising that West Germany even accepted his help.

These field marshals were only ordinary men whose skills and career hopes led them to ignore the moral ramifications in their pursuit of victory. They allowed themselves to be encased by the Nazi regime, to be wooed and won over by Hitler as they sought their own objectives of rising to the top of their power structure. They were not by nature evil men, but allowed themselves to put their careers first, using Prussian obedience as the excuse. They earned a vastly different place in history than they probably anticipated. They had their skills, but they lacked the perceptions and insights of men like General Hans von Seeckt and General Ludwig Beck, who recognised the amoral status of Nazism and stepped back.

Notes

Field Marshal Wilhelm Keitel

Chapter 1
1. Taylor Telford, *The Anatomy of the Nuremberg Trials* (New York: Alfred A. Knopf, 1992) p.30.
2. Gilbert G M, *Nuremberg Diary* (New York: Da Capo Press,1995) p.26.
3. Ibid., p.31.
4. Barnett Correlli, (Ed) *Hitler's Generals* (New York: Grove Weidenfeld,1989) p.140.
5. Goldensohn Leon (Ed, Gellately R, *The Nuremberg Interviews* (London: Pimlico, 2007) p.161.
6. Keitel Wilhelm, (Ed. Görlitz) *The Memoirs of Field Marshal Wilhelm Keitel* (New York: Cooper Square Press, 2000) p.12.
7. wwiigermandocsinrussia.org
8. See Messenger Charles, *The Last Prussian* (Barnsley: Pen & Sword, 2012) p.111.
9. See Knopp, Guido, *Hitler's Warriors* (Stroud: Sutton Publishing, 2005) p.78.
10. Goldensohn, *The Nuremberg Interviews*, p.159.
11. Ibid., p.162
12. Hassell, Ulrich von, *The Ulrich von Hassell Diaries, 1938—1944* (London: Frontline Books, 2011) p.2.
13. Barnett Correlli, (Ed) *Hitler's*, p.141.
14. See Knopp, *Hitler's Warriors*, p.81.
15. Keitel Wilhelm, *The Memoirs*, p.16.
16. Barnett Correlli, (Ed) *Hitler's*, p.143.
17. Keitel Wilhelm, *The Memoirs*, p.18.
18. Ibid., p.17.
19. See Knopp, *Hitler's Warriors*, p.87.
20. Keitel Wilhelm, *The Memoirs*, p.22.
21. Messenger, *The Last Prussian*, p.63.
22. See Barnett Correlli, (Ed) *Hitler's*, p.145.
23. See Goldensohn, *The Nuremberg Interviews*, p.162.
24. Keitel Wilhelm, *The Memoirs*, p.23.
25. Ibid., p.25.
26. Ibid., p.41.
27. Westphal, General Siegfried, *The German Army in the West* (London: Cassell & Company Ltd, 1951) p28.
28. Messenger, *The Last Prussian*, p.73.
29. Rees Laurence, *The Dark Charisma of Adolf Hitler* (London: Ebury Press, 2012) p.162
30. Keitel Wilhelm, *The Memoirs*, p.52.

31. Manstein, Field Marshal Erich von Manstein, *Lost Victories* (Minneapolis: Zenith Press, 1958) p.79.
32. Keitel Wilhelm, *The Memoirs*, p.57.
33. Manvell R, & Fraenkel H, *Goering* (London: Frontline Books, 2011) p.171.
34. Keitel Wilhelm, *The Memoirs*, p.29.
35. Bullock Alan, *Hitler, A Study in Tyranny* (London: Penguin Books, 1990) p.424.
36. Rees Laurence, *The Dark*, p.168.
37. Keitel Wilhelm, *The Memoirs*, p.29.
38. Ibid., p.69.
39. Ibid., p.75.
40. See Trial of The Major War Criminals before the International Military Tribunal, Vol III, (Published at Nuremberg, Germany, 1947) 5 December 1945.
41. Keitel Wilhelm, *The Memoirs*, p.85.

Chapter 2
1. Keitel Wilhelm, *The Memoirs*, p.92.
2. Trial of The Major War Criminals before the International Military Tribunal, Vol III, (Published at Nuremberg, Germany, 1947), 1 December 1945.
3. Knopp, *Hitler's Warriors*, p.104.
4. Gilbert G M, *Nuremberg*, p.92.
5. Keitel Wilhelm, *The Memoirs*, p.93.
6. Ibid., p.94.
7. Longerich Peter, *Heinrich Himmler* (Oxford: OUP, 2012) p.433.
8. Padfield Peter, *Himmler* (London: Macmillan, 1990) p.275.
9. Trial of The Major War Criminals, 1 December 1945.
10. Taylor, *The Anatomy*, p.189.
11. Longerich Peter, *Heinrich*, p.517.
12. Padfield Peter, *Himmler*, p.275.
13. Longerich Peter, *Heinrich*, p.590.
14. Hassell, *The Diaries*, p.148.
15. Keitel Wilhelm, *The Memoirs*, p107.
16. Ibid., p.110.
17. Ferris John, and Mawdsley Evan, *The Cambridge History of The Second World War*, Vol 1 (Cambridge: CUP, 2015) p.312.
18. Keitel Wilhelm, *The Memoirs*, p.114.
19. Westphal, *The German Army*, p.87.
20. See Liddell Hart B H, *History of the Second World War* (London: Book Club Associates, 1973) p.82.
21. Keitel Wilhelm, *The Memoirs*, p.112.
22. Roberts Andrew, *The Storm of War* (London: Allen Lane, 2009) p.74.
23. Michel Henri, *The Second World War* (London: Andre Deutsch, 1975) p.142.
24. *Ciano's Diary 1937-1943* (London: Phoenix Press, 2002) p.365.
25. Overy Richard, *Interrogations* (London: Penguin Books, 2002) p.274.
26. See Burleigh Michael, *Moral Combat A History of World War II* (London: Harper, 2010) p.98.
27. See Bullock, *Hitler*, p.594.
28. Keitel Wilhelm, *The Memoirs*, pp.117-8.

29. Bullock, *Hitler*, p.596.
30. Keitel Wilhelm, *The Memoirs*, p.124.
31. Ibid., p.136.
32. Ibid., p.137.
33. Ibid., p.146.
34. See Roberts Andrew, *The Storm*, p.170.
35. Keitel Wilhelm, *The Memoirs*, p.153.
36. Ibid., p.153.
37. Speer Albert, *Inside the Third Reich* (London: Weidenfeld & Nicolson, 1995) p.333.
38. Ibid., p.181.
39. Russian Archives: https://wwii.germandocsinrussia.org/de/nodes/2273#page/2/mode/grid/zoom/1
40. Ibid.
41. Ibid.
42. See Overy Richard, *Goering* (London: I. B. Taurus, 2012) p.207.
43. See Longerich Peter, *Goebbels* (London: Vintage Publishing, 2015) p.551 and p. 553.
44. Manvell R, *Goering*, p.278.
45. Keitel Wilhelm, *The Memoirs*, p.188.
46. Knopp, *Hitler's Warriors*, pp.118-9.
47. See Bullock, *Hitler*, p.747.
48. See Padfield Peter, *Himmler*, p.531.
49. See Guderian, General Heinz, *Panzer Leader* (London: Penguin Books, 1952) p.368.
50. See Kesselring, Field Marshal, *The Memoirs of Field Marshal Kesselring* (London: William Kimber, 1953) p.172.
51. Manvell R, *Goering*, p.313.
52. See Taylor, *The Anatomy*, p.464.
53. Manvell R, *Goering*, p.316.
54. Knopp, *Hitler's Warriors*, p.122.
55. See Padfield Peter, *Himmler*, p.599.
56. Padfield Peter, *Dönitz The Last Führer* (New York: Harper & Row, 1984) p.406
57. Bullock, *Hitler*, p.786.

Chapter 3

1. Goldensohn, *The Nuremberg Interviews*, p.327.
2. Gilbert G M, *Nuremberg*, p.112.
3. Ibid., p.48.
4. Overy Richard, *Interrogations*, p.37.
5. A copy of this interrogation may be found in Overy Richard, *Interrogations*, pp335 ff.
6. Overy Richard, *Interrogations*, p.341.
7. See Taylor, *The Anatomy*, p.228.
8. See Overy Richard, *Interrogations*, p.42.
9. Trial of The Major War Criminals before the International Military Tribunal, Vol III,)
10. Barnett Correlli, (Ed) *Hitler's*, p.153.
11. Trial of The Major War Criminals before the International Military Tribunal, Vol III.
12. Gilbert G M, *Nuremberg*, p.54.
13. Ibid., p.430.
14. See ibid., p.248.

15. Gilbert G M, *Nuremberg*, p.249.
16. Taylor, *The Anatomy*, p.355.
17. Ibid., p.492.
18. Gilbert G M, *Nuremberg*, p.239.
19. Ibid., p.245.
20. Trial of The Major War Criminals before the International Military Tribunal, Vol XVII, (Published at Nuremberg, Germany, 1947) 5 July 1946.
21. Taylor, *The Anatomy*, p.191.
22. Overy Richard, *Interrogations*, p.248.
23. Goldensohn, *The Nuremberg Interviews*, p.268.
24. Ibid., p.334.
25. Trial of The Major War Criminals before the International Military Tribunal, Vol XVII.
26. Ibid.
27. Ibid.
28. Taylor, *The Anatomy*, p.354.
29. Trial of The Major War Criminals before the International Military Tribunal, Vol XVIII.
30. Ibid.
31. Ibid.,
32. See Gilbert G M, *Nuremberg*, p.439.
33. Taylor, *The Anatomy*, p.598.
34. Gilbert G M, *Nuremberg*, p.93.
35. Goldensohn, *The Nuremberg Interviews*, p.158.
36. Ibid., p.159.
37. Ibid., p.161.
38. Ibid., p.160.
39. Goldensohn, *The Nuremberg Interviews*, p.165.
40. See Ibid., p.167.
41. Gilbert G M, *Nuremberg*, p.76.
42. Ibid., p.109.
43. Ibid., p.327.
44. Neave Airey, *Nuremberg* (London: Biteback Publishing, 2021) p.209.

Chapter 4
1. Hassell, *The Ulrich von*, p.2.
2. Ibid., p.4.
3. Ibid., p.61.
4. Ibid., p.175.
5. Taylor Fred Ed., *The Goebbels Diaries,1939–41* (London: Hamish Hamilton, 1982) p.54.
6. Ibid., p.77.
7. Ibid., p.93.
8. Ibid., p.255.
9. See Longerich Peter, *Goebbels*, p.415.
10. Taylor *The Goebbels Diaries*, p.177.
11. Overy Richard, *Goering*, p.73.
12. Ibid., p.221.
13. Ibid., p.221.
14. Bullock, *Hitler*, p.419.

15. Goldensohn, *The Nuremberg Interviews*, p.131.
16. Gilbert G M, *Nuremberg*, p.237.
17. Speer Albert, *Inside*, p.338.
18. Ibid., p.339.
19. Ibid., p.403
20. *Ciano's Diary*, p.432.
21. Ibid., p.516.
22. Overy Richard, *Interrogations*, p.533.
23. Knopp, *Hitler's Warriors*, p.91.
24. Messenger, *The Last Prussian*, p.111.
25. Ibid., p.245.
26. Liddell Hart B H (Ed) *The Rommel Papers* (New York: Da Capo Press, 1953) p.365
27. See Senger und Etterlin, General Frido von, *Neither Hope nor Fear* (London: Macdonald, 1963) p.147.
28. Göerlitz Walter, *Paulus and Stalingrad* (Westport: Greenwood Press, 1974) p.38.
29. Ibid., p.65.
30. Ibid., p.40.
31. Ibid., p.93.
32. Ibid., p.185.
33. Ibid., p.201,fn.
34. Manstein, *Lost Victories*, p.519.
35. Ibid., p.153.
36. See Ibid., p.154.
37. Guderian, *Panzer Leader*, p.320
38. See Ibid., pp.308-9.
39. Ibid., p.326-7.
40. Ibid., p.415.
41. Ibid., p.431.
42. Ibid., p.464.
43. Kesselring, *The Memoirs*, p.265.
44. Westphal, *The German Army*, p.27.
45. Ibid., p.46
46. Ibid., p.51.
47. Ibid., p.61.
48. Ibid., p.161.
49. Neitzel Sönke (Ed), *Tapping Hitler's Generals* (Yorkshire: Frontline Books, 2007)
50. Liddell Hart, *The German Generals Talk* (New York: Harper Perennial, 2002)
51. Overy Richard, *Goering* (London: I. B. Taurus, 2012) p.2.
52. Burleigh Michael, *Moral*, p.321.
53. Michel Henri, *The Second*, p.213.
54. Ibid., p.236.
55. Shirer L William, *The Rise and Fall of the Third Reich* (London: Book Club Associates, 1973) p.644 & 1041fn.
56. Evans Richard, *The Third Reich at War* (London: Allen Lane, 2008) p.638.
57. See Beevor Anthony, *The Second World War* (London: Weidenfeld & Nicolson, 2012) p.718.
58. Davies Norman, *No Simple Victory* (London: Penguin, 2007) p.242.
59. Roberts Andrew, *The Storm*, pp.6-7.

60. See Ibid., p.142.
61. Ibid., p.328.
62. Roberts Andrew, *The Storm*, p.51.

Chapter 5
1. Padfield Peter, *Himmler*, p.494.
2. Taylor, *The Anatomy*, p.334.

Field Marshal Friedrich Paulus

Chapter 1
1. Beevor Antony, *Stalingrad* (London: Penguin Books, 1999) p.53.
2. Göerlitz Walter, *Paulus and Stalingrad* (Westport: Greenwood Press, 1974) p.9.
3. Mitcham S & Mueller G, *Hitler's Commanders* (New York: Rowman and Littlefield, 2012) p.72.
4. Correlli, Barnet (Ed), *Hitler's Generals* (New York: Grove Weidenfeld, 1989) p.363.
5. See Göerlitz Walter, *Paulus*, p.11.
6. Wheeler-Bennett, John, *The Nemesis of Power: The German Army in Politics 1918-1945* (London: Macmillan, 1964) p.118, fn1.
7. Knopp, Guido, *Hitler's Warriors* (Stroud: Sutton Publishing, 2005) p.197.
8. Göerlitz Walter, *Paulus*, p.14.
9. Ibid., p.15.
10. Guderian Heinz, *Panzer Leader* (London: Penguin Books, 2009) p.49
11. See Mitcham, *Commanders*, p.73.

Chapter 2
1. Göerlitz Walter, *Paulus*, p.139.
2. See Beevor Antony, *The Second World War* (London: Weidenfeld & Nicolson, 2012) p.111.
3. See Göerlitz Walter, *Paulus*, p.24.
4. Göerlitz Walter, *Paulus*, p.39.
5. See Beevor Antony, *Stalingrad*, p.33.
6. Galante Pierre with Silianoff Eugène, *Hitler Lives, and the Generals Die* (London: Sidgwick & Jackson, 1982) p.98.
7. Messenger Charles, *The Last Prussian* (Barnsley: Pen & Sword, 2011) p.131.
8. See Göerlitz Walter, *Paulus*, p.26.
9. Ibid., p.28.
10. Manstein Erich von, *Lost Victories* (Minneapolis: Zenith Press, 1982) p.79.
11. Ibid., p.197.
12. Halder's War Diary, 8 March 1941.
13. Halder's War Diary, 26 March 1941.
14. Bullock Alan, *Hitler A Study in Tyranny* (London: Penguin Books, 1962) p.636.
15. Humble Richard, *Hitler's Generals* (London: Arthur Barker Ltd, 1973) pp.93-4.
16. Liddell Hart (Ed) *The Rommel Papers* (New York: Da Capo Press, 1953) p. 119.
17. Göerlitz Walter, *Paulus and Stalingrad* (Westport: Greenwood Press, 1974) p.32.
18. Halder's War Diary, May 1941.
19. Ibid., 21 May 1941.
20. Ibid., June 1941.

21. Ibid., October 1940.
22. Ibid., 29 August 1941.
23. Macksey Kenneth, *Why the Germans Lose at War* (London: Greenhill Books, 1996) p.126.
24. Halder's War Diary, 6, 21, July, 10,17 August 1942.
25. Ibid., 14 July 1942.
26. Göerlitz Walter, *Paulus*, pp.163-4.
27. Ibid., p.143.
28. Adam Wilhelm, Rühle Otto, *With Paulus at Stalingrad* (Barnsley: Pen & Sword, 2015) p.4.
29. Göerlitz Walter, *Paulus*, pp.47-8.
30. See Mitcham, *Commanders*, p.74.
31. See Göerlitz Walter, *Paulus*, p.49.
32. Adam Wilhelm, *With Paulus*, p.9
33. See Michel Henri, *The Second World War* (London: Andre Deutsch, 1975) p.403.
34. Roberts Andrew, *The Storm of War* (London: Allen Lane, 2009) p.319.
35. Evans J Richard, *The Third Reich at War 1939-1945* (London: Allen Lane, 2008) p.410.
36. Göerlitz Walter, *Paulus*, p.35.
37. Beevor Antony, *The Second World War*, p.329.
38. Liddell Hart B H, *History of the Second World War* (London: Book Club Associates, 1973) p.249.
39. Göerlitz Walter, *Paulus*, p.187.

Chapter 3
1. Glantz, David M, *Zhukov's Greatest Defeat* (Lawrence Kansas: University Press Kansas, 1999) p.2.
2. Adam Wilhelm, *With Paulus*, p.80.
3. Roberts Andrew, *The Storm*, p.329.
4. Davies Norman, *No Simple Victory* (London: Viking, 2006) p.107.
5. Quoted in Beevor Antony, *The Second World War*, p.359.
6. Ferris John, and Mawdsley Evan, *The Cambridge History of The Second Worlds War*, Vol 1 (Cambridge: CUP, 2015) p.345.
7. Quoted in Hastings Max, *All Hell Let Loose* (London: Harper Press, 2011) p.308.
8. Mitcham, *Commanders*, p.91.
9. Beevor Antony, *The Second World War*, p.396.
10. Göerlitz Walter, *Paulus*, p.272.
11. Beevor Antony, *The Second World War*, p.398.
12. See Ibid., p.336
13. Göerlitz Walter, *Paulus*, pp189-193.
14. Adam Wilhelm, *With Paulus*, p.68.
15. Gilbert G M, *Nuremberg Diary* (New York: Da Capo Press,1995) p.147.
16. Ibid., p.149.
17. Göerlitz Walter, *Paulus*, p.169.
18. Ibid., p.170.
19. Heer, Manoschek, Pollak, Wodak, (Editors) *The Discursive Construction of History* (London: Palgrave Macmillan, 2008) p.182.
20. Shirer L William, *The Rise and Fall of the Third Reich* (London: Mandarin, 1960) p.919.
21. Göerlitz Walter, *Paulus*, p.66.
22. See Beevor Antony, *Stalingrad*, p.210.

23. Göerlitz Walter, *Paulus*, p.67.
24. See Adam Wilhelm, *With Paulus*, p.83.
25. Ibid., p.85.
26. Beevor Antony, *The Second World War*, p.387.
27. See Adam Wilhelm, *With Paulus*, p.92.
28. Mitcham, *Commanders*, p.90.
29. Manstein Erich von, *Lost*, p.303.
30. Ibid., p.303.
31. Ibid.
32. Humble Richard, *Hitler's Generals* (London: Arthur Barker Ltd, 1973) p.107.
33. Göerlitz Walter, *Paulus*, p.238.
34. Ibid., p.241.
35. Hastings Max, *All Hell*, p.306.
36. See Adam Wilhelm, *With Paulus*, p.62.
37. Ibid., pp.123-4.
38. Manstein Erich von, *Lost*, p.302.
39. Goldensohn Leon, *The Nuremberg Interviews* (London: Pimlico, 2007) p.355
40. See Beevor Antony, *Stalingrad*, pp.269-70.
41. See: Russian Archives, p.48: https://wwii.germandocsinrussia.org/de/nodes/2273#page/2/mode/grid/zoom/1
42. Mitcham, *Commanders*, p.85
43. Galante, *Hitler*, p.150.
44. Liddle Hart, B H, *The German Generals Talk* (London: Harper Perennial, 2002) p.59
45. See Ferris John, *The Cambridge History*, p.345.
46. Shirer L William, *The Rise*, p.909.
47. Galante, *Hitler*, p.152.
48. Göerlitz Walter, *Paulus*, pp233-4.
49. Manstein Erich von, *Lost*, p.315.
50. Ibid., pp.551-554.
51. Adam Wilhelm, *With Paulus*, p.143.
52. Galante, *Hitler*, p.155.
53. Evans J Richard, *The Third Reich*, p.411.
54. Hastings Max, *All*, p.320.
55. Göerlitz Walter, *Paulus*, p.72.
56. Mitcham, *Commanders*, p.91.
57. Bullock Alan, *Hitler A Study in Tyranny* (London: Penguin Books, 1962) p.689.
58. Adam Wilhelm, *With Paulus*, p.155.
59. See Beevor Antony, *Stalingrad*, p.275.
60. Manstein Erich von, *Lost*, p.351.
61. Ibid., p.351.
62. See Beevor Antony, *Stalingrad*, p.314.
63. Galante, *Hitler*, p.157.
64. Quoted in Beevor Antony, *Stalingrad*, p.318.
65. Adam Wilhelm, *With Paulus*, p.174.
66. Göerlitz Walter, *Paulus*, p.271.
67. See Adam Wilhelm, *With Paulus*, pp.171ff.
68. Manstein Erich von, *Lost*, p.352.

Notes   233

69. Ibid., p.358.
70. Göerlitz Walter, *Paulus*, p.80.
71. Beevor Antony, *Stalingrad*. p.383
72. Uhl Matthias and Eberle Henrik, *The Hitler Book* (London: John Murray, 2005) p.97.
73. Longerich Peter, *Goebbels* (London: Vintage Publishing, 2015) p.556.
74. Liddell Hart B H, *History*, p.479.
75. Ibid.
76. Evans J Richard, *The Third Reich*, p.419.
77. Beevor Antony, *The Second World War*, p.399.
78. Der Spiegel: https://www.spiegel.de/geschichte/wehrmacht-general-friedrich-paulus-hitlers-feiger-feldherr-a-951010.html
79. Bartov Omer, *Hitler's Army* (Oxford: OUP, 1992) p.44.
80. Burleigh Michael, *Moral Combat* (London: harper Press, 2010) p.236.
81. Davies Norman, *No Simple Victory*, p.108.
82. Adam Wilhelm, *With Paulus*, p.218.
83. Heer, Manoschek, *The Discursive Construction*.
84. Ibid., pp.162-3.
85. Ibid., pp.162-3.
86. Ibid., p.180.
87. Ibid., p.185.
88. Ibid., p.191.
89. Ibid., p.193.

Chapter 4
1. See Davies Norman, *No Simple Victory*, p.273.
2. Adam Wilhelm, *With Paulus*, p.235.
3. Beevor Antony, *Stalingrad*, p.422.
4. Vassiltchikov Marie, *The Berlin Diaries 1940-1945* (London: Pimlico, 1999) p.80
5. Galante, *Hitler*, p.222.
6. Shirer L William, *The Rise*, pp.1014-15.
7. See Adam Wilhelm, *With Paulus*, p.262.
8. Göerlitz Walter, *Paulus*, p.168.
9. Beevor Antony, *Stalingrad*, pp.67-68.
10. Galante, *Hitler*, p.140.
11. See Messenger Charles, *The Last Prussian*, pp.263-4.
12. See Tusa Ann & Tusa John, *The Nuremberg Trial* (London: BBC Books, 1995) p.195.
13. Ibid.
14. Taylor Telford, *The Anatomy of the Nuremberg Trials* (New York: Alfred A Knopf, 1992) p.310
15. Shirer L William, *The Rise*, p.830.
16. Trial of The Major War Criminals before the International Military Tribunal, Vol XVIII, (Published at Nuremberg, Germany, 1948) 9 July 1946.
17. Taylor Telford, The Anatomy of the Nuremberg Trials (New York: Alfred A. Knopf, 1992) p.310.
18. Gilbert G M, *Nuremberg Diary* (New York: Da Capo Press,1995) p.146.
19. Taylor Telford, p.311.
20. See Gilbert G M, *Nuremberg Diary* (New York: Da Capo Press, 1995) pp.146-7.

21. Der Spiegel: https://www.spiegel.de/geschichte/wehrmacht-general-friedrich-paulus-hitlers-feiger-feldherr-a-951010.html
22. Knopp, Guido, *Hitler's Warriors*, p.229.
23. See Mitcham, *Commanders*, p.96.

Chapter 5
1. Beevor Antony, *Stalingrad*, p.17.
2. Galante, *Hitler*, p.158.
3. Bullock Alan, *Hitler*, p.733.
4. Uhl Matthias, *The Hitler Book*, p. 94.
5. Ibid., p. 95.
6. Macksey Kenneth, *Why*, p.167.
7. Shirer L William, *The Rise*, p.840.
8. Neitzel Sönke, *Tapping Hitler's Generals* (St Paul, USA: Frontline Books, 2007) p.35.
9. Ibid., p.252.
10. Heiber Helmut, *Goebbels* (New York: Hawthorn Books, 1972) pp.284-5.
11. Liddell Hart (Ed) *The Rommel Papers* (New York: Da Capo Press, 1953) p. 388.
12. Manstein Erich von, *Lost*, p.341.
13. Goldensohn Leon, *The Nuremberg*, p.355
14. Galante, *Hitler*, p.157.
15. Michel Henri, *The Second World War*, p.403
16. Ibid.
17. Beevor Antony, *Stalingrad*, p.54
18. Humble Richard, *Hitler's Warriors*, p.105.
19. Ibid., p.106.
20. Ibid., p.108.
21. Macksey Kenneth, *Why*, pp.170-171.
22. Evans J Richard, *The Third Reich*, p.410
23. Hastings Max, *All Hell*, p.316.
24. Roberts Andrew, *The Storm*, p.601.
25. Göerlitz Walter, *Paulus*, p.288.
26. Ibid., p.285.
27. Ibid., p.286.

Field Marshal Erich Von Manstein

Chapter 1
1. *Operatives Denken bei Clausewitz, Moltke, Schlieffen und Manstein*. Edited by the Militärgeschichliches Forschungsamt (Freiburg: MGFA, 1989).
2. Lemay, Benoît, *Erich von Manstein. Hitler's Master Strategist* (Newbury: Casemate, 2010) pp. 18-20 & Forczyk, Robert, *Erich von Manstein* (Oxford: Osprey, 2010) pp. 5-7.
3. Lemay, *Erich von Manstein*, pp. 20-27 & Forczyk, *von Manstein*, pp. 7-11.

Chapter 2
1. Lemay, *Erich von Manstein*, pp. 12-13.
2. Ibid.,pp. 13-20.

3. Lemay, *Erich von Manstein*, pp. 34-38 & Forczyk, *von Manstein*, pp. 20-22 & Ziemke, Earl F. and Magna E. Bauer, *Moscow to Stalingrad. Decision in the East* (Washington: Center of Military History U.S. Army, 1987) pp. 32-33.
4. Lemay, *Erich von Manstein*, pp. 38-41. Forczyk, *von Manstein*, pp. 22-25. Ziemke, Bauer, *Moscow to Stalingrad*, pp. 105-117. 261-269. 309-312.
5. Lemay, *Erich von Manstein*, pp. 41-44, 115-133, 142-155, 168-170. Forczyk, *von Manstein*, pp. 28-42. Ziemke, Bauer, *Moscow to Stalingrad*, pp. 478-490. Ziemke, *Stalingrad to Berlin*, pp. 90-97.

Chapter 3
1. Lemay, *Erich von Manstein*, pp. 44, 171-212. Forczyk, *von Manstein*, pp. 42-46. Ziemke, *Stalingrad to Berlin*, pp. 118-142.
2. Lemay, *Erich von Manstein*, p. 45. Ziemke, *Stalingrad to Berlin*, pp. 143-247.
3. Lemay, *Erich von Manstein*, pp. 213-250. Forczyk, *von Manstein*, pp. 46-57.
4. Lemay, *Erich von Manstein*, pp. 46-53, 251-285. Forczyk, *von Manstein*, pp. 58-60.

Chapter 4
1. War Journal of Generaloberst Franz Halder, Historical Division, SSUSA, 1950. Entries as per relevant date.
2. Engel, *At the Heart of the Reich*, p. 86.
3. Engel, *At the Heart of the Reich*, p. 87.
4. Joseph Goebbels Tagebücher, Vols. 4 and 5 (Munich and Zurich: Piper, 1999), relevant entries per date.
5. Lemay, *Erich von Manstein*, pp. 62-69.
6. Lemay, *Erich von Manstein*, pp. 6-15.
7. Liddell Hart, *The German Generals Talk*, pp. 113-4.

Cited Bibliography

Primary Sources
Bundesarchiv, *General Kartei*
Halder's Private War Diary. Accessible at the US Army Command and General Staff College, Fort Leavenworth, Kansas. See Ike Skelton Digital Library at: https://cgsc.contentdm.oclc.org/digital/search/searchterm/war%20journal%20of%20franz%20halder/page/1
International Military Tribunal, Vol III, (Published at Nuremberg, Germany, 1947) 5 December 1945.
International Military Tribunal, Vol III, (Published at Nuremberg, Germany, 1947), 1 December 1945.
International Military Tribunal, Vol XVII, (Published at Nuremberg, Germany, 1947) 5 July 1946.
International Military Tribunal, Vol XVIII, (Published at Nuremberg, Germany, 1948) 9 July 1946.
Russian Archives: wwiigermandocsinrussia.org and also https://wwii.germandocsinrussia.org/de/nodes/2273#page/2/mode/grid/zoom/1
War Journal of Generaloberst Franz Halder, Historical Division, SSUSA, 1950. Entries as per relevant date.

Diaries/Memoirs/Biographies
Adam Wilhelm, Rühle Otto, *With Paulus at Stalingrad* (Barnsley: Pen & Sword, 2015)
Ciano's Diary 1937–1943 (London: Phoenix Press, 2002)
Gilbert G M, *Nuremberg Diary* (New York: Da Capo Press,1995)
Goebbels Joseph, *Tagebücher, Vols. 4 and 5* (Munich and Zurich: Piper, 1999), relevant entries per date.
Goerlitz Walter, *Paulus and Stalingrad* (Westport: Greenwood Press, 1974)
Goldensohn Leon (Ed, Gellately R, *The Nuremberg Interviews* (London: Pimlico, 2007)
Guderian, General Heinz, *Panzer Leader* (London: Penguin Books, 1952)
Hassell, Ulrich von, *The Ulrich von Hassell Diaries, 1938—1944* (London: Frontline Books, 2011)
Heiber Helmut, *Goebbels* (New York: Hawthorn Books, 1972)
Keitel Wilhelm, (Ed. Görlitz) *The Memoirs of Field Marshal Wilhelm Keitel* (New York: Cooper Square Press, 2000)
Kesselring, Field Marshal, *The Memoirs of Field Marshal Kesselring* (London: William Kimber, 1953)
Liddell Hart B H (Ed) *The Rommel Papers* (New York: Da Capo Press, 1953)
Longerich Peter, *Heinrich Himmler* (Oxford: OUP, 2012)
Longerich Peter, *Goebbels* (London: Vintage Publishing, 2015)

Manstein, Field Marshal Erich von Manstein, *Lost Victories* (Minneapolis: Zenith Press, 1958)
Manvell R, & Fraenkel H, *Goering* (London: Frontline Books, 2011)
Messenger Charles, *The Last Prussian* (Barnsley: Pen & Sword, 2012)
Neave Airey, *Nuremberg* (London: Biteback Publishing, 2021)
Operatives Denken bei Clausewitz, Moltke, Schlieffen und Manstein. Edited by the Militärgeschichliches Forschungsamt (Freiburg: MGFA, 1989)
Overy Richard, *Goering* (London: I. B. Taurus, 2012)
Padfield Peter, *Himmler* (London: Macmillan, 1990)
Padfield Peter, *Dönitz The Last Führer* (New York: Harper & Row, 1984)
Senger und Etterlin, General Frido von, *Neither Hope nor Fear* (London: Macdonald, 1963)
Speer Albert, *Inside the Third Reich* (London: Weidenfeld & Nicolson, 1995)
Taylor Fred Ed., *The Goebbels Diaries,1939–41* (London: Hamish Hamilton, 1982)
Taylor Telford, *The Anatomy of the Nuremberg Trials* (New York: Alfred A. Knopf, 1992)
Vassiltchikov Marie, *The Berlin Diaries 1940–1945* (London: Pimlico, 1999)
Westphal, General Siegfried, *The German Army in the West* (London: Cassell & Company Ltd, 1951)

Other Published Works
Barnett Correlli, (Ed) *Hitler's Generals* (New York: Grove Weidenfeld,1989)
Bartov Omer, *Hitler's Army* (Oxford: OUP, 1992)
Beevor Antony, *Stalingrad* (London: Penguin Books, 1999)
Beevor Antony, *The Second World War* (London: Weidenfeld & Nicolson, 2012)
Bullock Alan, *Hitler, A Study in Tyranny* (London: Penguin Books, 1990)
Burleigh Michael, *Moral Combat A History of World War II* (London: Harper, 2010)
Correlli, Barnet (Ed), *Hitler's Generals* (New York: Grove Weidenfeld, 1989)
Davies Norman, *No Simple Victory* (London: Penguin, 2007)
Engel, Gerhard, *At the Heart of the Reich* (London: Greenhill, 2005)
Evans Richard, *The Third Reich at War* (London: Allen Lane, 2008)
Ferris John, and Mawdsley Evan, *The Cambridge History of The Second Worlds War*, Vol 1 (Cambridge: CUP, 2015)
Forczyk, Robert, *Erich von Manstein* (Oxford: Osprey, 2010)
Galante Pierre with Silianoff Eugène, *Hitler Lives, and the Generals Die* (London: Sidgwick & Jackson, 1982)
Glantz, David M, *Zhukov's Greatest Defeat* (Lawrence Kansas: University Press Kansas, 1999)
Göerlitz Walter, *Paulus and Stalingrad* (Westport: Greenwood Press, 1974)
Goldensohn Leon, *The Nuremberg Interviews* (London: Pimlico, 2007)
Hastings Max, *All Hell Let Loose* (London: Harper Press, 2011)
Heer, Manoschek, Pollak, Wodak, (Editors) *The Discursive Construction of History* (London: Palgrave Macmillan, 2008)
Humble Richard, *Hitler's Generals* (London: Arthur Barker Ltd, 1973)
Knopp, Guido, *Hitler's Warriors* (Stroud: Sutton Publishing, 2005)
Lemay, Benoît, *Erich von Manstein. Hitler's Master Strategist* (Newbury: Casemate, 2010)
Liddell Hart B H, *History of the Second World War* (London: Book Club Associates, 1973)
Liddell Hart, *The German Generals Talk* (New York: Harper Perennial, 2002)
Liddell Hart, Basil Henry, *The German Generals Talk* (New York: Quill, 1979)
Liddell Hart B H, *History of the Second World War* (London: Book Club Associates, 1973)
Longerich Peter, *Goebbels* (London: Vintage Publishing, 2015)

Macksey Kenneth, *Why the Germans Lose at War* (London: Greenhill Books, 1996)
Michel Henri, *The Second World War* (London: Andre Deutsch, 1975)
Mitcham S & Mueller G, *Hitler's Commanders* (New York: Rowman and Littlefield, 2012)
Neitzel Sönke (Ed), *Tapping Hitler's Generals* (Yorkshire: Frontline Books, 2007)
Overy Richard, *Interrogations* (London: Penguin Books, 2002)
Rees Laurence, *The Dark Charisma of Adolf Hitler* (London: Ebury Press, 2012)
Roberts Andrew, *The Storm of War* (London: Allen Lane, 2009)
Shirer L William, *The Rise and Fall of the Third Reich* (London: Book Club Associates, 1973)
Taylor Telford, *The Anatomy of the Nuremberg Trials* (New York: Alfred A Knopf, 1992)
Tusa Ann & Tusa John, *The Nuremberg Trial* (London: BBC Books, 1995)
Uhl Matthias and Eberle Henrik, *The Hitler Book* (London: John Murray, 2005)
Vassiltchikov Marie, *The Berlin Diaries 1940–1945* (London: Pimlico, 1999)
Wheeler-Bennett, John, *The Nemesis of Power: The German Army in Politics 1918–1945* (London: Macmillan, 1964)
Ziemke, Earl F. and Magna E. Bauer, *Moscow to Stalingrad. Decision in the East* (Washington: Center of Military History U.S. Army, 1987)
Ziemke, Earl F., *Stalingrad to Berlin: The German Defeat in the East* (Washington: Center of Military History U.S. Army, 2002)

Magazines

Der Spiegel: website - https://www.spiegel.de/geschichte/wehrmacht-general-friedrich-paulus-hitlers-feiger-feldherr-a-951010.html

Index

Adam, Colonel Wilhelm 107, 108, 109, 113, 115, 117, 123, 126, 130, 136, 140, 141, 142, 143, 145, 146, 147, 148, 154, 155, 156, 160, 167
Adenauer, Chancellor Konrad 147, 156
Anschluss 18, 19, 57, 99
Antonescu, Marshal 41

Bach-Zelewski, SS General Erich von dem 65
Badoglio, General Pietro 31, 32, 75
Barbarossa xvii, 33, 35, 36, 37, 58, 63, 84, 101, 102, 103, 104, 106, 109, 153, 165, 199
Beck, General Ludwig xiii, 17, 19, 20, 21, 28, 97, 149, 158, 175, 176
Behr, Captain Winrich 137
Blaskowitz, General Johannes 27
Blomberg, General von xi, xii, xiii, 7, 8, 9, 12, 13, 14, 15, 16, 17, 19, 20, 21, 22, 23, 71, 81, 176
Blumentritt, Colonel Günther 47, 178
Bock, General Fedor von 39, 44, 107, 109, 110, 112, 162, 165
Bormann, Martin 49, 51, 53, 54, 76
Brauchitsch, General Walther von xiii, xv, xviii, 17, 18, 19, 20, 21, 22, 24, 27, 36, 37, 42, 75, 79, 101, 176, 186, 214
Brooke, General Alan 42, 84, 85, 105
Busse, General 52

Canaris, Admiral xiii, 18, 27, 28, 35, 58, 63, 68
Chiang Kai-shek 14
Choltitz, General von 220
Chuikov, General 114, 115, 116, 121
Ciano, Galeazzo 31, 77, 226

Daladier, French Premier 21, 24
Dietl, General Eduard xiv
Dietrich, Sepp 41
Dönitz, Admiral 52, 54, 55, 60, 62, 76, 82, 154
Drebber, Major General von 138

Engel, Major Gerhard 214, 215

Flade, Dr Walter 107, 122
Flensburg government 55
Foerster, General 42
Franco 32, 33, 35
Free Germany Newspaper 144, 147, 148, 150, 154
Fritsch, General Werner von xii, xiii, 9, 12, 16, 17, 18, 20, 27, 120, 176
Fritzsche, Hans 120

German military rebuilt ix, xi
Germany Post Great War viii, 96, 173
Giraud, General Henri 27, 65
Gisevius, Hans 63
Gleiwitz incident 26
Goebbels, Joesph 49, 51, 54, 56, 75, 76, 82, 120, 124, 133, 138, 140, 143, 161, 215
Göring, Hermann xi, xii, xiv, xviii, 9, 11, 13, 14, 15, 16, 17, 18, 19, 21, 24, 32, 37, 47, 49, 51, 52, 53, 56, 59, 61, 62, 64, 65, 76, 77, 79, 81, 85, 122, 125, 126, 127, 137, 139, 141, 152, 153, 154, 163, 208
Guderian, General Heinz xiii, 38, 42, 78, 79, 80, 85, 98, 105, 155, 175, 176, 180, 181, 197, 198, 216, 219

Hacha, Emil 23
Halder, General Franz xiii, xiv, xv, xvi, xvii, xviii, 21, 22, 24, 35, 40, 44, 46, 49, 97, 101, 103, 104, 105, 106, 110, 119, 120, 121, 159, 162, 176, 179, 181, 183, 191, 213, 214
Hartmann, General von 138
Hassell, Ulrich von 7, 74
Heim, Colonel 79, 107, 110
Heinrichs, Finnish Chief of Staff General 40
Heusinger, General Adolf 102, 162
Himmler 11, 15, 16, 18, 27, 28, 36, 49, 51, 54, 55, 56, 64, 75, 76, 208
Hindenburg, Marshal Paul x, xi, 8, 10, 66, 172

Hitler in Control x, xiv, 10, 15, 16, 21, 36, 42, 57, 58, 84, 85, 101, 111, 119, 126, 159, 183, 186, 194, 204
Hoepner, General 42, 149, 182, 183
Horthy, Admiral Miklós 37, 41
Hoth, General 38, 118, 123, 125, 131, 132, 133, 134, 135
Hube, General Hans-Valentin 119, 130, 137
Huntziger, General 30

Jaenecke, General 130, 138
Jodl, General Alfred 13, 17, 20, 25, 29, 30, 32, 36, 37, 38, 44, 45, 46, 47, 48, 49, 52, 53, 54, 55, 60, 61, 62, 63, 64, 65, 67, 69, 74, 75, 77, 78, 80, 81, 82, 83, 87, 101, 121, 128, 152, 153, 154

Katyń massacres 28, 56
Keitel, Bodewin, Wilhelm's brother 4, 17
Keitel, Wilhelm
  As a young officer 7, 8, 9, 12
  As seen by contemporaries 56, 59, 70, 71, 72, 73, 74, 75, 76, 78, 79, 80, 81
  As viewed by historians 81, 82, 83
  At French Armistice 30
  Benefits by Hitler's gifts 31
  Character 9, 18, 20, 22, 24, 26, 34, 37, 38, 44, 46, 49, 50, 64, 66, 68, 70, 85, 86
  Clashes with Hitler 28, 29, 33
  Early life 4, 6
  Family life 6, 7, 10, 12, 15, 23, 29, 35, 39, 50, 71
  His execution 69
  In captivity 55, 56
  Knowledge of atrocities 27, 28, 36, 37, 39, 43, 58, 63, 65, 70, 86
  Later views on Hitler 26, 57, 64, 72, 73
  Nature of his memoirs 3
  On trial 61, 62, 63, 64, 65, 66, 67, 68
  Promotion 13, 17, 20, 24, 31
  Reactions to Hitler 10, 18, 19, 22, 29, 30, 32, 42, 46, 48, 50, 52, 54, 60
  Recorded conversation with Hitler 45, 47
  Visits Russia 9
Kleist, Field Marshal Ewald von 46, 65, 181, 202, 204
Kluge, General von 128, 165, 180, 198, 201, 203, 214, 216

Lahousen, General Erwin 58, 62
Lammers, Hans 31, 49, 76
Leeb, Field Marshal von 41, 176, 181, 182
Leopold, King of Belgium 100
List, Field Marshal 25, 36, 37, 44, 45, 47, 49, 74, 121

Lossberg, General von 174
Lüdwig Crüwell, General 161
Lutz, General 175, 176

Mannerheim, Field Marshal 51
Manstein, Erich von 218
  As a young officer 172
  As seen by contemporaries 213, 214, 215, 216
  As viewed by historians 217
  At Nuremberg 209
  Battlefield ability 182, 183, 185, 188, 189, 190, 196, 197, 206
  Battlefield ability fails 187, 193, 199, 200, 202, 204, 205
  Character 192, 209, 216, 220
  Clashes with Hitler 197, 201, 202, 206
  Early Life 172
  Family Life 174, 212
  His connection with July Plot 208
  His dismissal 207
  His trial 210, 211, 212
  Ignores Hitler 187, 202
  In captivity 209, 210, 211, 212
  Knowledge of atrocities 181, 210, 211, 217
  Later views on Hitler 208, 217
  Personal ambition 201, 206
  Post-war ambitions 212
  Promotion 173, 174, 175, 177, 180, 184, 190
  Reactions to Hitler 220
  Tendency to challenge 174, 175, 179, 182, 184, 185, 194, 195, 198, 199, 200, 201, 203
  The planner 176, 178, 179, 180, 188, 218
  Visits Russia 175
Marcks, General Erich 101
Mechelen Incident xv, 111
Milch, Field Marshal 137, 161
Molotov, Russian Foreign Secretary 34
Montgomery, Field Marshal 55, 103, 209, 210
Mussolini, Benito xi, 13, 14, 24, 26, 29, 31, 32, 34, 41, 74, 77, 105

Neave, Airey 73
Nelte, Dr Otto, Keitel's defence lawyer 61, 62, 63, 64, 65, 66, 67, 68, 69, 87, 153, 154
Neurath, Konstantin 13, 23
Night of the Long Knives 11

Operation *Blau* 110, 111
Operation *Felix* 32

Index

Operation *Little Saturn* 131
Operation *Sea Lion* 32, 60, 79, 101, 103
Operation *Winter Storm* 131, 133, 193
Operation *Zitadelle* 197, 198, 199, 200, 201

Papen, Franz von 18, 62, 77
Parparov, Lieutenant Colonel Fyodor Karpovich 151
Paulus, Elena Constance 78, 93, 100
Paulus, Friedrich 112
  After captivity 155, 156
  As a young officer 92, 93, 95
  As seen by contemporaries 160, 162
  As viewed by historians 162, 163, 164, 165
  Character 95, 98, 101, 107, 110, 111, 118, 122, 129, 147, 148, 165
  Early life 91, 92
  Eastern Front 106, 107, 108, 109, 113
  Family life 92, 93, 97, 102, 111, 126, 151, 156
  Germany Post Great War 95
  His own expressed view 167
  In captivity 140, 142, 143, 145, 146, 148, 149, 150, 152, 154
  Knowledge of atrocities 108, 109, 151, 166
  Later views on Hitler 149, 150, 151, 153, 158, 160
  Military diplomat for High Command 103, 104, 105
  Promotion 94, 96, 97, 100, 133, 139
  Reactions to Hitler 97, 119, 121, 129, 135, 140, 158
  Stalingrad Battle 112, 114, 115, 116, 118, 119, 120, 121, 122, 123, 124, 125, 126, 127, 129, 130, 131, 132, 134, 135, 136, 137, 139
  Takes over Sixth Army 107
  The Planner 102, 103
  With Manstein 124, 125, 126, 127, 130, 132, 133, 134
  Witness at Nuremberg 151, 152, 153, 154
Pétain, Marshal 33
Pfeffer, General Max 139
Pieck, Wilhelm 145, 146, 147
Plot to kill Hitler, 20 July 1944 50, 74, 82, 97, 150, 151, 160, 167

Raeder, Admiral 31, 60, 64, 69, 79
Reichenau, Field Marshal Walter von 12, 98, 100, 101, 105, 106, 107, 108, 109, 110, 162, 163, 167, 186
Reinhardt, General 181, 183
Ribbentrop, Joachim von 24, 33, 37, 51, 53, 64, 82
Richthofen, Wolfram von 118, 119, 125

Röhm, Ernst xi, 11
Rokossovsky, General Konstantin 135
Rudenko, Russian prosecutor 64, 152
Rundstedt, Field Marshal von 5, 12, 16, 41, 78, 80, 102, 106, 177, 178, 184, 210
Ruoff, General 46

Sauckel, Fritz 43, 59
Schacht, Hjalmar 64, 77
Schilze-Boyson, Lieutenant Colonel Harro 44
Schleicher, Kurt von x, xi
Schlieffen Plan xv, 171, 179, 219
Schmidt, Colonel Artur 110, 123, 125, 126, 127, 129, 136, 142, 145, 147, 163, 164
Schmundt, General 47, 179, 214
Schobert, General 184
Schuschnigg, Chancellor Kurt von 18, 57
Seeckt, General Hans von x, 9, 14, 78, 86, 95
Selle, Colonel 138
Senger, Genral von 78
Seydlitz, General 46, 127, 128, 129, 139, 148, 150, 151, 159, 164
Shumilov, General 143
Speer, Albert 43, 44, 55, 65, 76, 77
Stahmer, Dr, Nuremberg lawyer 67
Stalin 33, 102, 109, 111, 112, 115, 118, 121, 124, 128, 131, 142, 145, 152, 154, 190
Stalingrad Battle debates 143, 144
Stauffenberg, Claus von 50, 149, 150, 208
Szombathelyi, General, Hungarian Chief of General Staff 40, 41

Thoma, General Wilhelm Ritter von 161
Thomas, General Georg 36
Timoshenko, Russian Marshal 109, 110
Todt, Major General Fritz 21, 31

Ulbricht, Walter 134, 145

Versailles Treaty viii, ix, x, xi, xix, 9, 11, 20, 30, 72, 95, 96, 158, 159, 175
Voronov, Marshal 142

Warlimont, General 152
Weichs, Field Marshal Freiherr von 44
Weimar Republic viii, 8, 86, 96
Wenck, General 53
Westphal, General Siegfried 16, 30, 80, 81
Weygand, General 27
Wietersheim, General von 119, 164
Witzleben, General Erwin von 149, 175

Zeitzler, General Kurt 46, 49, 79, 120, 125, 128, 137, 141, 159
Zhukov, Marshal 114, 131

Dear Reader,

We hope you have enjoyed this book, but why not share your views on social media? You can also follow our pages to see more about our other products: facebook.com/penandswordbooks or follow us on Twitter @penswordbooks

You can also view our products at www.pen-and-sword.co.uk (UK and ROW) or www.penandswordbooks.com (North America).

To keep up to date with our latest releases and online catalogues, please sign up to our newsletter at: www.pen-and-sword.co.uk/newsletter

If you would like a printed catalogue with our latest books, then please email: enquiries@pen-and-sword.co.uk or telephone: 01226 734555 (UK and ROW) or email: uspen-and-sword@casematepublishers.com or telephone: (610) 853-9131 (North America).

We respect your privacy and we will only use personal information to send you information about our products.

Thank you!